Create Web Animations with Microsoft® Liquid Motion™

Send Us Your Comments:

To comment on this book or any other PRIMA TECH title, visit PRIMA TECH's reader response page on the Web at **www.prima-tech.com/comments**.

How to Order:

For information on quantity discounts, contact the publisher: Prima Publishing, P.O. Box 1260BK, Rocklin, CA 95677-1260; (916) 632-4400. On your letterhead, include information concerning the intended use of the books and the number of books you wish to purchase. For individual orders, visit PRIMA TECH's Web site at **www.prima-tech.com**.

Create Web Animations with Microsoft® Liquid Motion™

In a Weekend®

STEVE CALLIHAN

A Division of Prima Publishing

A Division of Prima Publishing

Prima Publishing and colophon, and In a Weekend are registered trademarks of Prima Communications, Inc., Rocklin, California 95677.

Publisher: Matthew H. Carleson

Managing Editor: Dan J. Foster

Senior Acquisitions Editor: Deborah F. Abshier

Project Editor: Kevin W. Ferns

Technical Reviewer: Emily Kim

Copy Editor: Robert Campbell

Interior Layout: Phil Quinn

Cover Design: Prima Design Team

Indexer: Emily Glossbrenner

Microsoft, Windows, Windows NT, Internet Explorer, Notepad, Liquid Motion, and FrontPage are trademarks or registered trademarks of Microsoft Corporation. Netscape is a registered trademark of Netscape Communications Corporation. LView is © 1998 Leonard Haddad Loureiro. All rights reserved.

Important: Prima Publishing cannot provide software support. Please contact the appropriate software manufacturer's technical support line or Web site for assistance.

Prima Publishing and the author have attempted throughout this book to distinguish proprietary trademarks from descriptive terms by following the capitalization style used by the manufacturer.

Information contained in this book has been obtained by Prima Publishing from sources believed to be reliable. However, because of the possibility of human or mechanical error by our sources, Prima Publishing, or others, the Publisher does not guarantee the accuracy, adequacy, or completeness of any information and is not responsible for any errors or omissions or the results obtained from the use of such information. Readers should be particularly aware of the fact that the Internet is an ever-changing entity. Some facts may have changed since this book went to press.

ISBN: 0-7615-1822-3

Library of Congress Catalog Card Number: 98-67578

Printed in the United States of America

99 00 01 02 DD 10 9 8 7 6 5 4 3 2

For Don and Michiko Callihan

CONTENTS AT A GLANCE

Introduction xiv

FRIDAY EVENING
Getting Started 1

SATURDAY MORNING
Working with the Easy-Authoring Templates 23

SATURDAY AFTERNOON
Creating Your First Web Animations 59

SATURDAY EVENING BONUS SESSION
Creating More Web Animations...95

SUNDAY MORNING
Creating Interactive Web Animations...131

SUNDAY AFTERNOON
Creating 3-D and Other Internet Explorer Animations.................203

SUNDAY EVENING BONUS SESSION
Using Liquid Motion Animations in Web Pages 267

APPENDIX A
Installing Liquid Motion 311

APPENDIX B
Using Liquid Motion with FrontPage 98 315

APPENDIX C
Placing Your Animation Files Up on a Web Server 321

APPENDIX D
What's on the CD-ROM..333

Glossary 339

Index 347

CONTENTS

Introduction xiv

FRIDAY EVENING
Getting Started 1
What Is Web Animation? 3
What Is Liquid Motion? 4
Why Create Dynamic and Interactive Web Content?.................5
Liquid Motion and HTML 6
What You Can Do with Liquid Motion Web Animations 7
Running Liquid Motion 8
Previewing the Easy-Authoring Templates............................9
Previewing More Liquid Motion Animations 20
Wrapping Up 21

SATURDAY MORNING
Working with the Easy-Authoring Templates 23
The Liquid Motion Model..26
Editing the Bluebar Banner 36
Take a Break?..47
Editing the Letters Banner...47
Editing the Waves Banner 54
Wrapping Up 57

SATURDAY AFTERNOON
Creating Your First Web Animations 59

Starting a New Animation 61
Working with the Colored Oval Shape 64
Adding Color-Animated Twirlers 65
Growing the "Welcome" Text 69
Inserting an Image 72
Shrinking the "To" Text 74
Inserting the "My Home Page" Text 75
More Fun with Your Animation 80
Take a Break? 82
Creating Your Second Web Animation 82
Adding an Eight-Pointed Star 83
Adding a Four-Pointed Star 86
Adding an Embossed Button Image 89
Wrapping Up 92

SATURDAY EVENING BONUS SESSION
Creating More Web Animations 95

Creating an Animated Color Bar 97
Adding a Sparkles Effect 101
Previewing Your Animation 103
More Fun with the ColorBar Animation 105
The Honking Car Animation 106
Previewing Your Animation in Your Browser 111
More Fun with the HonkingCar Animation 112
Take a Break? 113

Creating a Scrolling Marquee...113
Creating the First Marquee Message 116
Creating the Second Marquee Message 119
Setting the Animation to Repeat 124
Adding More Text Messages 125
More Options with the Scrolling Marquee Animation.................126
Using the ScrollingMarquee Animation in Other Web Pages.............127
Wrapping Up 128

SUNDAY MORNING
Creating Interactive Web Animations.................................131
Creating a "Click Me!" Animation 133
Creating a Flipping Navigation Bar...149
Take a Break? 172
Creating a Sidebar Menu Using Roll-Over Buttons 173
Creating the Running Man Animation 184
Wrapping Up 200

SUNDAY AFTERNOON
Creating 3-D and Other Internet Explorer Animations.................203
Only in Internet Explorer 4.0+...206
Creating a Swimming 3-D Fish Animation................................206
Take a Break?..230
Using Filters..230
Using Transitions 237
Take a Break?..248
Using 3-D Objects..248
Wrapping Up 266

SUNDAY EVENING BONUS SESSION
Using Liquid Motion Animations in Web Pages 267
Editing Liquid Motion HTML Files...269
Previewing HTML Files in Your Web Browser 272
Centering Liquid Motion Animations 273

Using Background Colors and Images 273

Using Liquid Motion Animations in Tables 280

Take a Break? 288

Using Liquid Motion Animations in Frames 288

Take a Break? 296

Creating Browser-Specific Animations 297

Creating Automatic Forwarding Links with the META Tag 298

Using Script Triggers 299

Tips for Publishing Multiple Animations 301

Wrapping Up 308

APPENDIX A
Installing Liquid Motion 311

Minimum Requirements 311

Which Browser Should You Use? 312

Installing Liquid Motion from the Web 312

If You Have Problems 313

Reading the Liquid Motion Newsgroups 313

Setting Internet Explorer 4.0+ as Your Default Browser 314

APPENDIX B
Using Liquid Motion with FrontPage 98 315

Checking for the Liquid Motion Component in FrontPage 98 315

Publishing Animations to a FrontPage Web 316

Moving Animations in a FrontPage Web 319

Getting FrontPage 98 Help 320

APPENDIX C
Placing Your Animation Files Up on a Web Server 321

Finding a Web Host 321

Connecting to a Web Server 322

Setting Up WS_FTP LE 324

Using WS_FTP LE 328

APPENDIX D
What's on the CD-ROM 333
Running the CD-ROM 334
Using Prima Tech's User Interface 334
Installing the Example Files 335
Using the Software on the CD-ROM 336

Glossary 339

Index 347

ACKNOWLEDGMENTS

I thank the folks at Prima Publishing for all their encouragement and assistance. Special thanks to Kevin Ferns, Emily Kim, and Bob Campbell for all the perspicacity, patience, and fortitude they showed in helping to bring this book to final fruition. Thanks to Tom Barich for the great job he did creating the CD-ROM for this book, and to Phil Quinn for a fine job laying out the book. And a very special thanks to Debbie Abshier, who proposed the idea for this book to me, and without whose diligent efforts this book would not have happened.

ABOUT THE AUTHOR

Steve Callihan is a freelance and technical writer from Seattle. He is the author of *Create Your First Web Page In a Weekend* and *Learn HTML In a Weekend* (both out in Revised Editions), also published by PRIMA TECH.

INTRODUCTION

Using Microsoft Liquid Motion, you can easily create sophisticated inter-active 3-D animations viewable by anyone on the Web with a Java-enabled Web browser. Because most Liquid Motion effects can be viewed in both Microsoft Internet Explorer and Netscape Navigator, you can be assured of the widest possible audience for your animations. Be the first on your block to create your very own animated Web site using Liquid Motion and do the following:

✿ Create animated banners, buttons, and rules to jazz up your Web pages.

✿ Add menu buttons to your Web pages that change color, grow and shrink, flip or spin, or play sound effects when the mouse is passed over or off of them.

✿ Learn how to add special AutoEffects, including sparkles, twirlers, bubbles, clouds, and smoke, that follow the mouse or are activated when the mouse is pressed.

✿ Create your own growing, shrinking, and spinning text messages with changing fill and drop shadow colors.

✿ Use a wide assortment of 2-D shapes in your animations, including ovals, circles, squares, rectangles, polygons, triangles, stars, speech balloons, arrows, and banners.

✿ Easily record complex motion paths for any object to have text or shapes move around or in and out of your animation.

✿ Use timing controls to time and start and stop effects, set their duration, and specify the number of play loops.

- ✿ Create interactive animation effects, such as playing a sound effect, making a shape appear out of the background, or flipping or spinning a button, that are keyed to mouse actions.

- ✿ Easily add URL links to objects (like menu buttons, for instance) that automatically launch Web pages, display images, or even play other Liquid Motion animations, when the mouse is clicked on the object.

- ✿ Import GIF animations or create your own image strips to add even more movement and animated pizazz to your animations.

- ✿ Include a wide range of sounds in your animations, including AU, WAV, MIDI, MPG, MP2, and MPA sound and music files. Set them to play automatically at any point in your animation, or key them to be triggered by user actions.

- ✿ Learn how to create a panning background, just like in the cartoons.

- ✿ Include 3-D shapes such as spheres, cubes, cones, and cylinders, plus an assortment of 3-D images.

- ✿ Apply realistic surface textures to 3-D shapes, and control 3-D light sources and ambient light effects.

- ✿ Combine 3-D shapes and motion paths with grow, shrink, and acceleration effects to create realistic movements of objects within a 3-D space.

- ✿ Use inner scenes to create animations within your animations.

- ✿ Use filters and transitions, including drop shadows, fade ins/fade outs, wipes, and other effects.

Who Should Read This Book

You should read this book if you want to learn to create and publish inter-active 3-D Web animations in the shortest possible time, in a single weekend! Whether you are a professional, salesperson, teacher, student, artist, or even a computer professional or programmer, this book teaches you *everything* that you need to know to start creating and publishing your own Java-based animations right away.

You don't need to know any programming languages. Knowing some HTML can be helpful but is not required, since this book provides you with starting HTML templates you can easily customize and use with your Liquid Motion animations.

Liquid Motion should be of special interest to Microsoft FrontPage 98 users. You can drag and drop Liquid Motion animations directly into FrontPage 98 Web pages, as well as publish your animations directly to a FrontPage Web server. Many of the Easy-Authoring Templates included with Liquid Motion complement FrontPage 98 Themes. This book con-tains a section dedicated specifically to using Liquid Motion with Front-Page 98.

You can try out Liquid Motion for free for 45 days. If you decide to buy the software, you'll find the price to be quite reasonable, especially considering the power of the program. The registered version is available for $149.

What You Can Do in a Weekend

How much you can learn in a weekend depends upon your learning style and speed, as well as the amount of time and effort you are willing to put into it. Because this book uses a graduated approach, anyone willing to dedicate the minimum amount of time required should be able to learn how to create Web animations, if not every single Web animation effect, in a single weekend. Of course, the more time you put in, the more you can learn. You are not, however, locked into having to complete everything that is in the book—two out of the seven sessions and many of the exercises in this book are optional.

The different sessions in this book walk you through editing Liquid Motion's Easy-Authoring Templates, as well as creating regular, interactive, and 3-D animations. Most of the sessions include optional bonus exercises that you can do if you have the time or skip if you are running short on time. So feel free to go at your own speed and according to your own learning style.

What You Need to Begin

Microsoft Liquid Motion is available to download for free from Microsoft's Web site in a 45-day trial version. See Appendix A, "Installing Liquid Motion," for information on downloading and installing Liquid Motion.

Liquid Motion requires Windows 95, 98, or NT 4.0. Microsoft recommends that you have at least a Pentium PC with 16MB of RAM, a super-VGA graphics board capable of 800x600 screen resolution and 16-bit color resolution ("hi-color"), and at least 30MB of free disk space.

While you can use any Java-enabled Web browser, such as Netscape Navigator 2.0+ or Microsoft Internet Explorer 3.02+, to preview animations created in Liquid Motion, you'll need to use Microsoft Internet Explorer 4.0+ to preview all the effects you can create in Liquid Motion. I recommend you download and install Internet Explorer 4.0+, if only to use it to preview Liquid Motion animations. Installing Internet Explorer 4.0+ will not interfere with your continuing to use Netscape Navigator as your main Web browser, if you wish to do so.

Who Can View Your Animations

To view 3-D effects, filters and transitions, and a few other effects in your animations, viewers will need Microsoft Internet Explorer 4.0+. The vast majority of effects that you can create in Liquid Motion, however, are fully viewable in any Java-enabled Web browser, such as Netscape Navigator 2.0+ or Microsoft Internet Explorer 3.02+, without the need to install a plug-in or player. In this book, I've split off all of the Internet Explorer 4.0+ effects into their own session. I also show you how you can create alternative versions of your animation, one for Internet Explorer 4.0+ (with 3-D effects, for instance) and the other for Netscape Navigator and other Java-enabled browsers (without the 3-D effects), that'll play automatically in the right browser.

Liquid Motion animations automatically detect the type of browser being used to download an animation. The Liquid Motion runtime is built into Internet Explorer 4.0+, so users of that browser need only to download the Liquid Motion animation file, and any included media files, to view it in their browser.

For users of other Java-enabled Web browsers such as Netscape Navigator 2.0+ or Microsoft Internet Explorer 3.02+, additional support files need only be downloaded the first time a Liquid Motion animation is played.

Users of Netscape Navigator are prompted the first time they play a Liquid Motion animation to install the Liquid Motion Accelerator to help speed up the playback of Liquid Motion animations in Navigator. The accelerator is automatically downloaded the first time a Liquid Motion animation is run and need not be downloaded subsequently, unless the user decides not to install the accelerator. Installation of the accelerator is not required in order to be able to play Liquid Motion animations, although their playback performance in Navigator won't be as smooth.

The only viewers who won't be able to view your animations are viewers who are not using Java-capable Web browsers or who have disabled Java in their browsers.

What this all means is that Liquid Motion is currently the Web animation tool of choice, due to its easy accessibility to all users (no programming or graphics experience is required) and the compatibility of its animations with any Java-enabled Web browser. Using Liquid Motion, you can easily create fantastic dynamic animated Web content for your Web pages that can be viewed by the widest possible audience on the Web. With the advent of Microsoft Liquid Motion, a whole new era in Web publishing has begun (and this is only the beginning).

How This Book Is Organized

This book breaks down the learning process into easily achievable steps:

Friday Evening: Getting Started. Learn about Web animation and Liquid Motion, and then preview the Easy-Authoring Animation Templates.

Saturday Morning: Working with the Easy-Authoring Templates. First read the quick overview of the Liquid Motion user interface, and then learn how to personalize the Easy-Authoring Templates with your own text messages.

Saturday Afternoon: Creating Your First Web Animations. Create your first Web animation, an animated "welcome" banner using color-animation, shrinking and growing 2-D shapes and text, a motion path, and an AutoEffect, as well as timing and sequence controls. Create an animation that uses shrinking, growing, and spinning star shapes combined with a throbbing button image to create a dynamically decorative element for your Web pages.

Saturday Evening Bonus Session: Creating More Web Animations. Create an animated color bar with sparkles, have fun with motion paths and sound effects, and learn how to use an inner scene to create a scrolling message marquee.

Sunday Morning: Creating Interactive Web Animations. Create Liquid Motion animations that use viewer-initiated triggers that can stop and start animation sequences, turn effects on and off, shrink or grow objects, start motion behaviors, or activate a link to another animation or Web page.

Sunday Afternoon: Creating 3-D and Other Internet Explorer Animations. Create 3-D and other advanced animations that are optimized for viewing in Microsoft Internet Explorer Version 4.0 (or higher), using 3-D shapes and objects, surface textures and light sources, spinning and rotating effects, moving objects within 3-D spaces, and filters and transitions.

Sunday Evening Bonus Session: Using Liquid Motion Animations in Web Pages. Learn how to integrate Liquid Motion animations with HTML Web pages and sites, including centering animations and adding background images, wrapping text and other elements around animations, creating animated two-column formats using tables, and creating complex multi-animation Web pages using frames.

Once you've learned how to create Liquid Motion animations this weekend, you can always come back at a later time to do any of the bonus or optional sessions or exercises you may have skipped. Additionally, I've included a number of appendixes that cover additional areas of interest:

Appendix A: Installing Liquid Motion. Look here for information on installing Liquid Motion, as well as other system configuration issues.

Appendix B: Using Liquid Motion with FrontPage 98. Look here for information on publishing animations directly to a FrontPage Web, publishing animations to a Web page open in the FrontPage editor, dragging and dropping Liquid Motion animations into FrontPage 98 Web pages, and other tips and techniques for using Liquid Motion with FrontPage 98.

Appendix C: Placing Your Animation Files Up on a Web Server. Once you create some Web animations, you'll want to put them up on the Web so all the world can see them. This appendix discusses finding a Web server for your animation files, then shows you how to use WS_FTP LE, an FTP program included on the CD-ROM, to transfer your animation and HTML files up onto a Web server.

Appendix D: What's on the CD-ROM? Look here for directions on how to use the CD-ROM and descriptions of the examples and software tools included on the CD-ROM.

Special Features of This Book

This book uses a number of special text formats and icons to make your job easier as you work through the sessions. They are used to call your attention to notes, tips, cautions, buzzwords, and programs or other resources included on the CD-ROM:

NOTE Notes are food for thought as you work through the tutorials. They bring up points of interest or other relevant information you might find useful as you develop your abilities with Liquid Motion.

TIP Tips offer helpful hints, tricks, and ideas to apply as you progress in the creation process.

CAUTION Cautions warn you of possible hazards and point out pitfalls that typically plague beginners.

BUZZ WORD Buzzwords are terms and acronyms that you should be familiar with and keep in mind as you develop and expand your Web animation skills.

  **ON THE CD-ROM** The CD-ROM icon marks resources or tools located on the accompanying CD-ROM that may be helpful to you in your Web animation endeavors.

Visit This Book's Web Site

You can visit the Web site for this book at **www.callihan.com /liquidmotion/** for links to useful tools and resources. If you don't have a CD-ROM drive, you'll find all the example files used in the book available there for download. In addition to what's included on the CD-ROM, you'll find additional collections of Web art images and sound files that you can download and use in creating Liquid Motion animations. And if something really stumps you, you can send me an e-mail message.

Getting Started

- ⚙ What Is Web Animation and Liquid Motion?
- ⚙ What Web Animations Can Do For You
- ⚙ Why Create Dynamic Content?
- ⚙ Previewing the Easy-Authoring Templates and Other Liquid Motion Animations

I t's Friday evening and you're champing at the bit, raring to go, ready to get a jump-start on your weekend. Before you begin to create Web animations, it will be helpful to get some background on Web animations and Microsoft Liquid Motion, as well as preview some Liquid Motion animations.

What Is Web Animation?

Simply put, Web animation is movement, and possibly interactivity, in a Web page. You may have already surfed Web pages where passing the mouse over a button causes it to change color, or where an animated banner plays when you first display a Web page in your browser. Animations can be simple non-interactive GIF animations that play a sequence of frames, or they can be more complex interactive animations that respond to mouse actions or other events. GIF animations are fairly easy for anyone to create using a GIF animation editor (I've included a couple on the CD-ROM).

Until recently, if you wanted to create more complex interactive Web animations, you needed the skills of a Java- or JavaScript-savvy programmer, or you were pretty much left out in the cold. There just weren't any software tools aimed at the general user for creating interactive Web animations for playback across the board in Java-capable Web browsers.

The few Web animation programs previously accessible to nonprogrammer users, such as Macromedia Flash (originally named Future Splash), required plug-ins or players for their animations to be viewable in a browser.

However, with the introduction of Microsoft Liquid Motion, ordinary users without programming experience no longer have to be satisfied with creating staid and static Web sites. Using Microsoft Liquid Motion, anyone can now create dynamic, interactive Web animations viewable in current browsers.

What Is Liquid Motion?

Microsoft Liquid Motion is the first Web animation program that allows users who aren't programmers to intuitively create their own dynamic and interactive Web animations viewable in any Java-capable Web browser. No plug-ins or players are required. A few effects included in Liquid Motion, such as 3-D effects, transitions, and filters, can only be displayed in Microsoft Internet Explorer 4.0 (or greater). However, the vast majority of animation effects available in Liquid Motion, including growing and shrinking objects, spinning 2-D shapes, color animation, timing controls, and mouse action triggers, can automatically be viewed in any Java-capable Web browser, such as Netscape Navigator 2.0 (or greater) or Internet Explorer 3.0 (or greater).

NOTE Both Java and JavaScript must be enabled in a Java-capable Web browser, such as Netscape Navigator, to view Liquid Motion animations. To check what these settings are in Navigator 4.0+, select Edit, Preferences, and then select Advanced. If Java or JavaScript are disabled, Liquid Motion animations will not be displayed. For this reason, you may not want to use a Liquid Motion animation as the front page to a Web site. One solution is to set up a front page that allows a visitor the option of displaying your Liquid Motion page or another page if their browser is not up to snuff. For more information on doing this, see the Sunday Evening session, "Using Liquid Motion Animations with Web Pages."

Even animations using Internet Explorer 4.0-only effects can easily be made Navigator-friendly, so there is no need to fear that your Web animations will not be viewable in all current Java-capable browsers. Liquid Motion actually creates two separate animations: A Java animation that is displayed in Java-capable Web browsers and a DirectX animation that can only be displayed in Internet Explorer 4.0 (or greater). A JavaScript automatically directs the browser to the correct animation file. See the Sunday Evening session, "Using Liquid Motion Animations with Web Pages," for some pointers on how to use this feature to create alternative animations for display in Java-capable Web browsers.

◄ ◄

Java is an object-oriented programming language developed by Sun Microsystems that is designed to create programs that can be run securely on any platform, making it the ideal programming language for the World Wide Web. Because programs distributed across the Web need to be small due to bandwidth constraints, Java programs are often called "applets."

JavaScript is a scripting language developed by Netscape and Sun Microsystems that is loosely based on Java. It is particularly useful for adding dynamic behaviors, such as mouse-over effects, to a Web page.

DirectX is a software technology for Windows that allows applications to directly access a computer's graphics and sound hardware. Liquid Motion's 3-D effects, for instance, make use of DirectX technology. Currently, Internet Explorer 4.0+ is the only Web browser that supports displaying DirectX animations.

◄ ◄

Why Create Dynamic and Interactive Web Content?

The days of primarily static Web sites are rapidly coming to an end. Cutting edge Web sites are presenting increasingly richer content, including dynamic, interactive user interfaces and navigation facilities.

The Web is all about competition for visitors. While the number of people surfing the Web continues to increase rapidly, so is the number of new Web sites. To get noticed on today's (and especially tomorrow's) Web, you'll need more than a plain Web site.

Using Microsoft Liquid Motion, you can create a Web site that will make your visitors think you spent thousands of dollars developing it. The kicker, of course, is that you have free use of Liquid Motion for 45 days, and with this book you can learn everything you need to know to create dynamic, interactive, and 3-D Web animations that'll amaze visitors to your Web site! With the aid of this book, you should be able to create the dynamic, interactive Web site of your dreams before your 45 days run out.

True, you still need to deliver the goods. Even the snazziest animated Web site won't attract return visitors if its content is weak or unoriginal. The battle is simply getting visitors to come in your front door in the first place, and then keeping them coming back for more.

Liquid Motion and HTML

You can create stand-alone Web animations with Liquid Motion and transfer them to your Web site. If you know some HTML, you can go a step further and easily integrate Liquid Motion animations into your Web pages. It is as simple as cutting and pasting the animation code from the HTML file Liquid Motion creates to your own HTML file. With a

---

THE CUTTING EDGE LOOK

When I worked as a word processor (years ago!), we used to print form letters on a daisy wheel printer to try to make them look like they were typed, rather than produced on a computer. But when we got our first laser printer, our marketing head told us to ditch the daisy wheel. When I asked him why, he said it was more important for potential clients to know we had a laser printer (which cost several thousand dollars back then) than it was for them to not know the letter was produced on a computer. The same holds true today.

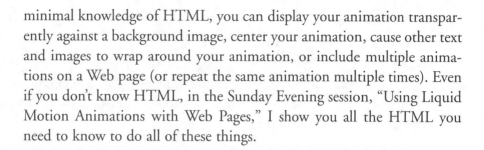

minimal knowledge of HTML, you can display your animation transparently against a background image, center your animation, cause other text and images to wrap around your animation, or include multiple animations on a Web page (or repeat the same animation multiple times). Even if you don't know HTML, in the Sunday Evening session, "Using Liquid Motion Animations with Web Pages," I show you all the HTML you need to know to do all of these things.

 NOTE If you want to learn HTML, I've got two books out, both also published by PRIMA TECH: *Create Your First Web Page In a Weekend* and *Learn HTML In a Weekend.* They are both available in revised versions that cover the latest in HTML, including HTML 4.0. To find out more about these books, just go to my Web site at **http://www.callihan.com /booksidx.htm** or go to PRIMA TECH'S Web site at **http://www.prima-tech.com/**.

What You Can Do with Liquid Motion Web Animations

There are many different ways that you can use Liquid Motion Web animations in your Web site or Web pages. The following are some of the highlights:

- ✿ Publish stand-alone animations directly to the Web that can easily be linked from your other Web pages. Anyone using a Java-capable Web browser will be able to view your animations.

- ✿ Create an animated front-end to your Web site that'll function like an image map, but with dynamic interactive responses to different mouse actions included.

- ✿ Create dynamic and interactive Web page objects, such as banners, buttons, menus, navigation bars, icons, rules, and much more. With Liquid Motion, it is easy to add roll-over effects to your buttons and menus, so passing the mouse over them will cause their appearance or colors to change, as well as play a sound effect, pop up a text box, and so on. Web page objects can also be set to shrink and grow, flip and spin, or slide and move in response to mouse actions. Clicking one Web page object can set off chain reactions in other objects.

✪ Create fully-interactive animated Web presentations, including sound effects (such as voice-over introductions to your Web presentation slides).

✪ Add animated illustrations and pop-ups to product descriptions and catalogs. Instead of looking at a static image of your product, visitors move through an interactive animation to discover exactly what they want to know. Responses can be pop-up boxes providing information details or technical specifications, or mini-animations illustrating a particular feature of your product.

✪ Use Liquid Motion to explore and investigate the possibilities of a whole new medium of artistic expression. Web animations are works of art, after all, and nothing says they can't be just that.

✪ Create new learning experiences for students. Educators and teachers can create an animated anatomy lesson, for instance, or a tour of the Sistine Chapel. You can create animated multiple-choice quizzes with crash-and-burn sound and animation effects for wrong answers, and applause sounds for right answers.

These are some of the ways you can use Liquid Motion Web animations to enhance your presence on the Web. As you develop and grow as a Web animator, I'm sure you'll figure out many other new ways to apply your Web animation talent.

Running Liquid Motion

If you have not yet downloaded and installed Liquid Motion, please see Appendix A, "Installing Liquid Motion," for instructions on how to download and install this software from the Web.

To run Liquid Motion:

✿ Click on the Start button, then <u>P</u>rograms, then Microsoft Liquid Motion, and then Microsoft Liquid Motion again.

Or:

✿ Double-click the Microsoft Liquid Motion shortcut icon on the Desktop.

The Getting Started dialog box provides you with a number of options, including opening or previewing an Easy-Authoring Template, opening an existing animation file, or creating a new animation (see Figure 1.1).

Previewing the Easy-Authoring Templates

Included with Liquid Motion is a selection of Easy-Authoring Templates that you can easily edit to add your own text or images. To get an idea of what Liquid Motion can do, click the <u>P</u>review button to preview Liquid Motion's Easy-Authoring Templates (see Figure 1.2). The Easy-Authoring Templates included with the trial version of Liquid Motion are organized in three categories: Banners, Buttons, and Extras. You'll learn more about each of the following examples in the Saturday Morning session, "Working with the Easy-Authoring Templates."

Figure 1.1

The Getting Started dialog box is displayed when you first run Liquid Motion.

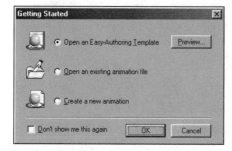

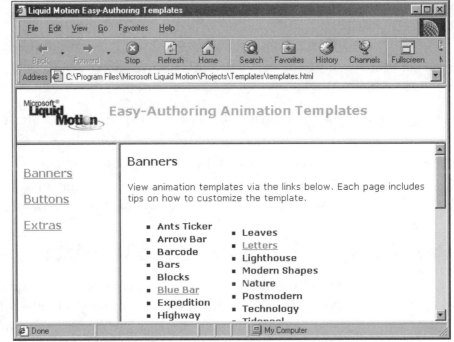

Figure 1.2

To view some of Liquid Motion's capabilities, you can preview the Easy-Authoring Templates.

If clicking the Preview button does not display the Easy-Authoring Web page, you may need to specify Internet Explorer as your default browser. To find out how to do this, see Appendix A, "Installing Liquid Motion." To specify Netscape Navigator 4.0+ as your default browser, you'll have to re-install Communicator and then specify it as your default browser. Ultimately, you'll want to install both main browsers on your computer so you can thoroughly check out how your animations run in both of them. If you do have Internet Explorer 4.0+ and Navigator 4.0+ installed, for the sake of using Liquid Motion, I recommend that you specify Internet Explorer as your default browser—it won't interfere with Navigator.

The Blue Bar Banner

To preview the Blue Bar banner, click the Blue Bar link (see Figure 1.3). When you pass the mouse over a shape, it'll light up and emit a clicking sound (see Figure 1.4).

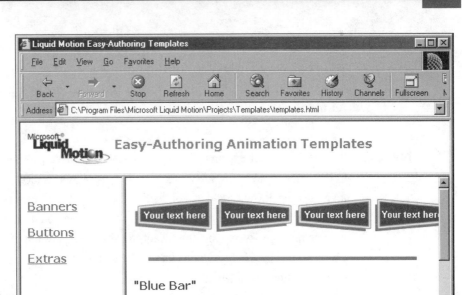

Figure 1.3

The Blue Bar banner is a series of 2-D shapes with boilerplate text.

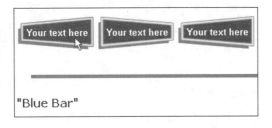

Figure 1.4

When you pass the mouse over one of the shapes, it lights up and emits a sound.

 NOTE Some animations, such as the Blue Bar banner animation shown in Figure 1.3, may be cropped inside of your browser's default window dimensions. Feel free to adjust your browser's window dimensions to see all of an animation or to maximize the browser window—or you can just use the scroll bars to bring unseen parts of an animation into view.

Each of the shapes in the Blue Bar banner also function as a hypertext link, in this case to Microsoft's Liquid Motion Web site. Go ahead and click one of the shapes (you'll be prompted to connect to the Internet if you are not already connected) to go to the Liquid Motion Web site. Since you don't have a whole lot of time tonight, resist for now the temptation to go exploring the Liquid Motion site and click the Back button to return to the Easy-Authoring Animation Templates page.

NOTE By default, Internet Explorer only tries to connect to a Web page the first time you link to that page in a Windows session. After that, it will automatically load the Web page from its cache. If you clicked one of the Blue Bar shapes just described and connected to the Internet to open the Liquid Motion Web site, you can go ahead and disconnect from the Internet if you want (you don't want to consume bandwidth unless it is necessary). Wait until the page is finished loading, however, before clicking the Back button or disconnecting from the Internet.

The Letters Banner

To preview the Letters banner, click the Banners link in the sidebar, and then click the Letters link (see Figure 1.5). When you pass the mouse over the animation, the boilerplate text, "Your Text Here," expands from within the animation (see Figure 1.6). You'll also notice that the color of the text changes from black to white as it grows.

The Waves Banner

To preview the Waves banner, click the Banners link in the sidebar, and then click the Waves link (you may need to scroll down to see it. See Figure 1.7).

The Abstract Button

To preview the Abstract button, click the Buttons link in the sidebar, and then click the Abstract link (see Figure 1.8). When you pass the mouse over the middle of the Abstract button, its contents change from gray to white, and the text "[home]" is displayed (see Figure 1.9), accompanied by a buzzer sound.

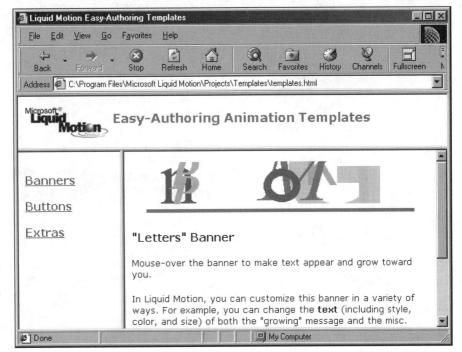

When you click on the Abstract button, a link to Microsoft's Liquid Motion Web site will be activated. In the Saturday Morning session, "Working with the Easy-Authoring Templates," you'll learn how to substitute your own text here in place of "[home]." You'll also learn how to substitute the address of your own home page (if you have one) for the Liquid Motion link.

"Letters" Banner

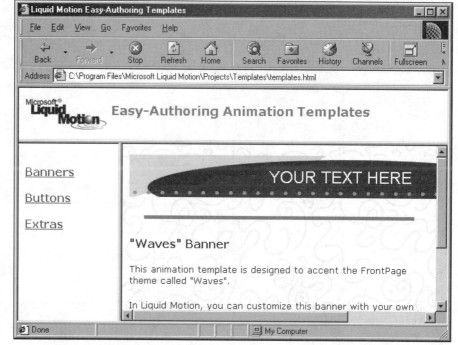

Figure 1.7

The Waves banner transparently displays one shape over another, a line of sequential dots, and some boilerplate text that flows in from the left.

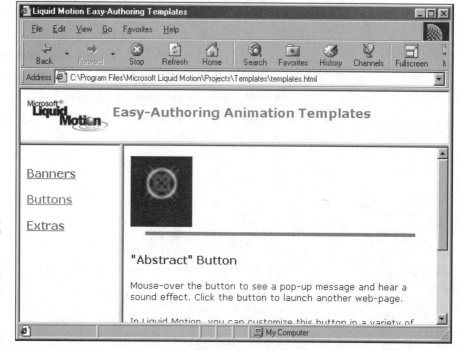

Figure 1.8

The Abstract button doesn't look like much to start out with, just a black and gray button with a circle and an *x* in the middle.

Figure 1.9

When you pass the mouse over the middle of the Abstract button, the contents change from gray to white, and a sort of "buzzing" sound is emitted.

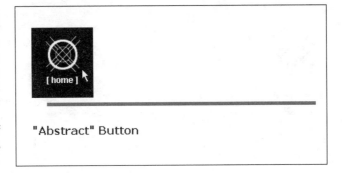

"Abstract" Button

The Help Button

To preview the Help button, click the Buttons link in the sidebar, and then click the Help link (see Figure 1.10). When you pass the mouse over the question mark, the animation comes to life. Small floating question marks and sparkles appear, and a series of clicking sounds emerge from your speakers, while the "Info" text grows and shrinks (see Figure 1.11).

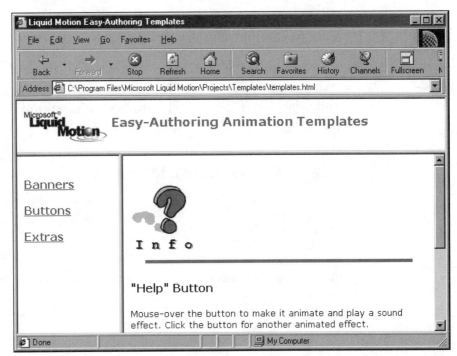

Figure 1.10

The Help button displays a question mark and the word "Info."

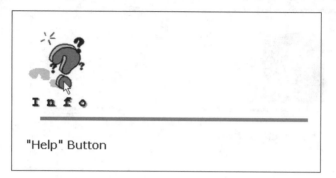

"Help" Button

You can click the question mark to connect to Microsoft's Liquid Motion Web site. In the Saturday Morning session, "Working with the Easy-Authoring Templates," you'll learn how to substitute your own text here. You'll also learn how to substitute a different address for the Liquid Motion link.

The Waves Button

To preview the Waves button, click the Buttons link in the sidebar, and then click the Waves link (see Figure 1.12). When you pass the mouse over the button, some balls roll down the contour of the wave (see Figure 1.13).

You can click the Waves button to connect to Microsoft's Liquid Motion Web site. In the Saturday Morning session, "Working with the Easy-Authoring Templates," you'll learn how to substitute your own text here and substitute a different address in place of the Liquid Motion link.

The Skydiver Extra Template

To preview the Skydiver extra template, click the Extras link in the sidebar, and then click the Skydiver link. You may need to scroll down to see the falling skydiver in the animation (see Figure 1.14). When you click the skydiver, his parachute deploys (see Figure 1.15). You'll also notice that a boilerplate text banner periodically scrolls across the screen after the parachute deploys.

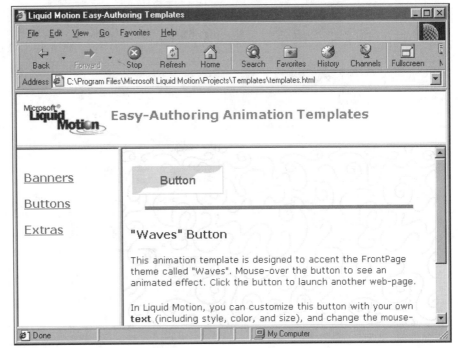

Figure 1.12

The Waves button displays a wave contour behind the word "Button."

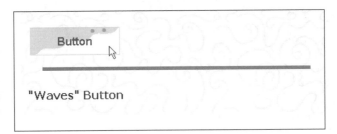

Figure 1.13

Passing the mouse over the Waves button causes some balls to roll down the contour of the wave.

The Valentine Extra Template

To preview the Valentine extra template, click the Extras link in the sidebar, and then click the Valentine link. You may need to scroll down a bit to see the animation (see Figure 1.16). When you pass the mouse over the package, a "Click me" call-out balloon is displayed (see Figure 1.17). When you click on the package, it opens and a beating heart rises from it (see Figure 1.18). If you click on the beating heart, it bursts open and displays the Valentine message, "(I love you!)" (see Figure 1.19).

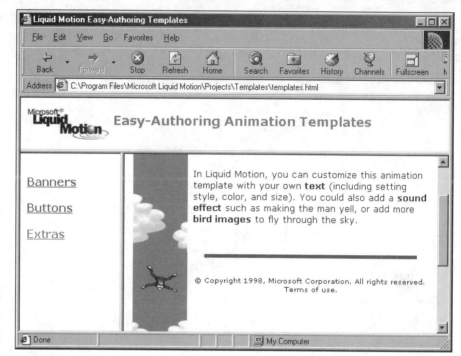

Figure 1.14

The Skydiver extra template displays a falling skydiver.

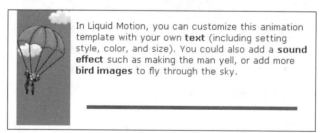

Figure 1.15

Clicking on the skydiver causes his parachute to deploy.

The Waves Extra Template

To preview the Waves extra template, click the Extras link in the sidebar, and then click the Waves link (see Figure 1.20). When you pass the mouse over the animation, the waves rise to the top of the animation (see Figure 1.21).

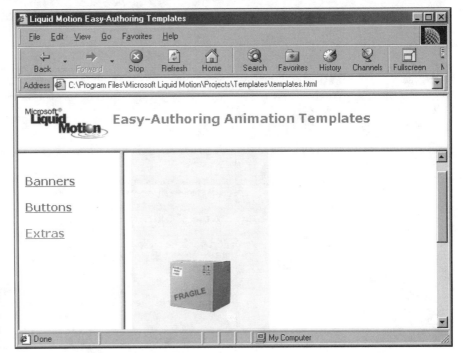

Figure 1.16

The Valentine extra template displays a surprise package.

Figure 1.17

When you pass the mouse over the package, a "Click me" call-out balloon is displayed.

Figure 1.19

Clicking on the beating heart causes it to display the Valentine message.

Figure 1.18

Clicking on the package causes a beating heart to rise from it.

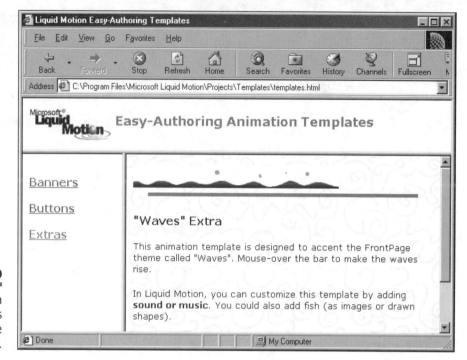

Figure 1.20

The Waves extra template displays some moving blue waves.

Figure 1.21

When you pass the mouse over the animation, the waves rise to the top of the animation.

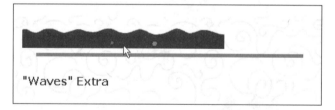

Previewing More Liquid Motion Animations

The rest of the Easy-Authoring Animation Templates are available for preview at the Liquid Motion Web site. To view them, open the Liquid Motion home page in your browser (**www.microsoft.com/liquidmotion/**), and then click "Downloads" in the sidebar menu. Scroll down the page, and then click on the Banner Templates, Button Templates, or Template Extras link.

Microsoft also has a gallery of Liquid Motion animations available online. To view it, open the Liquid Motion home page in your browser (**www .microsoft.com/liquidmotion/**), and then click the "Gallery" link in the sidebar menu.

You can also preview some sample animations included with Liquid Motion. In Internet Explorer, select File, Open, and Browse; in Netscape Navigator, select File, Open Page, and Choose File. Go to `C:\Program Files\Microsoft Liquid Motion\Samples\` and double-click on `samples_frame.html`.

You must purchase the licensed version of Liquid Motion to get access to the remaining Easy-Authoring Templates not included with the trial version. Three additional animation templates optimized for use with specific FrontPage 98 themes (although you don't need FrontPage 98 to make use of the templates) are available for download from Microsoft. To get them, just go to the Liquid Motion Web site at **www.microsoft.com/liquidmotion/** and click the Downloads option in the sidebar. Just click on the links to download the templates to your computer. They are included in self-extracting .exe files, so after downloading them, just use the Windows Run command to extract the templates to folders of your choosing. These templates are full HTML Web pages, so to see them in action, you should pull them up in your browser (open the HTML file that matches the name of the animation template).

ON THE CD-ROM

Check out the CD-ROM for a selection of sample Liquid Motion animations that you can easily customize for your own uses.

Wrapping Up

The next session will give you a quick rundown on the Liquid Motion user interface and then show you how to easily customize the Liquid Motion Easy-Authoring Templates with your own text messages. Get a good night's sleep, and I'll see you bright and early tomorrow!

Working with the Easy-Authoring Templates

- ✿ Using the Liquid Motion Interface
- ✿ Customizing the Easy-Authoring Templates
- ✿ Adding Your Own Text and Colors
- ✿ Changing Fonts and Adding Drop Shadows
- ✿ Playing, Previewing, and Saving Animations

The quickest and easiest way to get started creating Liquid Motion animations is to learn to customize the Easy-Authoring Templates, replacing their boilerplate text with your own, as well as changing a font here, a color there, and so on. This morning, you'll have a brief overview of Liquid Motion's user interface, and then you'll begin to edit the Easy-Authoring Templates.

As you do the examples in the following sessions, you'll become quite familiar with Liquid Motion's user interface. For starters, however, it is helpful to go over the basics. First, run Liquid Motion:

✿ Click the Start button, then click Programs, Microsoft Liquid Motion, and Microsoft Liquid Motion again.

OR

✿ Double-click the Microsoft Liquid Motion shortcut icon on the Desktop.

With Liquid Motion's Getting Started window displayed, do the following:

1. The Open an Easy-Authoring Template radio button should be selected. Click the OK button.

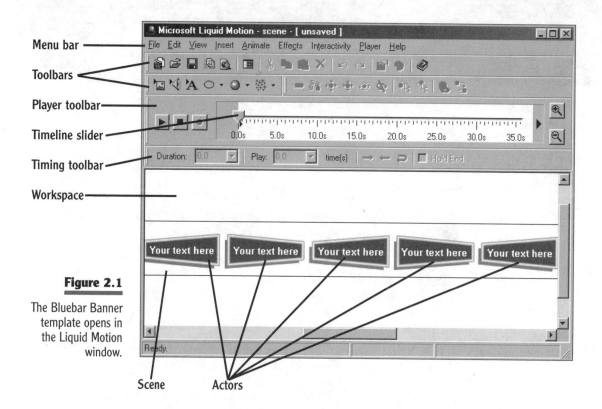

Menu bar

Toolbars

Player toolbar

Timeline slider

Timing toolbar

Workspace

Figure 2.1

The Bluebar Banner
template opens in
the Liquid Motion
window.

Scene   Actors

2. Double-click the Banners folder, double-click the bluebar folder,
   and then double-click navbar.jcz. The Bluebar Banner template is
   shown in the Liquid Motion window (see Figure 2.1).

The Liquid Motion Model

In Liquid Motion, you create an animation by inserting actors into a
scene and assigning behaviors to those actors. An actor (also called an
object) can be an image, text, a 2-D or 3-D shape, or an audio clip. A
behavior might be shrinking, growing, spinning, rotating, color animation, and motion. Additionally, you can assign properties to scenes, actors,
and behaviors, such as background and foreground colors, timing effects,
and sizes.

NOTE Actors are objects, such as images, text, audio clips, and shapes, to which behaviors, such as shrinking, growing, spinning, and motion, can be assigned. Both actors and behaviors are objects to which properties, such as color, size, duration, and start time, can be assigned.

Using the Menu Bar

The Liquid Motion menu bar is quite similar to those in other Windows programs. Here's a brief rundown of some of the features located on the menu bar:

- ⚙ **File:** Perform file operations, such as starting, opening, or saving an animation. You can also preview or publish an animation.

- ⚙ **Edit:** Perform edit operations, such as undo, redo, cut, copy, paste, and delete. Creating new objects by copying and pasting previous animation actors or behaviors can save you time. Additionally, you can bring an animation object to the foreground so it shows in the scene in front of other animation objects. You can also choose to focus on an inner scene, so that it is brought to the foreground to allow easier editing.

- ⚙ **View:** Toggle the display of toolbars, structure view, the status bar, auto-preview, and motion points. You can also refresh any updated media (after hopping out to edit an image in your graphics editor, for instance).

- ⚙ **Insert:** Insert an actor (image, audio, text, drawing, 2-D/3-D shape, and AutoEffect). You can also insert an inner scene and import a Liquid Motion animation.

- ⚙ **Animate:** Record motions and animate colors. Select Jump, Shrink, Grow, Spin, and Rotate 3-D behaviors.

- ⚙ **Effects:** Control 3-D Light, Filters, and Transitions.

- ⚙ **Interactivity:** Set URL (hypertext) links and interactive triggers.

⚙ **Player:** Play, pause, and stop an animation, as well as step forward or back.

⚙ **Help:** Access the Liquid Motion help system, including a user's guide, tutorials, how-to's, Q & A's, and more. You can also view the sample animations, the Easy-Authoring Templates, and an index of available clip art.

Using the Toolbars

You can see three toolbars in two rows just below the menu bar. These are the *Standard, Object,* and *Behavior* toolbars (see Figure 2.2).

NOTE When you first open a Liquid Motion animation, many of the toolbar buttons are grayed out. To see all the toolbar buttons, click on any of the button objects in the animation.

⚙ **Standard toolbar:** The Standard toolbar is the top toolbar, just below the menu bar. It is composed of tools that allow you to start, open, save, publish, and preview an animation; toggle the structure view on and off; cut, copy, paste, and delete; undo and redo; edit properties; access the color palette; and get help.

⚙ **The Object toolbar:** The Object toolbar is composed of the first six tools in the second row just below the menu bar. It allows you to insert an image, an audio clip, text, a 2-D shape, a 3-D shape, and an AutoEffect.

⚙ **The Behavior toolbar:** The Behavior toolbar is composed of the last ten tools in the second row below the menu bar. It allows you to attach to an object a behavior such as color animation, jumping, growing, shrinking, spinning, rotating, avoiding, following, a URL link, and an event trigger.

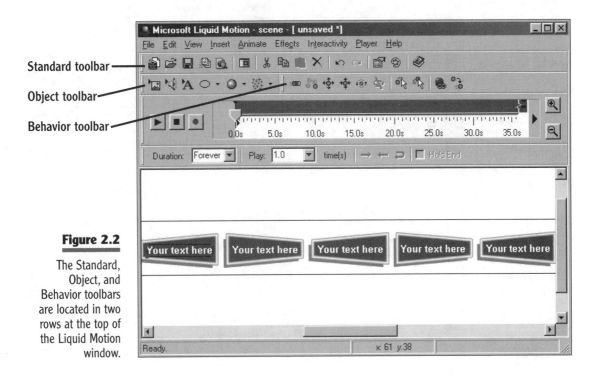

Figure 2.2

The Standard, Object, and Behavior toolbars are located in two rows at the top of the Liquid Motion window.

The Player toolbar is composed of three tools located on the left of and below the Behavior toolbar. These tools are used to play an animation, stop an animation, and record a motion path (see Figure 2.3).

Using the Timeline Slider

The Timeline slider is located to the right of the Player toolbar. It displays the timeline of an animation, as well as the start and end of an animation object (actor or behavior). The Timeline slider can also be used to set the start and end of an animation event (see Figure 2.3).

The Slider Button is located at the start of the Timeline when you first open an animation. When you play an animation, it moves from the left to the right, showing you the progress of the animation, from start to finish. It also displays the elapsed time in a small box to the right of the Slider Button while the animation plays.

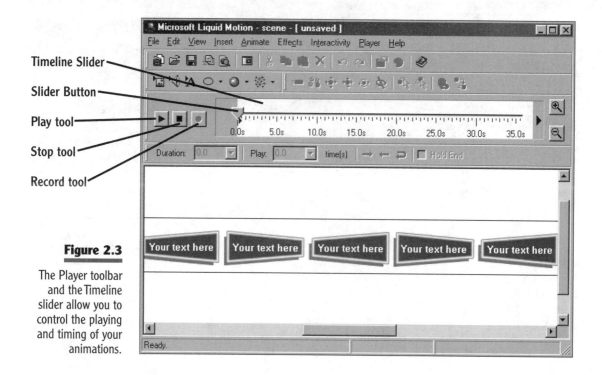

Timeline Slider

Slider Button

Play tool

Stop tool

Record tool

Figure 2.3

The Player toolbar and the Timeline slider allow you to control the playing and timing of your animations.

 When you play an animation, the Record tool on the Player toolbar changes into the Pause tool. For instance, go ahead and click the Play tool, let the animation play for a few seconds, then click the same tool (now the Pause tool). The animation and Slider Button pause.

Now, click on the Slider Button to select it (you'll see it outlined by a box). With the Slider Button selected, you can now use the left and right cursor keys on your keyboard to step backward or forward through the animation. You won't see any change in the animation scene, but in other animations with objects using more of the timing controls, you may see actors or behaviors turn on or off at different points along the Timeline as you step forward or backward through the animation.

You can also use your mouse to move the Slider Button to a new location on the Timeline. For instance, you could slide the Slider Button to a point midway along the Timeline, and then click the Play button to play just the second half of the animation. You can also use this feature to insert an actor or behavior that you want to start playing at a certain point in an animation.

To return the Slider Button to the start of the Timeline, just click the Stop tool on the Player toolbar.

Using the Timing Toolbar

The Timing toolbar is located directly below the Player toolbar and the Timeline Slider. As its name implies, it allows you to control the timing and visibility of an actor or behavior on the Timeline and set the duration, number of times, and direction that an animation will play. Click the mouse on the lower-left edge of the first button shape—you want to select the shape, but not the text (see Figure 2.4).

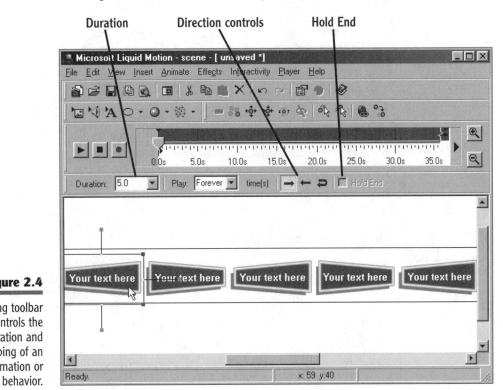

Figure 2.4

The Timing toolbar controls the duration and looping of an animation or behavior.

The Duration Control

The Duration control allows you to select or type in a duration for an object. In Figure 2.4 (and on your screen), the selected object is set to play for a duration of five seconds. By clicking the pull-down handle for the Duration control, you can select from a list of time durations, or you can type a duration directly in the Duration box (such as 2.5 to set the duration to two and a half seconds).

The Play Control

The Play control allows you to select or type in the number of times you want an object to play in an animation. In Figure 2.4 (and on your screen), the selected object is set to repeat playing forever (or until the end of the animation). By clicking the pull-down handle for the Play control, you can select from a list of play times or type the number of play times for the object directly in the Play box.

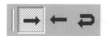

Direction Arrows

The Direction arrows control the direction in which an object plays. These are the three arrow tools located just to the right of the Play control (the Play Forward, Play Backward, and Play Forward then Backward tools). You can use these controls to cause an object to play forward or backward. By clicking the Play Forward or Play Backward tool in combination with the Play Forward then Backward tool, you can cause an object to play either forward and backward or backward and forward.

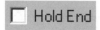

Hold End Check Box

The Hold End check box is only available if the number of Play times is set to a value other than "Forever." Right now, it is grayed out. (If you want to see what it looks like when active, just click the pull-down handle for the Play control and select one of the number values. Change it back to "Forever" when you're through.) This check box is used to control whether an object (actor or behavior) remains visible or disappears at the end of its duration. For instance, if you set a discrete duration (not "Forever") for an actor and select the Hold End check box, the "end state" of the selected object will remain visible at the end of the duration, but any behaviors assigned to the actor will stop playing. If the Hold End check box is selected for a growth behavior, the affected actor remains visible at its increased size at the end of the growth behavior's duration. If the Hold End check box is not selected, the affected object snaps back to its original size at the end of the growth behavior.

Using the Structure View

Although you can add actors and assign behaviors entirely within the Liquid Motion workspace view, using Liquid Motion's structure view can make it a lot easier to see what you are doing. Most instructions in this book involve using the structure view. To turn on the structure view, click the Structure View tool on the Standard toolbar (or select View and Structure View on the menu bar; see Figure 2.5).

Structure view

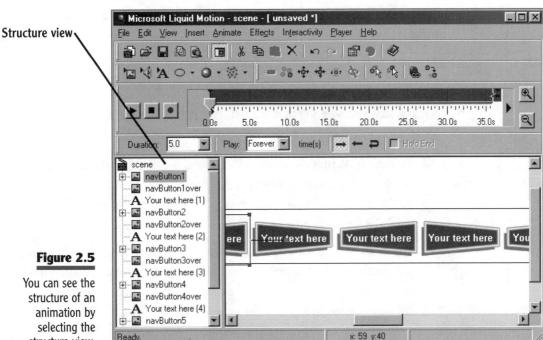

Figure 2.5

You can see the structure of an animation by selecting the structure view.

NOTE With the structure view turned on, the display of animations in the scene window may be cropped, as is the case here with the Blue Bar banner animation. Feel free to redimension or maximize the Liquid Motion window to make all or more of an animation visible in the workspace view. You can use the horizontal or vertical scroll bars to move down and up or to the left or right in the workspace view. You can also grab the divider between the structure view window and the Workspace view with the mouse and drag it to the left or right to adjust their relative sizes.

You'll notice that the items listed in the structure view are presented in a tree hierarchy. The top item represents the entire "scene," under which are arrayed the different actors that are included in the scene. If you click the "+" boxes to the left of any of the actors, you'll see the behaviors that are assigned to them.

The different actors can be identified by means of their icons, which are the same as those displayed on the Object toolbar. In the structure view of the Bluebar banner animation, three different object types are represented by these icons: the Insert Image, Insert Text, and Insert Audio icons.

The behaviors listed in the structure view can also be identified by their icons, which are the same as are shown in the Behavior toolbar.

Since you'll spend a lot of time using this feature, it's worthwhile to take some time to cover the basics of working in the structure view:

🟊 **Selecting Actors.** You can select any actor listed in the structure view by clicking on it. When you select an actor in the structure view, you'll also see the object selected in the workspace view. (For instance, click the "navbutton2" actor in the structure view to select it.)

🟊 **Expanding and Collapsing Behavior Lists.** Right now, only actors are displayed in the structure view. If any behaviors are assigned to an actor, you'll see a "+" box to the left of the actor. To expand the list of assigned behaviors for any actor, just click the "+" box. When

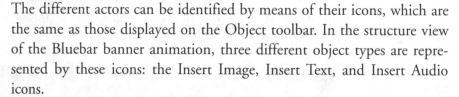

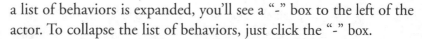

a list of behaviors is expanded, you'll see a "-" box to the left of the actor. To collapse the list of behaviors, just click the "-" box.

✿ **Selecting Behaviors.** Once you expand a list of behaviors, you can select any behavior in it by clicking on it. When you select a behavior in the structure view, you'll see the behavior's icon displayed at the upper-right corner of the object to which it is assigned.

✿ **Editing Object Properties.** Actors and behaviors have properties defined for them that you can edit. There are two ways to edit the properties of an object in the structure view. The first is to simply double-click the object you want to edit. The second is to right-click the object you want to edit, then select Properties. Alternatively, you can also double-click or right-click an actor that is not overlapped by other actors in the workspace view (or press Ctrl+F to bring an actor to the front, and then double-click it), or you can double-click or right-click the behavior icon displayed next to a selected behavior's actor.

✿ **Cutting, Copying, Pasting, and Deleting Objects.** It is often useful to cut, copy, paste, or delete an object in the structure view. For instance, you might want to move an actor from one position to another position in the structure view, make copies of an actor (and its assigned behaviors), or copy a behavior from one actor to another actor. To cut or copy a selected object to the Clipboard, select it and press Ctrl+X or Ctrl+C. To paste an object you cut or copied from the Clipboard, select an object and press Ctrl+V. If you paste in an actor, it will be inserted following the currently selected actor. If you paste in a behavior, it will be inserted at the end of the listed behaviors for a selected actor or it will be inserted immediately following a selected behavior. To delete an object, select it and press the Delete key. You can also cut, copy, paste, or delete an object by right-clicking on the object and selecting Cut, Copy, Paste, or Delete.

NOTE You can also drag and drop actors and behaviors in the structure view list. Just click and hold the mouse button on the object, drag it to its new position, and then lift off the mouse button. The only trouble with doing this is that it takes some practice to learn how to get the object to drop exactly where you want it, instead of falling one object up or down.

The order in which actors are displayed in the structure view determines the precedence they have in the animation scene. The second actor in the list is displayed in front of the first, the third in front of the second, and so on. It is important to understand that the position of an actor in the structure view doesn't determine the sequence in which an actor will play in the animation. An actor at the top of the structure view list can play at the end of the animation, and an actor at the bottom can play at the start. However, if you want one actor to be displayed in front of another actor in the animation scene, the first actor needs to follow the second in the structure view list. For behaviors, on the other hand, it doesn't matter in which order they are listed under their respective actors.

Editing the Bluebar Banner

You can edit any of the actors or behaviors in the Bluebar banner template, but to keep things simple starting out, you'll learn how to replace the boilerplate text ("Your text here") with some text of your own. Because the Bluebar banner is also a navigation bar, I'll show you how to substitute your own URLs (Web addresses) as well.

Adding Text

Just to get the hang of substituting your own text, replace the boilerplate text ("Your text here") with "Page 1," "Page 2," "Page 3," and so on.

To add your own text to the first button, follow these steps:

1. First, if the first button in the animation scene isn't displayed inside the workspace view, use the horizontal scroll bar to reposition the first button so that it is visible within the workspace view.

2. To edit the text for the first button, double-click the "Your text here (1)" actor in the structure view (or use any of the other methods described previously; see Figure 2.6).

NOTE Text actors are listed using whatever name is assigned to them, which can be different in every case. You can identify a text actor in the structure view by the Insert Text icon, a large capital A.

3. Replace the text, "Your text here," with text of your choosing. For instance, type **Page 1** as your text. Since "Page 1" takes up less space than "Your text here," increase the Size from 10 to 12 points.

NOTE Feel free to come back later and experiment with changing the other text properties. You could do such things as select a different font, color the text or the background, or add a drop shadow.

Leave everything else as it is. Click the Close button (the "⊠" button in the window's upper-right corner) to close the Edit window (see Figure 2.7).

Figure 2.6

In the Edit window for text actors, you can type text and specify its properties.

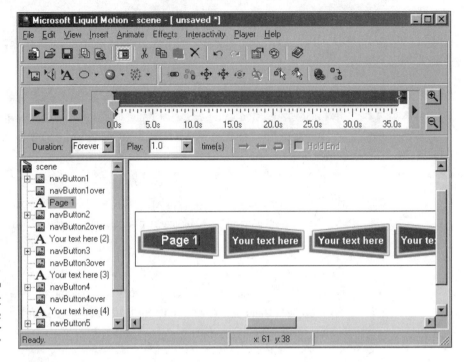

Figure 2.7

The text in the first
button in the
Bluebar banner
changes to "Page 1."

Follow the steps shown in the previous section to edit the remaining five buttons in the Bluebar banner. Just double-click each of the text actors in the structure view ("Your text here (2)," Your text here (3)," and so on), or you can double-click the actual text in the workspace. Replace "Your text here" in each instance with "Page 2," "Page 3," and so on, increasing the font size in each case to 12 points. When you are done, your new Bluebar banner should look like what is shown in Figure 2.8.

Adding URLs

The Bluebar banner has URLs (Web addresses) assigned to the buttons. Once you publish your animation and open it in a Web browser, you jump to the corresponding URL by clicking on a button.

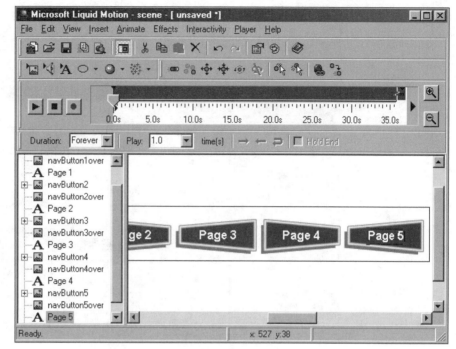

Figure 2.8

The Bluebar banner buttons now read "Page 1," "Page 2," and so on, up to "Page 5" in the last button.

I'll cover this in more depth when you get around to doing interactive animations in the Sunday morning session. For this session, it is pretty simple. To add your own URLs, follow these steps:

1. Scroll back to the top of the structure view and click the "+" box to the left of "navButton1" (see Figure 2.9).

2. Double-click the "URL Link" behavior under the "navButton1" actor. The Edit URL Link window is displayed.

NOTE

Behaviors are listed using whatever name is assigned to them, which can be different in every case. You can identify a URL link behavior in the Structure View by the URL Link icon. (A little later in this exercise, you'll run into a URL link behavior that doesn't use "URL Link" as its name.)

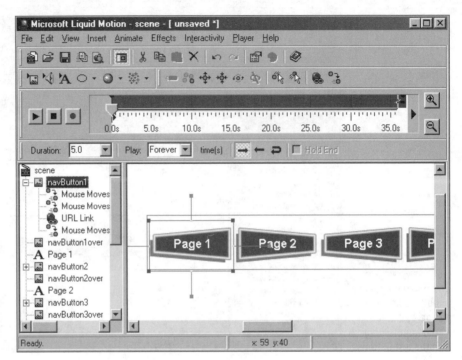

Figure 2.9

The list of behaviors
for the navButton1
actor expands.

3. In the URL text box, delete the URL (http://www.microsoft.com/...)
   that is there and type **page1.html** in its place (see Figure 2.10).
   Click the Close button to close the window.

NOTE

What you're doing here is substituting what is called a "relative URL" (**page1.html**) for
an "absolute URL" (**http://www.microsoft.com/...**). By just including the file name,
page1.html, here, you indicate that the file will be found in the same folder as your animation file (in the folder where your animation is published, which you'll get around to
doing a little further on in this section). If, on the other hand, you were to substitute a
URL such as subpages/page1.html, that would indicate that the linked file is in the subpages folder inside of the animation's publish folder.

You could also just as easily substitute another absolute URL here (such as the URL to
the Web site for this book, **http://www.callihan.com/liquidmotion/**)

Figure 2.10

In the Edit URL
Link window,
page1.html is
inserted as the URL.

4. Repeat steps 2 and 3 for "navButton2," "navButton3," "navButton4," and "navButton5," substituting **page2.html**, **page3.html**, **page4.html**, and **page5.html** as the URLs. (For the "navButton4" actor, see the following note.)

NOTE You won't find a "URL Link" behavior listed under the "navButton4" actor. Instead, the behavior you want to edit is listed as "http://www.microsoft.com/liquidmotion/." Just double-click it, instead of "URL link," to substitute your own URL (page4.html).

If you want to edit this behavior so it matches the other URL Link behaviors you are editing, just click the Detail tab in the properties window and then type URL Link in the URL Link box in place of the Liquid Motion URL. Click the Close button.

TIP When editing the properties for an object, you don't have to open and close the Edit window for each one. When you finish editing the properties for one object, just click a second object to edit its properties, then click a third object, and so on.

If your screen resolution is large enough (1024 x 768, for instance), so the Edit window won't obscure the animation scene, you can leave it open all the time to make editing object properties a snap.

Playing Your Animation

Do you want to test the changes you made to the BlueBar banner animation? Hey, you can't tell if something will work until you play it:

1. If you can't see all of the animation in the workspace view, click the Structure View tool to turn off the structure view (or you can redimension or maximize the Liquid Motion window).

2. To play the animation, just click the Play tool on the Player toolbar.

3. With the animation playing (the Slider button moves from left to right on the Timeline slider), move the mouse over any of the buttons. The color of the button's border should change to red, and you should hear an audible click (see Figure 2.11).

4. To stop playing the animation, click the Stop tool.

NOTE   Even if you inserted some real URLs for your buttons, you can't check them out when you play the animation in Liquid Motion. To check out a URL link that you assigned to an actor, you need to preview your animation in your browser.

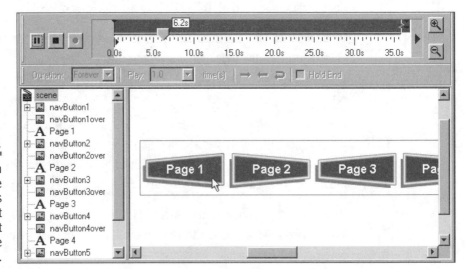

Figure 2.11

When you play an animation, the Slider button moves from left to right and you can test the behavior of the animation.

Previewing Your Animation

Once you edit and play your animation, you want to preview it in your browser, right? Of course you do. Previewing your animation for the first time is actually a three-step process. First you're prompted to save your animation, and then you're walked through publishing your animation, before you actually preview your animation in your browser. Don't worry, it's a lot easier than it sounds.

 To preview your animation, click the Preview in Browser tool on the Standard toolbar.

The first time you preview your animation, you're prompted to save it in Liquid Motion's Projects folder. Type **Bluebar_banner** as the new file name, and then click Save.

Publishing Your Animation

After you save your animation, the Publish Wizard comes up to walk you through the steps of publishing your animation. The Publish Wizard's first window has three options that allow you to publish your animation to your local disk (the default), an FTP server on the Web, or a FrontPage 98 web.

 NOTE I discuss using the second two options later in this book. For information on publishing to an FTP server (transferring your Web pages to a Web server using FTP), see Appendix C, "Placing Your Animation Files on the Web." For information on publishing to a FrontPage 98 web, see Appendix B, "Using Liquid Motion Animations with FrontPage 98."

To publish your animation, follow these steps:

1. Click Next to publish to your local disk.

2. The next window of the Publish Wizard prompts you for the folder where you want to publish your animation. By default, Liquid Motion publishes an animation to a folder based on the animation's name that it creates within its publish folder. Although you can't see

the whole folder path in the input box, you can click the mouse in
the box and use the right cursor key to see the whole path
(C:\Program Files\Microsoft Liquid Motion\publish
\Bluebar_banner\).

NOTE You're not limited to publishing only to the folder Liquid Motion suggests. You can change
the folder name for the animation (to Bluebar_banner2) or use the Browse button and
select a base folder other than Liquid Motion's publish folder. If you want to publish your
animation in a \Bluebar_banner folder (that you haven't created yet) inside of a
C:\pages\ folder (that you have created), click the Browse button and select the
C:\pages\ folder. Type **Bluebar_banner** at the end of the input box to publish your
animation to the C:\pages\Bluebar_banner\ folder.

3. Click Next to accept the suggested publish location (C:\Program
    Files\Microsoft Liquid Motion\publish\Bluebar_banner\).

4. The next window of the Publish Wizard prompts you for the name
    of your animation's HTML file.

NOTE You can also select a background color for your animation's HTML file at this point. For
instance, you might want to choose black as the background color for your Web page,
rather than the default white. You can also edit the HTML file later and insert the code for
a background color in the BODY tag, or you can insert the code for a background image.
I cover using background colors or images in your animations' Web page files in more
detail in the Sunday Evening session, "Using Liquid Motion Animations with Web Pages."

5. Click Next to accept the suggested HTML file name
    (Bluebar_banner.html).

6. The next window of the Publish Wizard allows you to specify a
    splash image for your animation. A splash image is displayed while
    your animation downloads, so a viewer of your animation won't be
    left staring at nothing until your animation is completely down-

loaded. You might specify a splash image that would display the words, "Please wait," for instance. The default when you first publish an animation is to not include a splash image.

NOTE There are also a couple radio button options you can select in this window. In most cases, you should just leave the first radio button (<u>N</u>o other animated elements) selected. However, if you're planning on publishing more than one animation to the same Web page, selecting the second radio button (<u>O</u>ther animated elements...) will reduce the frame rate for your animation (putting less of a stress on the host system). You might also want to consider selecting this second radio button option if your animation is a particularly large or complicated animation.

7. To not include a splash image and finish publishing your animation, click Finish.

TIP You followed the steps in the Publish Wizard so you'd be familiar with the different options it presents. However, if you don't plan on changing any of the suggested or default options, you can just click Finish at the first Publish Wizard window (or at any subsequent window in the wizard).

Previewing Your Animation in Your Browser

Your animation should now be displayed in your Web browser. Figure 2.12 shows how it should look when displayed in Internet Explorer.

Go ahead and check out the animation, passing the mouse over the buttons. Because page1.html, page2.html, and so on don't actually exist, you can't check out the URL links assigned to the buttons. If you are at all familiar with HTML, however, you could easily create these files—just save them in the same folder as your animation.

The Publish Wizard only comes up the first time you preview an animation. Unless you save and reopen your animation file, when you subsequently

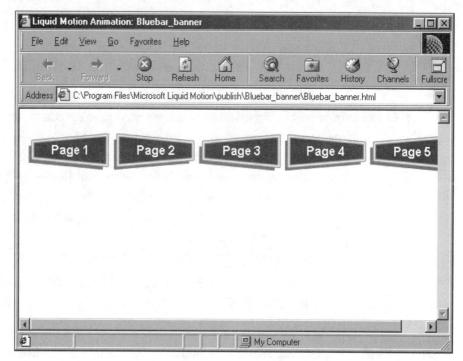

Figure 2.12

The Bluebar banner
in Internet Explorer.

click the Preview in Browser tool, your animation will be directly opened and displayed in your browser, without going through the Publish Wizard.

NOTE You can also use the Publish tool to publish an animation. It works exactly the same as the Preview in Browser tool, except it won't display the animation in your browser. However, if you previewed your animation and it is still displayed in your browser, you can just click the Publish tool and then hop out to your browser and click the Refresh (or Reload) button to see any changes to your animation. This can be especially handy where your animation is displayed inside a window of a frame page (see the Sunday Evening session, "Using Liquid Motion Animations in Web Pages" for a more detailed discussion of this).

Hooray! You created your first Liquid Motion animation. You could include the Bluebar_banner animation in any other Web page you want to create (see the Friday Evening session, "Using Liquid Motion

Animations in Web Pages"), or you could edit Blue_banner.html and add additional HTML codes, text, or images.

TIP After you publish a Liquid Motion animation to your local drive, you can use an FTP program such as WS-FTP to transfer your animation to your server on the Web or to another location on your local drive. In either case, you need to transfer or move your animation's entire folder, including all its subfolders.

NOTE If you are a FrontPage 98 user, when you select to publish your animation to a FrontPage 98 web, you can publish to either a local or remote FrontPage 98 web. For instance, you could first publish your animation to your local FrontPage web and then import it into a FrontPage Web page. Once you're through tweaking, you can then use FrontPage 98 to publish both your FrontPage Web page and your Liquid Motion animation up onto your remote FrontPage web (if your server has the FrontPage 98 server extensions installed).

Take a Break?

How about getting up and taking a stretch? If you skipped breakfast to get a head start, you might want to pour yourself a bowl of Cocoa Puffs and put a new pot of coffee on.

Editing the Letters Banner

The next Easy-Authoring Template is the Letters banner. This animation is a jumble of moving letters and numbers, a kind of animated alphabet soup. If you pass the mouse over the animation, some boilerplate text ("Your Text Here") grows from large to small from out of the other jumbled moving elements in the scene.

To open the Letters banner template, do one of the following:

✪ If you are still in Liquid Motion after editing the Bluebar banner animation, click the Open tool on the Standard toolbar, and then double-click the Templates folder.

✪ If you exited Liquid Motion, run Liquid Motion and click OK at the Getting Started window (the Open an Easy-Authoring Template radio button is already selected by default).

1. Double-click the Banners folder, and then double-click the Letters folder.

2. Double-click Letters.jcz to open it in Liquid Motion.

NOTE As long as you save your animation file to the Projects folder when you preview or publish an animation, clicking the Open tool later will take you back to that folder. However, if you should save your animation file somewhere else, clicking the Open tool later will take you back to that folder. If for any reason you should get lost there, you can find the Projects folder inside the Microsoft Liquid Motion folder, which is inside the Program Files folder.

Adding Text

The Letters banner template only has one text actor that you can edit. Go ahead and edit it to add your own text:

1. In the structure view, double-click "Your Text Here."

2. In the Edit window, substitute whatever text you want for "Your Text Here." For instance, type **I Love New York!** (Or change "New York" to your own home town or other locale; see Figure 2.13.) Click the Close button.

Figure 2.13

"I Love New York!" is substituted in the Edit window for "Your Text Here."

Playing Your Animation

The text actor you just edited is set so that it is triggered when you pass the mouse over the animation scene. (I'll explain more about using triggers later in the Sunday Morning session, "Creating Interactive Web Animations.") If you click the Play tool at this point, with the "Your_Text_Here" text actor selected, the text actor will play without you moving the mouse over the scene to trigger the action.

To play the animation without the selected text actor playing at the start, first click the "scene" actor and then click the Play tool. Alternatively, you can first click the Stop tool on the Player toolbar and then click the Play tool.

With the animation playing, move the mouse over the animation. You'll see the text you just added emerge and grow out of the jumble of moving letters and numbers in the animation (see Figure 2.14). To stop playing the animation, click the Stop tool.

Figure 2.14

When you play an animation, the Slider button moves from left to right and you can test the behavior of the animation.

Previewing Your Animation

To preview your animation for the first time:

1. Click the Preview in Browser tool on the Standard toolbar. Type **Letters_banner** as the new file name, and then click Save.

2. At the Publish Wizard's first window, click Finish to accept the default settings (your animation will be published as Letters_banner.html to the C:\Program Files\Microsoft Liquid Motion\publish\Letters_banner\ folder).

You should see your animation playing in your Web browser. Figure 2.15 shows the jumble of moving letters and numbers as they are displayed in Internet Explorer.

Go ahead and check out the animation. When you move the mouse over the animation, the text you added will emerge and grow out of the animation.

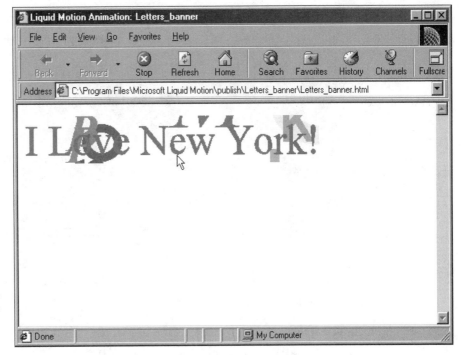

Figure 2.15

The Letters banner is displayed here in Internet Explorer.

Gussing Up the Letters Banner Animation

How about a black background for a really dramatic look? How about a bright red color for your emerging text, and a drop shadow? How about a different font face? Sometimes, making really dramatic changes to an animation can be done in a few fairly simple steps.

Back in Liquid Motion, do the following to assign a black background to the animation's scene:

1. At the top of the structure view, double-click the "scene" actor.

2. Click the Fill Color button and select the black color (bottom-left corner) in the Edit Colors window (see Figure 2.16). Click OK and then click the Close button.

The color of your text is controlled by a color animation behavior, which changes the color of the text gradually from black to white as it emerges

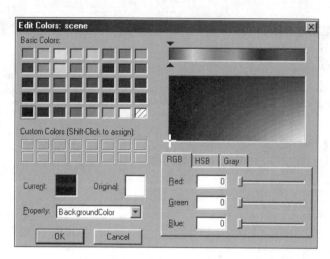

Figure 2.16

The black color
(bottom-left corner)
is selected in the
Edit Colors window
as the background
color for the
root scene of the
animation.

out of the animation scene. Follow these steps to have the text color gradually change from red to orange:

1. Click the "+" button to the left of the "Your_Text_Here" text actor to expand its list of assigned behaviors.

2. Double-click the "Cycle TextColor" color animation behavior.

3. Click the Initial button and select the bright red color (second color down in the first column) as the initial color. Click OK

4. Click the Final button and select the bright orange color (second color down in the second column) as the final color. Click OK.

5. Leave the Clockwise radio button selected. Click the Close button.

Next, change the font and style for your text and set a drop shadow:

1. Double-click the "Your_Text_Here" text actor again.

2. Click the Font control's pull-down handle and select Helvetica as the font. Click the Style control's pull-down handle and select Bold as the font. Leave the Size as it is.

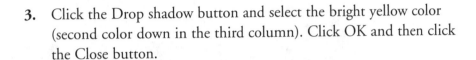

3. Click the Drop shadow button and select the bright yellow color (second color down in the third column). Click OK and then click the Close button.

NOTE You might think when you preview your animation again that it gets resaved to the Projects folder. While your animation does get republished to your animation's publish folder, the project file you saved when you first previewed your animation is not updated. If you exit Liquid Motion or open a new animation, you'll be prompted to save your unsaved changes, so there's little danger that you'll lose anything, unless of course you click No when prompted to save. Even if you do click No, you can always open your published animation file and edit it.

This feature allows you some free reign if you want to just experiment with an animation. If you don't like the result but can't figure out how to get back to where you started experimenting, just reopen your last saved project file (without saving your unsaved changes). When you get what you want, click Yes to save any unsaved changes when you exit Liquid Motion or open a new animation (or you can click the Save tool to resave your project file).

To play the animation, without playing the selected text actor at the start, first click the Stop tool and then click the Play tool. You'll see the jumble of moving letters and numbers moving against a black backdrop. If you move the mouse over the scene, your text will emerge out of the background in a different font face, all decked out in its new colors, and with a drop shadow added as well (see Figure 2.17).

If you want to see what the new animation looks like in your browser, click the Preview in Browser tool. Because you already previewed your animation, your animation comes up directly in your browser. To see your new text effect, just move the mouse over the animation scene.

Figure 2.17

The gussied up Letters banner animation plays with new text colors in front of a black background.

Editing the Waves Banner

The next Easy-Authoring Template is the Waves banner. This banner doesn't use any mouse effects, but among other animation effects, it uses a motion path to flow the text, "YOUR TEXT HERE," from the left to the center of the banner. In this exercise, you'll edit the animation to add your own text. To open the Waves banner template, do one of the following:

⚙ If you are still in Liquid Motion after editing the Letters banner animation, click the Open tool on the Standard toolbar, and then double-click the Templates folder.

⚙ If you've exited Liquid Motion, run Liquid Motion and click OK at the Getting Started window (the Open an Easy-Authoring Template radio button is already selected by default).

1. Double-click the Banners folder, and then double-click the wave folder.

2. Double-click wave02.jcz to open it in Liquid Motion.

Adding Your Text

To add your own text, follow these steps:

1. In the structure view, double-click "YOUR_TEXT_HERE."

2. In the Edit window, substitute whatever text you want for "YOUR TEXT HERE." For instance, you might type **Jane's Home Page!** (substituting your own name for "Jane").

3. While you're at it, change the Font to TimesRoman, the Style to Bold, and the Size to 24 (see Figure 2.18).

Coloring Your Text and Adding a Drop Shadow

To get a little fancier here, go ahead and change the color of your text and add a drop shadow:

1. While still in the Edit window for the text actor, click the Color button and select a color for your text (since the background object is dark blue, select a light color that'll contrast with it, such as the light violet pink color, the first color in the last column). Click OK.

Figure 2.18

"Jane's Home Page!" is substituted for "YOUR TEXT HERE," and the Font, Style, and Size settings are changed in the Edit window.

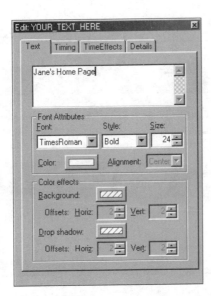

2. Click the Drop shadow button and select a color for your drop shadow (if you're at a loss, try the bright red color, second color down in the first column). Click OK. Click the Close button.

Playing Your Animation

The situation here is somewhat similar to the triggered text actor in the Letters banner animation, except here the text actor's start time is offset so that it doesn't start playing until 15 seconds into the animation. If you now click the Play tool, with the "YOUR_TEXT_HERE" text actor still selected, the animation starts playing at the point where the text actor starts (at 15.0 on the Timeline). This is a handy feature, because if an object starts playing part way through an animation, you don't want to have to play the animation from the very start just to check out that one part. If you do want to replay the animation from the start, just click the Stop tool first, then click the Play tool.

Go ahead and click the Play tool (without first clicking the Stop tool). You'll see your edited text immediately scroll into the animation scene, rather than waiting 15 seconds for it to appear (see Figure 2.19). To stop playing the animation, click the Stop tool.

Figure 2.19

The text, "Jane's Home Page," violet pink with a red drop shadow, after scrolling in from the left into the Wave banner animation scene.

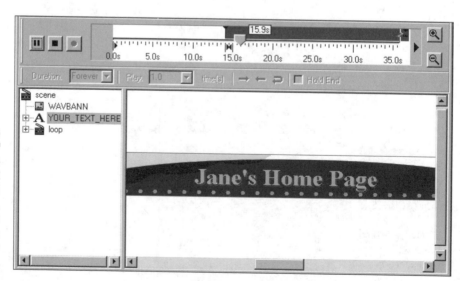

You should be pretty familiar with previewing an animation by now. Just click the Preview in Browser tool, save your project file, and then click the Finish button at the opening window of the Publish Wizard. If you saved your project file as Wave_banner, for instance, your animation will be published to C:\Program Files\Microsoft Liquid Motion\publish \Wave_banner\Wave_banner.html.

Wrapping Up

So far, you've edited three of the Easy-Authoring Templates included with Liquid Motion. You should now know how to do these things:

- Open an Easy-Authoring Template, both from the Getting Started menu and from within Liquid Motion.

- Edit the text in an animation, substituting your own text.

- Insert your own Web address in a URL link.

- Set the font, font style, and font size of text in an animation.

- Set the color of text in an animation.

- Add a drop shadow to text in an animation and assign a color to it.

- Set a background color in the scene.

- Change the colors in a color animation behavior.

- Play, preview, and publish an animation.

Feel free to go back and experiment with the animations you created, changing the text, font, font style, and font size settings. You can also play around with different text and drop-shadow colors. Try selecting an italic font, for instance, or define a background color for a text actor.

Go ahead and experiment with the remaining Easy-Authoring Templates, adding your own text and URLs. If you don't have the time for this, take a lunch break. I'll see you back here first thing this afternoon, when you'll create your first animation.

Creating Your First Web Animations

- ✪ Setting Scene Dimensions and Background Colors
- ✪ Inserting 2-D Shapes, AutoEffects, Text, and Images
- ✪ Using Shrinking, Spinning, Growing, and Motion Path Behaviors
- ✪ Color Animating Backgrounds, 2-D Shapes, and Text.

This morning you learned how to edit the Easy-Authoring Templates and add your own personalized text and color combinations. This afternoon, you'll create your first Web animation from scratch, and you can also try out the bonus animation if you have time before dinner.

Starting a New Animation

The animation example you'll follow is a "welcome" banner designed to run at the top of a Web page. It displays the words "WELCOME," "to," and "My Home Page" in sequence, along with a 2-D shape, an AutoEffect, and an image. The example introduces you to using many of the most useful animation effects, such as growing and shrinking, color animation, and motion paths.

To start your first animation:

1. If you exited Liquid Motion, click the Start button, then click Programs, Microsoft Liquid Motion, and then Microsoft Liquid Motion again.

    If you are still in Liquid Motion, click the New tool on the Standard toolbar (or select File, then New Animation.)

If you get the prompt, "Save this scene before closing it?," the animation currently open in Liquid Motion has changes in it that aren't saved to its project file. If you made changes to your current animation after previewing it in your browser, you should click Yes if you want to save those changes to your animation's project file. If you don't care to keep the changes, just click No."

2. At the Getting Started window, select the third radio button (Create a new animation), and then click OK.

3. If the structure view is not turned on, click the Structure View tool.

Setting the Background

You can set either a background color or image for your scene. For this example, set a purple-blue background color for the scene:

1. Double-click the "scene" actor in the structure view (or double-click inside the scene in the workspace view).

2. Click the Fill Color box. Select the purple-blue color, third down in the sixth column. Click OK. (Don't close the Edit window yet.)

Setting the Scene Dimensions

It is easy to reset the scene dimensions for your animation. If you want, you can just grab one of the red handles at the corners of the scene and pull it to a new position. That's not very exact, however, and Liquid Motion doesn't give you any feedback to tell you what your new dimensions are. To reset your scene dimensions exactly, do the following:

1. While still in the Edit window for the scene, click the Details tab.

2. In the bottom row, labeled Size, type **400** as the width and **75** as the height. Click the Close button in the upper-right corner.

NOTE Just to reiterate, there is no button labeled "Close" in Liquid Motion's window for editing the properties of actors and behaviors. The Close button referred to here and elsewhere in this book is the "x" button in the upper-right corner of the dialog window.

Setting the Duration and End State

The default duration for a Liquid Motion animation is 30 seconds. Reset that to 20 seconds and set the final frame of the animation to remain visible at the end of the animation:

1. On the Timing toolbar, change the Duration value to 20.0.

2. Click the Hold End check box so that it is checked (see Figure 3.1).

NOTE You may have noticed that when you selected the Hold End check box for the scene, the Timeline Slider display changed. The timeline scale (with the rule marks) extends beyond the 20-second mark. Also the top bar of the Timeline Slider (the duration bar) is solid green up to the 20-second mark, marking the duration of the scene, while it is filled with green and white lines after the 20-second mark, indicating that the selected object (the scene itself) holds its end state (remains visible) at the end of its duration.

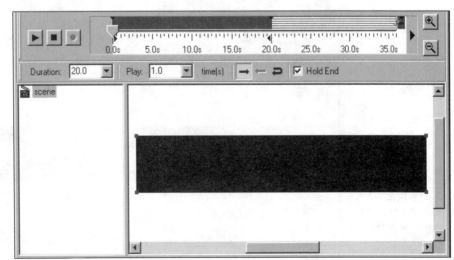

Figure 3.1

The background color, dimensions, duration, and end state are set for the animation.

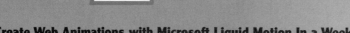

Working with the Colored Oval Shape

For the first effect, insert a 2-D shape and then set it to shrink to zero:

1. Click the pull-down handle of the Insert 2-D tool on the Object toolbar.

2. Click the oval shape (in the upper-left corner).

3. On the Timing toolbar, change the value in the Duration box to 3.0. Leave the Play amount as it is.

Change the color of the shape:

1. Double-click the "Oval" actor in the structure view (or double-click inside the oval shape in the workspace view)."

2. Click the Fill box and choose a color for the oval shape (try the violet color, second down in the seventh column). Click OK. Click the Close button (see Figure 3.2).

Shrink the oval from 500 percent to zero percent of its original size:

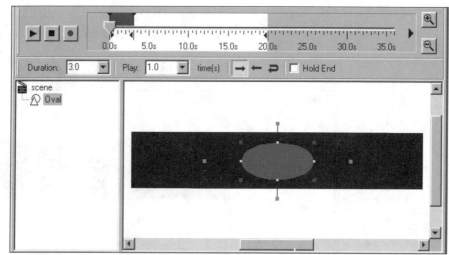

Figure 3.2

An oval shape is added with its color set to violet and its duration set to three seconds.

 1. With the oval shape still selected, click the Shrink tool on the Behavior toolbar. (A preview is played of the default Shrink action.)

2. Double-click the "Shrink" behavior in the structure view (or double-click the Shrink icon next to the upper-right corner of the oval shape in the workspace view).

3. In the Edit window, change the Initial value to 500, then change the Final value to 0 (you'll have to type this value, since 0.0 is not available from the pull-down list). Click the Close button (see Figure 3.3).

To play the animation, click the Play tool on the Player toolbar. You'll see the Oval shape shrink to nothing. To stop the playing of the animation, just click the Stop tool.

NOTE Because you set the initial size to 500 percent for the shrink behavior, you may not be able to see its outline in the workspace view. In this book you primarily use the structure view to design your animations, so you don't see everything in the workspace view. If you want to see the shrink behavior outline in the workspace view, feel free to redimension or maximize the Liquid Motion window.

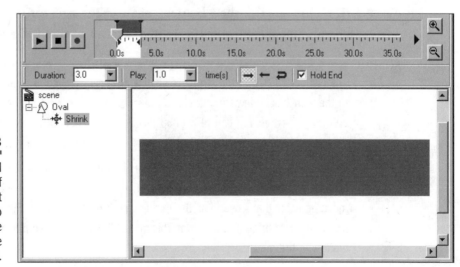

Figure 3.3

The initial preshrunk size of the oval shape is set to 500 percent, so that it fills the entire scene before beginning to shrink.

Adding Color-Animated Twirlers

Next, add an Autoeffect to spice up your animation:

1. Click the pull-down handle of the Insert AutoEffect tool.

2. Select Twirlers from the menu.

3. Click and hold the mouse down on one of the red corner handles of the AutoEffect, and then pull to expand it to fill most of the scene (see Figure 3.4).

4. On the Timing toolbar, click the mouse inside the Duration box, and type **19** as the value.

NOTE   The duration of the Twirlers effect is set to one second less than the duration of the scene. Since you want the end to remain visible, setting the Twirlers' duration to one second less will ensure that they aren't also visible at the end of the animation.

Setting the Gravity and Float Properties

To have the Twirlers float up and to the right in your animation, you need to set the Gravity and Float properties:

1. Double-click the "Twirlers" actor in the structure view (you can also double-click inside the Twirlers border in the workspace view).

TIP   The last actor listed in the structure view is always displayed in front of any other actors in the workspace view, so you can always just double-click it in the workspace view to edit its properties. You can also double-click on any part of an actor in the workspace view that is not overlapped by later actors listed in the structure view.

Where actors are overlapped by other actors in the workspace view, it is usually easier to edit their properties by double-clicking on them in the structure view. If you want to move an actor that's overlapped by others, click on the actor in the structure view and press Ctrl+F to bring it to the front. This makes the actor temporarily available to manipulate with the mouse.

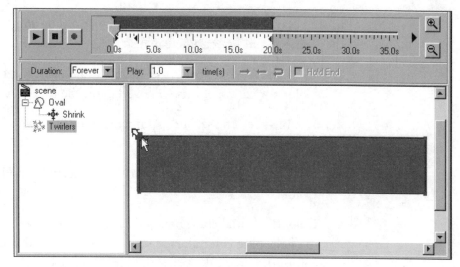

Figure 3.4

To activate the Twirlers throughout the scene, you need to resize the AutoEffect to fill most of the scene.

2. In the Edit window, move the Gravity slider up slightly (just a smidgen) toward Floats. Move the Wind slider slightly toward Right. Click the Close button.

To play the animation, click the Play tool. In addition to the Oval shape shrinkage, the Twirlers float up and to the right in the scene (see Figure 3.5). To stop the animation, just click the Stop tool.

Animating Colors

Your Twirlers are still a bit bland, displaying only in a single color. To animate the color of your Twirlers, do these things:

1. With the Twirlers AutoEffect selected, click the Animate Color tool on the Behaviors toolbar.

2. The color animation is set to only three seconds. On the Timing toolbar, click the mouse inside the Duration box and type **19** as the value.

Now when you play the animation, you should see the "glow" characteristic of the Twirlers change colors for 19 seconds. Click the Stop button to stop playing the animation. Besides color animating the Glow effect of the Twirlers AutoEffect, you can also color animate the Gleam effect:

1. Click the Animate color tool again. You'll be prompted that the two Color animation effects will overlap on the timeline. Just click OK.

2. Double-click the second "Animate Color" behavior in the structure view.

3. Click the pull-down handle for the Property list and select Gleam Color.

4. Click the Initial color box and select any color you want, other than the light blue color already set (try red, second down in the first column). Click OK. Click the Final color box and select the same color you selected for the Initial color. Click OK. Click the Close button.

5. On the Timing toolbar, click the mouse in the Duration box and type **19** as the value.

When you play the animation, you should see both the Glow and the Gleam colors animated using different color sequences.

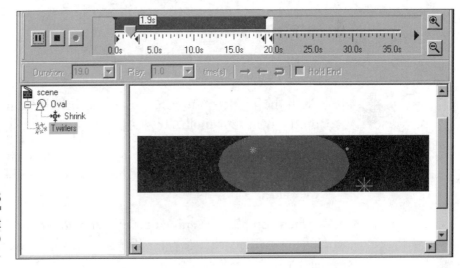

Figure 3.5

The Twirlers are set to float up and to the right.

NOTE Setting the two color animation's durations to 19 seconds causes them to cycle through the color spectrum only once. To make them cycle more than once, set a shorter duration (5.0, for instance), and set the number of Play times to forever. (The color animations won't actually play forever, however, since they'll be turned off when the Twirlers turn off after 19 seconds.)

Growing the "WELCOME" Text

Add the first text actor, the word "WELCOME" that grows out of the background of the animation once the 2-D oval shape has shrunk:

1. Click the Insert Text tool.

2. Backspace to delete the text ("Your text here") and type WELCOME to replace it.

3. In the Font box, select Helvetica. In the Style box, select Bold. In the Size box, type **48**.

4. Click the Color box and select a color for the text. (Try the lime-green color, second down in the fourth column.) Click OK.

5. Click the Drop Shadow box to add a drop shadow, and select a color for it. (Try the orange color, second down in the second column.) Click OK.

6. In both the Horiz and Vert boxes, change the settings to 4 to increase the horizontal and vertical offsets for the drop shadow to four pixels. Click the Close button (see Figure 3.6).

◆◆◆

CAUTION For the examples in this book, text actor names inserted in the structure view by Liquid Motion are called "Text," "Text (2)," "Text (3)," and so on. Liquid Motion may behave differently on some computers, however, and the text message may become the text actor name. When inserting a text actor, you may need to mentally substitute the text actor names Liquid Motion displays on your computer ("WELCOME," for instance) for the text actor names shown in this book. Just remember that "Text (2)" refers to the second text actor (marked with the "A" icon) listed in the structure view tree, and "Text (3)" refers to the third, and so on.

◆◆◆

Setting the Start Time and Duration

The "WELCOME" text now starts at the beginning of the animation and remains in the scene until it is finished. Go ahead and offset the text actor's start time so that it starts one second before the oval shape finishes shrinking and only remains in the scene for five seconds:

1. Double-click the "Text" actor in the structure view (or double-click within the borders of the actor in the workspace view).

2. Select the Timing tab in the Edit window.

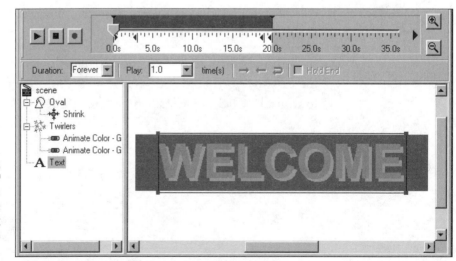

Figure 3.6

A 48-point green and orange "WELCOME" text actor is added to the scene.

3. At the bottom of the Edit window, delete the contents of the Offset box and type **2.0** to cause the "WELCOME" text to first appear two seconds after the animation starts. Click the Close button.

4. On the Timing toolbar, change the Duration value to 5.0.

Because you reset the start offset for your text actor so it no longer plays at the beginning of the scene, you can no longer see the text in the scene (because the Timeline Slider button is still at the start of the scene). You'll also notice that the dark green duration bar for the currently selected object (your text actor) now starts two seconds after the beginning of the scene.

Growing "WELCOME" out of the Background

To cause the "WELCOME" text to grow out of the background, you'll need to set a grow behavior to expand the "WELCOME" text from zero percent to 100 percent of its original size:

1. Click the Grow tool on the Behavior toolbar.

2. Double-click the "Grow" behavior in the structure view."

3. To set the text to grow from zero percent to 100 percent of its original size, type **0** for the Initial value and select **100** as the final value. Click the Close button.

To play the animation from the start (so you can see the grow behavior you just added play in context with the other actors and behaviors you defined), first click the Stop tool, then the Play tool.

Now when playing the animation from the start, one second before the 2-D oval shape finishes shrinking to nothing, the word "WELCOME" grows out of the background to fill most of the scene. Click the Stop tool to stop playing the animation.

Inserting an Image

You haven't inserted an image into an animation yet. Go ahead and do that now:

1. Click the Insert Image tool on the Objects toolbar.

2. In Liquid Motion's Image folder, double-click btn_flower2.gif to insert it into the animation scene.

3. On the Timing toolbar, select 10.0 as the Duration value. Leave the number of Play times set to 1.0.

4. Double-click the "btn_flower2" actor in the structure view, and then click the Timing tab. Select When Previous Ends as the Start value. Type **7.0** as the Offset value. Click the Close button.

Recording a Motion Path for the Image

Now, record a motion path for the image so that it will appear to move and float through the scene:

1. Click the Record Motion tool on the Player toolbar.

2. Click and hold down the mouse button on the center of the flower image, and then drag it around the scene to create the motion path. (Feel free to drag it in and out of the scene.) When finished creating the motion path, just release the mouse button to stop recording the motion (see Figure 3.7).

3. On the Timing toolbar, select a value of 5.0 in the Duration box. (This changes the duration of the motion path from three to five seconds.)

4. Click the Hold End check box so it is unchecked (you don't want the image to remain visible and stationary once the motion path completes.)

Shrinking and Growing the Image

A good way to give your animation even more of a three-dimensional look is to combine shrinking and growing with a motion path. The motion

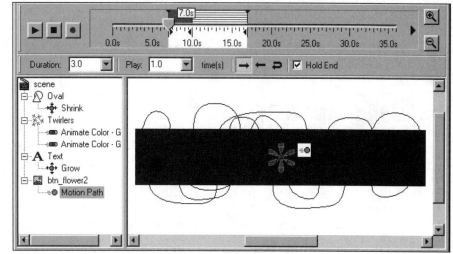

Figure 3.7

A motion path is recorded for the image, with its duration set to ten seconds.

path will seem to move within the space of the animation, rather than merely around the scene. To do this, you'll add a "two-way" shrinking behavior that'll cause the image to shrink into and then regrow out of the background as it follows the motion path:

1. With the "Motion Path" behavior still selected, click the Shrink tool on the Behavior toolbar.

2. On the Timing toolbar, select 5.0 as the Duration. Leave 1.0 set as the number of Play times.

3. Click the Play Forward and Backward arrow on the Timing toolbar to cause the image to shrink and then regrow.

NOTE You'll notice when you click the Play Forward and Backward arrow that the Duration of the behavior doubles. Keep this in mind when you set the duration of an object or behavior that you want to have play forward and backward. You'll also notice that the Play Forward arrow remains selected. If you select the Play Backward arrow in combination with the Play Forward and Backward arrow, the behavior plays backward and then forward.

When you play the animation and the "WELCOME" text disappears, the flower image appears, shrinking and then regrowing, as it moves through the scene.

Shrinking the "To" Text

For your next effect, add the second part of the text message for the animation (the "to" that comes between "WELCOME" and "My Home Page"):

1. Click the Insert Text tool.

2. Backspace to delete the text ("Your text here") and type **to**.

3. In the Font box, select Courier, just to give it a little bit of a different look. In the Style box, select Bold. In the Size box, type **48**.

4. Click the Color box and select a color for the text. (Try the blue color, second down in the sixth column.) Click OK.

5. Click the Drop Shadow box to add a drop shadow, and select a color for it. (Try the green color, third down in the fourth column.) Click OK.

6. In both the Horiz and Vert boxes, change the settings to 4 to increase the horizontal and vertical offsets for the drop shadow to four pixels. (Don't close the window yet.)

Setting the Duration and Start Time

Set the "to" text so that it starts one second before the previous text actor (the "WELCOME" text) disappears from the scene:

1. Select the Timing tab in the Edit window.

2. In the Offset box, type **6.0** to cause the "to" text to first appear one second before the previous text effect ends. Click the Close button.

3. On the Timing toolbar, change the Duration to 5.0.

Shrinking the "to" Text into the Background

You made the "WELCOME" text grow out of the background. Now make the "to" text shrink back into the background. To do this, you'll shrink the text from 200 percent of its original size to nothing:

1. Click the Shrink tool.

2. Double-click the "Shrink" behavior in the structure view (under the "Text (2)" actor).

3. To set the text to shrink from 200 percent of its original size, select 200.0 as the Initial value and type **0** as the Final value. Click the Close button (see Figure 3.8).

4. On the Timing toolbar, select 5.0 as the Duration value.

To play the animation from the start, first click the Stop tool, then click the Play tool. You'll see the "WELCOME" text grow out of the background and then disappear one second after the "to" text shrinks. Click the Stop button to stop playing the animation.

Inserting the "My Home Page" Text

For your next effect, add the third part of the text message for the animation, "My Home Page":

1. Click the Insert Text tool.

2. Backspace to delete the text ("Your text here") and type **My Home Page** to replace it.

3. Leave TimesRoman set as the Font, but select Bold for the Style and type **44** as the Size.

4. Click the Color box and select a color for the text. (Try the orange color, second down in the second column.) Click OK.

5. Click the Drop Shadow box to add a drop shadow, and select a color for it. (Try the brick red color, third down in the first column.) Click OK.

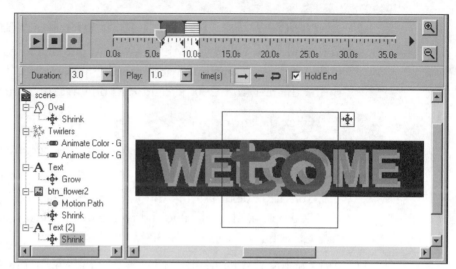

Figure 3.8

The "to" text shrinks from 200 percent of its original size.

6. Increase the horizontal and vertical offset values (Horiz and Vert) for the drop shadow to 4 to offset the drop shadow from the text by four pixels. (Don't close the window yet.)

Setting the Duration and Start Time

Set the "My Home Page" text so that it starts one second before the previous text actor (the "to" text) disappears from the scene:

1. Click the Timing tab in the Edit window.

2. Change the Start value to When Previous Ends.

3. Type **-1.0** as the Offset value. Click the Close button.

NOTE This is the first time you've set a negative Offset value for an object's start time. You can't use negative Offset values for objects with When Scene Plays set as the Start value, but you're free to do so with When Previous Starts, When Previous Ends, and When Triggered. You'll learn more about these on Sunday morning.

4. Change the Duration to 5.0 on the Timing toolbar. Click the Hold End check box to select it (since this is the last text actor you'll add, you want it to remain visible after it is through running).

Growing "My Home Page" out of the Background

Now cause the "My Home Page" text to grow out of the background from zero percent to 100 percent of its original size:

1. Click the Grow tool.

2. Double-click the "Grow" behavior you just added in the structure view.

3. Type **0** as the Initial value and select 100.0 as the Final value to cause the text to grow from nothing to 100% of its original size. Click the Close button.

4. On the Timing toolbar, set the Duration value to 5.0 so the duration of the grow behavior matches the "Text (3)" actor.

To play the animation from the start, click the Stop tool, then click the Play tool. Now when you play the animation, the text, "My Home Page," grows out of the background starting one second before the end of the previous text effect (see Figure 3.9). Click the Stop tool to stop playing the animation.

Animating the "My Home Page" Text Colors

Adding color animation to actors is a great way to give your animation some extra pizzazz. Go ahead and animate the colors of the "My Home Page" text actor:

1. With the last grow behavior still selected in the structure view, click the Animate Color tool.

2. On the Timing toolbar, type **2.5** as the Duration. Select 2.0 as the number of Play times.

3. Click the Animate Color tool again. At the prompt warning you about overlapping behaviors, click OK.

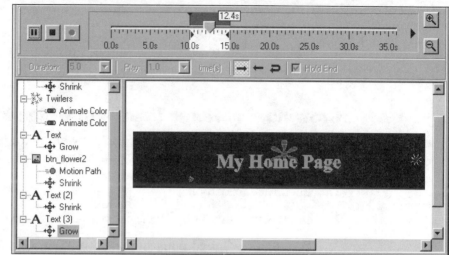

Figure 3.9

The "My Home Page" text is set to grow from zero percent to 100 percent of its original size.

4. Double-click the second "Animate Color" behavior (under the "Text (3)" actor).

5. In the Property box, select DropshadowColor.

6. Click the Initial box and select an initial color for animating the text actor's drop shadow (try the brick red color, third down in the first column). Click OK.

7. Click the Final box and then select the same color you chose for the Initial box. Click OK and Close.

8. On the Timing toolbar, type **2.5** as the Duration. Select 2.0 as the number of Play times.

Animating the Background Colors

For a final touch, animate the colors of the scene background and then set the color animation to play only for the last 10 seconds of the animation:

1. Click the "scene" actor at the top of the structure view.

2. Click the Animate Color tool. The animation plays a sample of the background color animation.

NOTE The Animate Color behavior you added is set to start playing at the ten-second mark of the animation. When you go back up the tree and insert an actor or behavior, it has the same start time as the last actor or behavior you inserted (determined by the current position of the Slider Button on the timeline). If the Slider Button isn't located at 10.0s on the timeline for the scene's color animation behavior, double-click the "Animate Color" actor, click the timing tab, and then type **10.0** as the Offset value.

3. Change the Duration value to 10.0 on the Timing toolbar.

Now when you play the animation, the background color for the scene as well as the colors for the third text effect are animated for the last ten seconds of the animation. Click the Stop tool to stop playing the animation.

Previewing Your First Animation

Now that you've finished your first Liquid Motion animation, preview it in your browser:

1. Click the Preview in Browser tool on the General toolbar.

2. Type **Welcome** as the file name of the animation, and then click Save.

3. At the Publish Wizard window, just click Finish to publish your animation to your local disk (your animation will be published to C:\Program Files\Microsoft Liquid Motion\publish\Welcome \Welcome.html). Your Web browser will run and play your Web animation (see Figure 3.10).

NOTE If your animation isn't automatically displayed in your Web browser after you choose to preview it, see Appendix A, "Installing Liquid Motion," for a discussion of browser configuration issues.

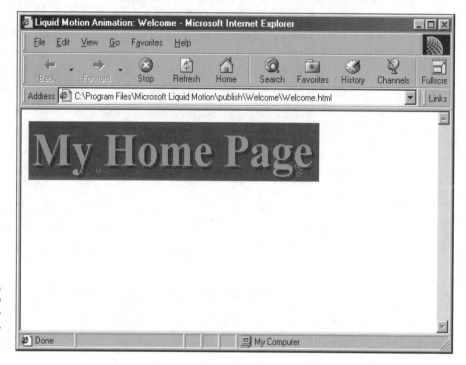

Figure 3.10

You can preview your animation in your browser at any time.

More Fun with Your Animation

You might try experimenting with some different color combinations for the scene background, text actors, and oval shape (I'm sure you can probably improve on some of the colors I chose). Also, you only added an Animate Color behavior to the last text actor—you could just as easily add the same behavior to the other text actors, or to the oval shape. Make sure, however, that you set different Initial and Final colors in the Animate Color behaviors, so you don't cycle through the same colors each time.

If you want to get really creative, you can try adding some additional 2-D shapes. For instance, to insert another 2-D shape following the oval shape:

1. Click the "Oval" actor in the structure view to highlight it.

2. Click the pull-down handle of the Insert 2-D tool to display the menu of 2-D shapes.

3. Select any of the 2-D shapes you want to use (the hexagon shape, for instance, which is the fifth one over in the second row).

4. Change the Duration from Forever to 6.0.

5. Double-click the 2-D shape actor you just added (the "Hexagon" actor, if you chose the hexagon shape) in the structure view and change its Start value to When Previous Ends. (This causes it to automatically start playing when the preceding "Oval" actor stops playing.) Click the Close button.

6. Click the Animate Color tool to animate your 2-D shape's color. Also change its Duration to 6.0.

7. Click the Grow tool. To cause your 2-D shape to both grow out of and then shrink back into the background, click the Play Forward then Backward arrow on the Timing toolbar. (You'll notice that the Duration has changed to 6.0.)

8. Double-click the "Grow" behavior you just added in the structure view and type **0** as the Initial size and select 500.0 as the Final size. Click the Close button.

9. To do something you haven't done yet, try spinning your 2-D shape. Just click the Spin tool on the Behaviors toolbar. Change its Duration to 6.0 to match your 2-D shape's duration.

NOTE A Spin behavior applied to a 2-D shape displays in any Java-capable Web browser (in both Navigator and Internet Explorer). Spin behaviors applied to text or image actors, however, can only be displayed in Internet Explorer 4.0 (or greater).

Now, if you click the Stop tool and then the Play tool to play the animation from the beginning, immediately after the oval shape shrinks into the background, the 2-D shape grows out of the background (behind the growing "WELCOME" text) with its colors animated. Click the Stop tool to stop playing the animation.

If you want, go ahead and edit the properties of your 2-D shape's "Animate Color" behavior, changing its Initial and Final colors. If you want the colors to cycle through the whole spectrum, you need to set the same color for both your Initial and Final color (and have the Full Circle radio button selected).

Take a Break?

The following animation is optional and the Saturday Evening session is filled with bonus projects, so if it's too late today to do any more, feel free to pack it up for now.

If, however, the afternoon is still young, and you're hot to keep on truckin', go ahead and grab a quick snack. Get some chips or pretzels, or throw a bag of popcorn in the microwave. I'll see you back in five or ten minutes, raring to go, for the rest of the Saturday Afternoon session.

Creating Your Second Web Animation

In this bonus example, you'll create an animation that functions primarily as a decorative element. It combines overlapping spinning 2-D star shapes with a throbbing button image to create a spinning and throbbing button animation. As with the first animation you created from scratch, this animation plays for only a set period of time, but its end state remains visible after it stops playing.

To start a new animation:

1. If you exited Liquid Motion, click the Start button, then click Programs, Microsoft Liquid Motion, and then Microsoft Liquid Motion again.

     If you are still in Liquid Motion, click the New tool on the Standard toolbar (or select File, then New Animation).

 If you get the prompt, "Save this scene before closing it?," you've made changes to your current animation that haven't yet been saved to its project file. If you want to save the changes, click Yes. If not, click No.

2. At the Getting Started window, select the third radio button (Create a new animation), and then click OK.

 3. If the structure view is not turned on, click the Structure View tool.

Adding an Eight-Pointed Star

Insert one of the 2-D shapes, the Eight-Pointed Star, into your animation:

1. Click the pull-down handle on the 2-D Shapes tool.

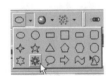 2. Click the Eight-Pointed Star shape, third down in the second column.

You may notice that the 2-D shape does not fit inside the scene. That's because the starting scene dimension is determined by the previous animation you created and saved (the Welcome animation). (If you do this example out of sequence, you will see different starting dimensions here.) For this example, resize the scene dimensions to match the dimensions of the eight-pointed star shape:

1. Double-click the "scene" actor in the structure view (or just double-click in the scene, but outside of the borders of the 2-D shape, in the workspace view).

2. Click the Resize to Contents button. Click the Close button (see Figure 3.11).

Animating the Eight-Pointed Star's Colors

For starters, go ahead and animate the colors of the star:

1. Click the "8 Point Star" actor in the structure view.

2. Click the Animate Colors tool.

3. Select Forever as the number of Play times on the Timing toolbar.

4. Double-click the "Animate Colors" behavior in the structure view.

5. Click the Initial box and change the color to red (second color down in the first column). Click OK.

6. Click the Final box and also change that color to red. Click OK. Click the Close button.

Shrinking (and Growing) the Eight-Pointed Star

This star shape falls behind the other actors in the animation. By assigning a two-way shrink behavior to it, you can cause it to shrink and grow from behind the actors you'll add later. Go ahead now and add a two-way shrink behavior to your eight-pointed star shape:

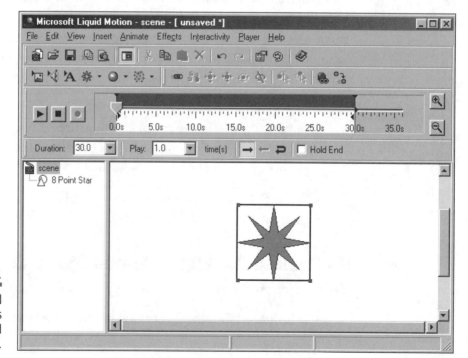

Figure 3.11

The scene is resized to fit the contents (the eight-pointed star shape).

1. Click the Shrink tool.

2. Change the number of Play times to Forever on the Timing toolbar.

3. Click the Play Forward then Backward tool on the Timing toolbar. (This causes the star shape to shrink into and emerge from the background. You'll notice that the Duration increases from 3.0 to 6.0.)

4. Double-click the "Shrink" behavior in the structure view.

5. Type **0** as the Final size. Click the Close button.

When you play the animation, you'll see the star's colors change continually as it shrinks back into and emerges out of the scene every six seconds. (Click the Stop tool to stop playing the animation.)

Spinning the Eight-Pointed Star

For your next effect, why don't you spin the star:

1. Click the Spin tool.

2. Double-click the "Spin" behavior in the structure view.

3. Select the Counterclockwise radio button to cause the star shape to spin in the opposite direction. Click the Close button.

Now, when you play the animation, the star will spin in a counterclockwise direction, in addition to changing colors while shrinking into and reemerging from the scene. (Click the Stop button to stop playing the animation.)

Adding a Four-Pointed Star

Now, add the 2-D shape, a four-pointed star, that'll play on top of the eight-pointed star, and set its start time so it'll wait one and a half seconds before starting to play:

1. Click the pull-down handle on the 2-D Shapes.

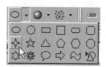

2. Click the four-pointed star shape, second down in the first column (see Figure 3.12).

3. Double-click the "4 Point Star" actor in the structure view.

4. Click the Timing tab and type **1.5** as the Offset value. Click the Close button.

NOTE

You'll notice that the four-pointed star disappears from the scene after you reset the Offset value. That's because the Slider Button is still positioned at the start of the animation, but the four-pointed star is not set to appear until 1.5 seconds after the start of the animation.

Animating the Four-Pointed Star's Colors

Go ahead and animate the colors of the four-pointed star:

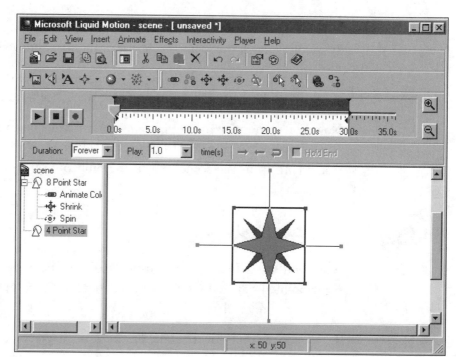

Figure 3.12

The four-pointed star shape on top of the eight-pointed star.

 1. Click the Animate Colors tool.

 NOTE You'll notice that the four-pointed star reappears in the workspace view, and the Slider Button automatically resets to 1.5 seconds. That's because a behavior or actor is automatically inserted at the point on the timeline indicated by the Slider Button. Whenever you offset the start time of an actor, the Slider Button remains at its new position, unless you do something to reset its position (such as clicking the Stop tool to stop playing the animation).

2. Select Forever as the number of Play times on the Timing toolbar.

3. Double-click the "Animate Colors" behavior in the structure view.

4. Click the Initial box and change the color to blue (second color down in the sixth column). Click OK.

5. Click the Final box and also change that color to the same blue color you set for the Initial color. Click OK. Click the Close button.

Growing (and Shrinking) the Four-Pointed Star

Now, apply a two-way grow behavior so that the star first grows out of, and then shrinks back into, the scene's background:

 1. Click the Grow tool.

 NOTE Don't worry if the four-pointed star grows beyond the borders of the scene in the preview that Liquid Motion plays. You'll change the initial and final percentages later so the star won't grow beyond its original size.

2. Select Forever as the number of Play times on the Timing toolbar.

3. Click the Play Forward then Backward arrow on the Timing toolbar. (This will cause the star to grow out of and shrink into the background).

4. Double-click the "Grow" behavior in the structure view.

5. Change the Initial size to **0.0**. Change the Final size to **100.0**. Click the Close button.

Now, if you play the animation, you'll see the star's colors change continually while it shrinks back into and emerges from the scene every six seconds. (Click the Stop tool to stop the animation from playing.)

Adding an Accelerating Spin Behavior

You want to set this star to spin like the first star, but in the opposite direction. To add some variety to the spin, add the accelerating spin behavior by following these steps:

1. Click the Spin tool.

2. Leave the number of Play times set to Forever.

3. Double-click the "Spin" behavior you just added in the structure view.

4. Leave the <u>C</u>lockwise radio button selected (you want this star to spin in the opposite direction from the first star).

5. Click the TimeEffects tab. Select **100.0** as the Accelerate percentage. Click the Close button.

Go ahead and play the animation from the beginning. The first star will shrink and spin (counterclockwise) into the background. The second star will then grow and spin (clockwise) out of the background, after which it will shrink and spin back into the background, while the first star re-emerges out of the background. Also, notice the accelerated spin rate of the second star. Click the Stop tool to stop playing the animation.

Adding an Embossed Button Image

Add an image to the animation by using one of the button images that comes with Liquid Motion:

1. Click the Insert Image tool.

2. Double-click btn_emboss_dot.gif to open it (or click it to highlight it, and then click open (see Figure 3.13.).

Since the four-pointed star is set to start playing 1 1/2 seconds from the start of the animation, set the start time for the button image you just inserted so it starts playing even later in the animation. Go ahead and set its start offset so it'll start playing 2 1/2 seconds from the start of the animation:

1. Double-click the "btn_emboss_dot" actor in the structure view.

2. Click the Timing tab, and then type **2.5** as the Offset value. Click the Close button.

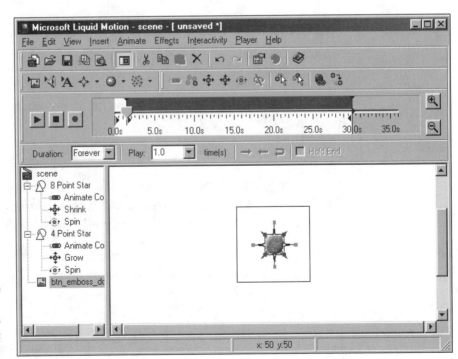

Figure 3.13

An image of an embossed button is added to the animation.

Growing (and Shrinking) the Button

The button is round, so spinning it won't do a whole lot (it would only be viewable in Internet Explorer 4.0+, anyway). You can use a grow behavior, however, to make it pulsate:

1. Click the Grow tool.

2. Click the Play Forward then Backward arrow on the Timing toolbar.

3. Set the Duration to **2.0**. Select Forever as the number of Play times.

4. Double-click the "Grow" behavior for the button image you just added in the structure view.

5. Select **25.0** as the Initial size, and **150.0** as the Final size. (Don't click the Close button.)

Accelerating the Button's Growth Rate

Set an acceleration rate for the grow behavior so that it speeds up as it grows (and shrinks):

1. While still in the Edit window for the grow behavior, click the TimeEffects tab.

2. Select **100.0** as the Accelerate value. Click the Close button.

Now, when you play the animation, you'll see the button grow out of and shrink back into the scene starting 2 1/2 seconds into the animation (see Figure 3.14). Notice also the button's accelerated growth rate.

Right now, if you were to play your animation in a browser, the animation would disappear at the end of its 30-second run. To set the end of the animation to remain visible after the animation is through playing, do the following:

1. Click the "Scene" actor at the top of the structure view.

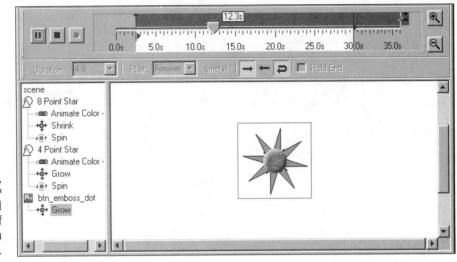

Figure 3.14

The embossed button grows out of the animation scene.

2. Click the Hold End check box on the Timing toolbar so that it is checked.

Previewing Your Animation

Preview your animation in your Web browser:

1. Click the Preview in Browser tool.

2. Type **SpinAndThrob** as the file name for your animation. Click Save.

3. At the Publish Wizard, leave the Local Disk radio button selected. Click Finish. (Your animation will be published as C:\Program Files\Microsoft Liquid Motion\publish\SpinAndThrob \SpinAndThrob.html.)

The SpinAndThrob animation will play in your Web browser for thirty seconds, as shown in Figure 3.15. When it finishes playing, its end state will remain visible.

If you want to play around some more with the SpinAndThrob animation, go ahead. Try changing the Initial and Final colors for the color animation

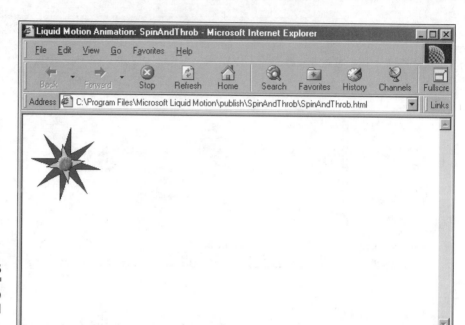

Figure 3.15

The SpinAndThrob
animation, with all
three objects visible,
in Internet Explorer

behaviors. Move the different start times up or down. To increase the speed of any of the grow or spin behaviors, just adjust their Duration settings up or down. If you want to get adventurous, try adding some additional 2-D shapes or images into the mix.

Wrapping Up

If you managed to do both of the example animations in this session, you've covered a lot of ground. You should now know how to do these things:

- ✪ Set the background color and dimensions of an animation scene.
- ✪ Resize the scene dimensions to fit its contents.
- ✪ Insert 2-D shapes, AutoEffects, text, and images.
- ✪ Apply shrinking and growing behaviors to 2-D shapes, text, and images.

✿ Apply a two-way shrinking or growing behavior.

✿ Apply clockwise and counterclockwise spinning behaviors to 2-D shapes.

✿ Record a motion path for an actor.

✿ Set durations and start times for objects and behaviors.

✿ Animate the colors of scene backgrounds, 2-D shapes, and text effects.

✿ Hold the end of an animation so it remains visible after the animation stops playing.

If you've got time and energy left, I've prepared some more animations you can learn to create in tonight's bonus session, "Creating More Web Animations." In addition to many of the techniques covered in the animation you just created, the animations scheduled for tonight cover using sounds, background images, two-part motion paths, inner scenes, and other effects.

Bonus Session: Creating More Web Animations

- ✪ Creating a Color-Animated Bar with Sprinkles
- ✪ Grooving with Motion Paths and Sound Effects
- ✪ Using an Inner Scene to Create an Animated Window in the Animation Scene
- ✪ Drawing a Two-Part Motion Path

This afternoon, you created your first Liquid Motion Web animation, an animated banner graphic. You may also have created a second bonus example, a spinning logo graphic. The following bonus session will give you some more practice using the animation effects from the earlier examples, as well as introduce you to some effects that you haven't tried yet, such as inserting sound effects or using inner scenes.

The following examples are "straight" animations, meaning that they don't include interactive or 3-D effects. I'll cover creating interactive and 3-D animations in the Sunday Morning and Sunday Afternoon sessions.

Creating an Animated Color Bar

This is a simple animation you can create to spiff up your Web pages. The animation is 500 pixels wide and 50 pixels high, with a color animation behavior assigned to a 2-D shape. For an extra touch, you'll include a sparkle effect.

Setting the Scene Dimensions

You should be familiar with how to start a new animation. From inside Liquid Motion, select File and New Animation. If you've exited Liquid Motion, run Liquid Motion and choose to create a new animation. If the Structure View is off, be sure to click the Structure View to turn it back on.

First, you need to set the duration of the animation and the dimensions for the scene, 500×50 in this case:

1. Double-click the "scene" actor in the structure view.

2. In the Edit window for the scene, click the Details tab.

3. In the bottom row, type **500** as the width and **50** as the height. Click the Close button in the upper-right corner.

Setting the Scene Duration

An animation's default duration is 30 seconds, with the animation set to play one time. For this animation, go ahead and change the duration to 10 seconds and set it to play forever:

1. Select **10.0** as the scene's Duration on the Timing toolbar.

2. Select Forever as the number of Play times.

Inserting a 2-D Shape

For this example, you'll first insert a 2-D shape to create the bar shape and then apply a color animation behavior to animate the bar's colors. Insert the 2-D shape:

1. Click the pull-down handle for the Insert 2-D tool and select the rounded rectangle shape (the fifth shape over in the first row).

2. Double-click the "Rounded Rectangle" actor in the structure view (or double-click the rounded rectangle shape in the workspace view).

3. You'll use a color animation behavior to control the color of your bar, so leave the fill color as it is. To make the corners of the rectangle even rounder, increase the Rounding radius value to 20.

4. Click the Details tab. In the bottom row, change the width to **375** and the height to **20**. Click the Close button.

Animating the Bar Shape's Colors

Just a bar by itself doesn't do very much (especially displaying Liquid Motion's default pea green). To animate the colors of your bar, go ahead and apply a color animation behavior:

1. Click the Animate Color tool. You'll see a preview of the rectangle's colors being animated.

2. On the Timing toolbar, leave the Duration set to 3.0. For the number of Play times, select Forever.

3. Double-click the "Animate Color - Fill" actor you just added to the structure view (or you can double-click the Animate Color icon in the workspace view).

4. Click the Initial box and select a color (try the orange color, second down in the second column). Click OK. Click the Final box and select the same color you selected in the Initial box. Click OK.

5. Leave the Full Circle radio button selected (see Figure 4.2).

6. Click the Close button.

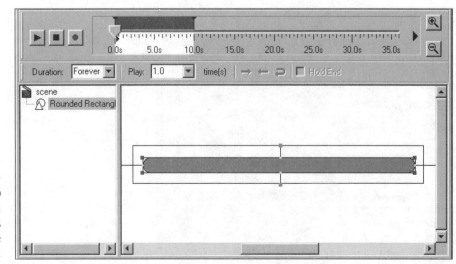

Figure 4.1

A bar shape with rounded ends is added to the animation scene.

7. On the Timing toolbar, change the Play value to Forever (otherwise, the color animation will stop playing after three seconds).

When you play the animation, the bar's colors cycle through the color spectrum every three seconds. Click the Stop tool to stop playing the animation.

The Duration value controls the rate at which the color animation plays. To cause the colors to cycle at a slower rate, just increase the Duration value for the color animation behavior (to 5.0, for instance). To cause the colors to cycle at a quicker rate, decrease the Duration value.

Adding a Sparkles Effect

To add an extra touch to your animation, add a Sparkles effect, which is one of the AutoEffects included with Liquid Motion:

Full Circle radio
button

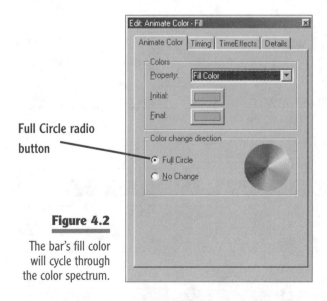

Figure 4.2

The bar's fill color
will cycle through
the color spectrum.

CONTROLLING COLOR CHANGES

Because you've selected the same color for both your initial and final color, selecting the Full Circle radio button, as shown in Figure 4.2, causes the animation to cycle through the whole spectrum on the color wheel. In this case, selecting the No Change radio button would simply display the selected color when the behavior plays.

If you select two different colors, you have the option of selecting the Clockwise or Counterclockwise radio button to cause the color animation to cycle from the initial to the final color on the color circle in either a clockwise or counterclockwise direction.

If you select two different shades of the same color, selecting the No Change radio button causes the color animation to fade from the initial to the final color. The same is true if one of your colors is black, white, or one of the gray shades. Selecting the Full Circle radio button causes the animation to cycle through the color spectrum (the long way around, between the bright red and dark red color).

1. Click the pull-down handle of the Insert AutoEffect tool and select Sparkles.

2. Grab the upper-left corner handle for the Sparkles effect with the mouse and drag it to fill the scene (or you can double-click the "Sparkles" actor in the structure view and change the width to 500 and height to 50 under the Details tab.

The Sparkles effect is automatically set to play Forever, so you don't need to change anything on the Timing toolbar. If you play the animation, you'll see the colors of the bar shape cycle through the color spectrum every three seconds, while the Sparkles effect plays in the foreground.

TIP

If you select a darker shade color for your initial and final colors, the color animation will cycle through colors of the same darker shade. If you select a lighter shade color, the animation will cycle through colors of the same lighter shade.

Changing the Sparkles' Behavior

Right now, the Sparkles just sparkle. Edit the properties of the Sparkles effect to change its behavior:

1. Double-click the "Sparkles" actor in the structure view.

2. To have your sparkles stay visible longer, nudge the Lifespan slider to the right (further toward Longer).

3. To create larger sparkles, nudge the Size slider to the right (toward Larger).

4. To increase the rate at which the sparkles appear, nudge the Rate slider to the right (toward Quicker).

5. To have the sparkles float upward, nudge the Gravity slider slightly upward (toward Floats).

6. To have the sparkles also move from left to right, nudge the Wind slider slightly to the right (toward Right). Click the Close button.

When you play the animation, you'll see the changes you just made to the behavior of the sparkles. Click the Stop tool to stop playing the animation.

Color Animating the Sparkles Effect

For an additional touch, animate the colors of both the Gleam and Glow properties of the Sparkles effect:

1. With the "Sparkles" actor still selected in the structure view, click the Animate Colors tool.

2. On the Timing toolbar, change the Play value to Forever.

3. Click the Animate Colors tool again. At the prompt warning you that your behaviors will overlap, just click OK.

4. After the preview finishes playing, double-click the second "Animate Color" behavior under the "Sparkles" actor in the structure view.

5. Click the pull-down handle of the Properties window and select Gleam Color.

6. Right now, your second "Animate Color" behavior has the same initial and final colors as your first one. Click the Initial box and select any color other than the one currently selected. Make it a bright one, though (try the lime green color, second down in the fourth column). Click OK.

7. Click the Final box and select the same color you selected for the initial color. Click OK. Leave the Full Circle radio button selected. Click the Close button.

8. Change the number of Play times to Forever on the Timing toolbar.

Now, when you play the animation, you'll see that the colors of the Sparkles' gleam and glow effects are also animated. Click the Stop tool to stop playing the animation.

Previewing Your Animation

Preview your animation in your Web browser:

1. Click the Preview in Browser tool on the Standard toolbar.

2. Type ColorBar as the file name for your animation. Click Save.

3. At the Publish Wizard, leave Local Disk selected. To accept the other default settings on the following windows, just click Finish. (Your animation will be published as C:\Program Files\Microsoft Liquid Motion\publish\ColorBar\ColorBar.html.) Your ColorBar animation plays in your Web browser, as shown in Figure 4.3.

TIP Often when previewing an animation in your browser, you'll see something that you want to change. You can just leave your animation playing in your browser and hop back to Liquid Motion (hold down the Alt key and tap the Tab key one or more times to select the Liquid Motion icon), make the change, and then click the Preview in Browser tool— your browser will pop back into the foreground, playing your animation with the change you made.

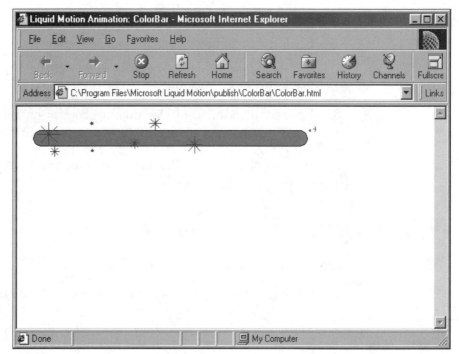

Figure 4.3

The ColorBar animation, with Sparkles, in Internet Explorer.

More Fun with the ColorBar Animation

The ColorBar animation is an easy example of using a color animation behavior, plus an AutoEffect actor, to create an animated element that you can include in your Web pages.

Try using some of the other AutoEffects. Change the colors used in the color animation behavior to get a different look. You can also resize the 2-D shape, making it thinner or wider, for instance.

The ColorBar animation is not an animation that can stand on its own. To put it to good use, you'll need to include its codes inside any HTML file where you want to use it. For right now, you should concentrate on learning how to create Liquid Motion animations, and you'll add them to your other Web pages later. In the Sunday Evening session, I'll show you how to include Liquid Motion animations in other Web pages you have already created or may want to create. However, for a taste of things to come, see the example in Figure 4.4 of the ColorBar animation in another Web page.

THE PUBLISH TOOL

If you pasted the codes for your animation into another Web page (such as those in Figure 4.4), you can't just click the Preview in Browser tool to see the updated changes reflected in that Web page. You'll instead see the animation's HTML file, not the HTML file into which you pasted the animation code.

The trick here is to open in your browser the HTML file into which you've copied your animation code (as shown in Figure 4.3). Hop back over to Liquid Motion and make any changes you want to make to your animation. Then, instead of clicking the Preview in Browser tool, click the Publish tool (next to the Preview in Browser tool) to republish your animation. The Publish tool works just like the Preview in Browser tool, except it won't reopen the animation in your browser. After republishing your animation, just hop back over to your browser and click the Refresh (or Reload) button to see your updated changes in your Web page.

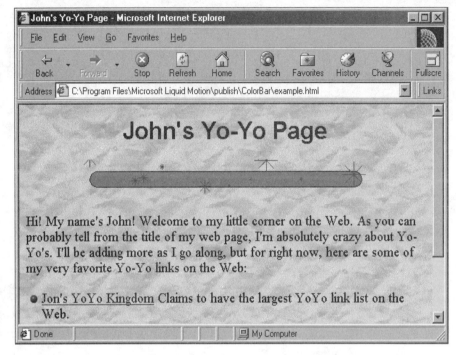

Figure 4.4

The ColorBar
animation as it
might appear in a
Web page.

The Honking Car Animation

I had a lot of fun creating this simple animation. It will give you some more practice using a motion path, and you'll insert some sound effects for the first time.

This example combines an image of a car, a motion path, and two sound clips to create an animation in which a car seems to drive out of the background into the scene and then stops and honks its horn.

You should be pretty familiar by now with starting a new animation, so I won't go over the steps again here to create a new animation. If you earlier turned the structure view off, be sure to click the Structure View tool to turn it back on.

Setting the Scene Dimensions

If you do this example in sequence, the scene dimensions left over from the previous example are a bit small for this animation. Go ahead and resize the scene dimensions to a width of 400 pixels and a height of 100 pixels:

1. Double-click the "scene" actor in the structure view (or double-click the scene in the workspace view).

2. In the Edit window for the scene, click the Details tab.

3. In the bottom row, type **400** as the width and **100** as the height. Click the Close button in the upper-right corner.

4. On the Timing toolbar, leave the duration, 30 seconds, set as it is. To have the end state of the animation remain visible at the end of the animation, select the Hold End check box.

Inserting the Car Image

You'll use one of the images included with Liquid Motion for this animation. To insert the image of a 1940s car:

1. Click the Insert Image tool on the Object toolbar.

2. Double-click the car_1940s.gif file to insert the image (see Figure 4.5).

Creating a Motion Path for the Car

In this example, you want the car to appear to drive into the scene from the upper-right corner. Just follow these steps to create the car's motion path:

1. Click and hold down the mouse cursor on the car, and then drag the image just outside the upper-right corner of the scene so that the image of the car is no longer visible inside the scene. Don't worry if only the bottom-left corner of the car image's border is still

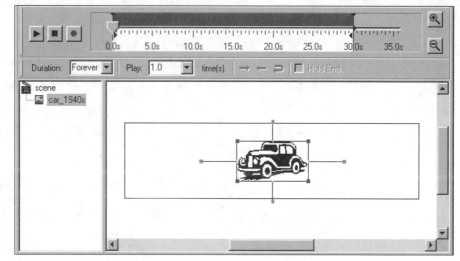

Figure 4.5

A black-and-white image of a 1940s-style car is inserted into the scene.

visible inside the workspace view (as shown in Figure 4.6). You only need to grab the corner to be able to be able to drag it back into the scene and create the motion path. Feel free to expand or maximize Liquid Motion's window to see more of the workspace.

2. Click the Record Motion tool on the Player toolbar.

3. Click and hold down the mouse button inside the border of the car image (just outside the upper-right corner of the scene), and then drag the car image with a smooth motion into the center of the scene, as shown in Figure 4.7. Release the mouse button to end the motion path. The animation preview will play.

Adding a Grow Behavior to the Car

To make the car look as if it emerges out of the background while moving into the scene, add a grow behavior:

1. Click the Grow tool on the Behavior toolbar.

2. Double-click the "Grow" behavior in the structure view.

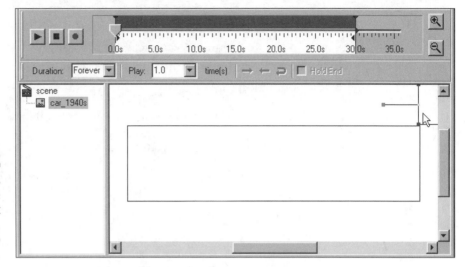

Figure 4.6

The car image is dragged just outside the upper-right corner of the scene, where it is no longer visible.

3. For the Initial value, select 50.0 from the pull-down list. For the Final value, type **125** in the box (you can't select 125.0 from the pull-down list). Click the Close button.

Now, if you play the animation, you'll see the car grow in size as it drives into the scene. Click the Stop tool to stop playing the animation.

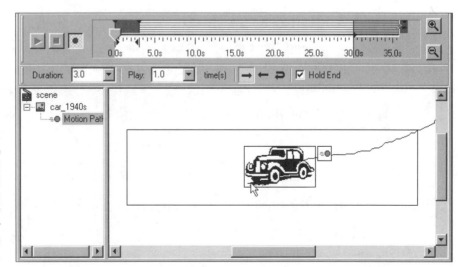

Figure 4.7

With the Record Motion tool selected, a motion path is created by dragging the car image back into the center of the scene.

Adding the Car Engine Noise

Now, add the first sound effect, a car engine noise. It just so happens that a handy car engine noise sound clip comes with Liquid Motion. To add it to your animation:

1. Click the Insert Audio tool on the Object toolbar.

2. Double-click on carengine.au to insert it.

3. Change the number of Play times to 3.0 on the Timing toolbar. (Otherwise, the car engine will stop running before the car stops.) When you play the animation, you'll hear a car engine noise as the car drives into the scene.

NOTE You can insert a number of different types of sound files in Liquid Motion, including .au, .wav, .mid, .mpg, .mp2, and .mpa sound files. Most of these sound file formats play only in Internet Explorer 4.0 (or greater). Only .au format sound files play in all Java-capable browsers, and they need to be a specific kind of .au file: Sun mu-Law 8000 Hz sample rate, 8-bit, mono. If your .au sound file is not in this format, it'll only play in Internet Explorer. (This is not a Liquid Motion limitation, but a Java limitation.)

Adding the Car Honk

Next, add the car honk. And what do you know, Liquid Motion just happens to come with an .au file of a car horn honking. To add it to your animation:

1. Click the Insert Audio tool again.

2. Double-click carhonk.au to insert it into your animation.

3. Double-click the "carhonk" actor in the structure view.

4. Click the Timing tab, and then change the Offset value to 4.0. Click the Close button.

ON THE CD-ROM

Only a handful of .au format sound files are included with the trial version of Liquid Motion. While it is easy to find sources on the Web where you can find .wav format sound files, .au format sound files are a lot harder to find (and mu-Law, 8000 Hz, 8-bit, mono .au files are even harder to find).

A shareware sound editor, CoolEdit 96, is included on the CD-ROM that you can use to convert other sound file formats (such as .wav files) to a mu-Law, 8000 Hz, 8-bit, mono .au format. In CoolEdit 96, this is a two-step process:

1. With the sound file you want to convert open in CoolEdit 96, select Edit, Convert Sample Type. Select 8000 as the Sample Rate. The Mono radio button (under Channels) and the 8-bit radio button (under Resolution) should be selected. Click OK.

2. Select File, Save As. In the Save as type box, select Next/Sun (*.au;*.snd). Click the Options button, then select the mu-Law 8-bit radio button. Click OK. Change the folder to where you want to save your sound file, then click Save.

Now, if you play the animation from the start (click the Stop tool, then the Play tool), you'll see and hear the car drive into the scene, seemingly at an angle out of the background, and stop. After the engine sound shuts off, the car horn honks. To stop playing the animation, click the Stop tool. If you want the horn to honk before the car engine sound shuts off, just change the start offset for the "carhonk" actor to 3.0.

Previewing Your Animation in Your Browser

Now, go ahead and preview your animation in your Web browser:

1. Click the Preview in Browser tool.

2. Type HonkingCar as the file name for your animation. Click Save.

3. At the Publish Wizard, leave Local Disk selected. Click Finish. (Your animation will be published to C:\Program Files\Microsoft Liquid Motion\publish\HonkingCar\HonkingCar.html.)

You should see and hear the car drive into your browser window, stop and turn off its engine, and then honk its horn (see Figure 4.8). Just click the Refresh button (or the Reload button in Navigator) to replay the animation.

More Fun with the HonkingCar Animation

There are a lot of different things you could do to further gussy up the HonkingCar animation. You could add a message at the end of the animation that drops down from the top of the animation or scrolls in from the left or right of the animation. You could also use a Grow behavior to cause the text to grow out of the scene. You could also start up the car engine noise again after the car honk, and then use a motion path and a Grow behavior to drive the car out of the bottom-right corner of the

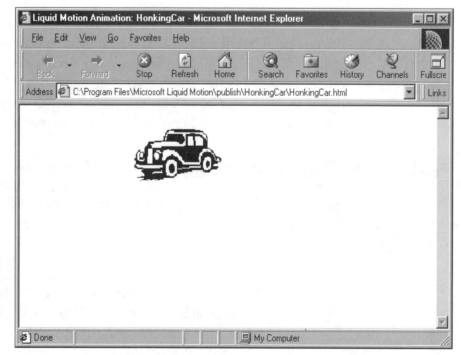

Figure 4.8

The HonkingCar animation is shown after it finishes playing in Internet Explorer.

scene. Although I haven't covered creating interactive effects yet (that'll be in the next session), you could trigger another animation when the car is clicked on, or you could have it bring up another Web page.

The HonkingCar animation is primarily an attention-getter. You could incorporate it into a Welcome page, for instance. Or you could put it at the top of your regular home page or other Web page. See the Sunday Evening session for instructions and pointers on including Liquid Motion animations in other Web pages.

Take a Break?

Since this is an evening session, if you're getting an attack of the munchies, feel free to break here and go raid your refrigerator or cupboards for a snack. If you're starting to get drowsy (it's been a long day!), you can save the rest of this session until another weekend. Better that you get to bed early enough to get a good night's sleep, so you'll be wide awake for the Sunday Morning session.

If, however, you're still fired up and ready to create another animation, go grab those munchies, and I'll see you back here in five or ten minutes, when you'll create a scrolling message marquee in Liquid Motion.

Creating a Scrolling Marquee

You've probably run into scrolling marquees on the Web, where a series of messages scroll through a long rectangular box. Well, with a little ingenuity, you can do the same thing in Liquid Motion. First create a new animation.

For this example, you need to set the scene dimensions to a width of 360 pixels and a height of 60 pixels (you'll see why in a bit):

1. Double-click the "scene" actor in the structure view (or double-click the scene itself in the workspace view).

2. Click the Details tab. In the bottom row, change the width to **360** and the height to **60.** Click the Close button.

Inserting the Drop Shadow Shape

To give your marquee more of a 3-D look, first insert a rectangular shape that'll serve as a drop shadow behind your marquee box:

1. Click the pull-down handle of the Insert 2-D tool and click the rectangle shape (third shape over in the first row).

2. Double-click the "Rectangle" actor in the structure view.

3. Click the Line box and select the transparent color (the diagonally striped box at the bottom-right corner). This will make the border line for the rectangle invisible. Click OK.

4. Click the Fill box and select one of the gray shades (try the fifth color over in the fifth row). Click OK.

5. Click the Details tab. In the bottom row, change the width of your rectangle to **350** and the height to **50.** Click the Close button.

6. Click and hold the mouse button on the rectangle shape and drag it so it lines up with the bottom and right borders of the scene, as shown in Figure 4.9.

Inserting the Marquee Window

For inserting the marquee window through which your marquee text message will scroll, you'll use an inner scene. Inner scenes work just like the root scene of your animation, but anything you include in your inner scene will only be displayed inside of the inner scene borders, and not in the surrounding root scene. Inner scenes are therefore a good way to create "windows" in your animation that include objects that don't play beyond their borders (as with the scrolling marquee text you'll create here).

You can add as many inner scenes as you want. You can even nest inner scenes inside of an inner scene. Although this isn't what you'll do in this example, they can also be a very handy way to create a group of actors and behaviors that can be turned on, as a group, by a single trigger (more about this in the next session). To create the marquee "window" through which your message will scroll, insert an inner scene inside of your root scene:

1. From the menu bar, select Insert, Inner Scene.

2. Double-click the "Inner scene" actor in the structure view.

3. Click the Fill Color box and select a color for your marquee window (try the blue color, second color down in the sixth column). Click OK.

4. Click the Details tab. In the bottom row, change the width of the inner scene to **350** and the height to **50.** Click the Close button.

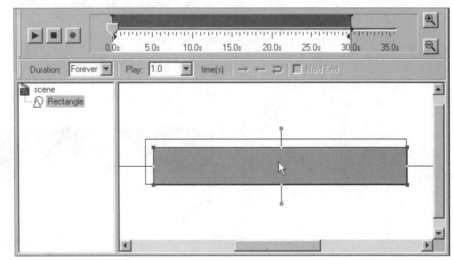

Figure 4.9

The rectangle shape for the drop shadow is dragged to the lower-right corner of the scene.

5. Click and hold the mouse button on the inner scene you just added and drag it so it lines up with the top and left borders of the root scene, as shown in Figure 4.10.

Creating the First Marquee Message

You need to insert the text for your first marquee message into the inner scene you just added:

1. With the inner scene still selected, click the Insert Text tool.

2. Type any message that you want, or just type **Type your first message here** if you can't think of a message. (Keep the message fairly short, not more than four or five words.)

3. Select Helvetica as the Font, and Bold as the Style. Select (or type) 17 as the Size.

Figure 4.10

The inner scene (the marquee window) is dragged to the upper-left corner of the root scene.

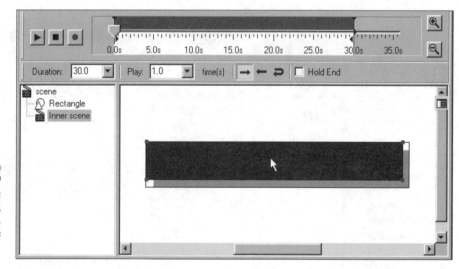

4. Click the Color box and select a color for your text (try the bright yellow color, second down in the third column). Click OK.

5. Click the Drop shadow box and select a color for the drop shadow (try the brick red color, third down in the first column). Click the Close button.

Because you inserted your text message inside the inner scene, it should automatically be centered in the inner scene, as shown in Figure 4.11.

Scrolling the Marquee Message

Scrolling the marquee message through the marquee window can be a bit tricky. Even if you created a straight motion path that long, you might not have room enough on the screen to pull the marquee message from completely outside of the right end of the inner scene to completely outside of the left end of the inner scene.

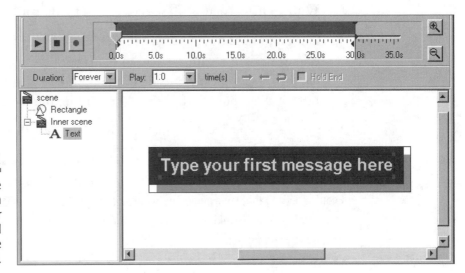

Figure 4.11

The first marquee message has been added to the inner scene that'll function as the marquee message.

The trick is to record two motion paths, but you can't just record one motion path and then pick up the second motion path where the first one ends. Record the first motion path from the center of the inner scene to completely outside the right end of the inner scene. Then you record the second motion path from the center of the inner scene to completely outside of the left end of the inner scene. Finally, for the first motion path, you reverse its direction by clicking the Play Backward arrow (you also need to uncheck the Hold End check box). Set the second motion path to start when the first motion path ends. Now, your two motion paths will dovetail perfectly. All you need to do is record two fairly straight, but not too long, motion paths.

Recording the First Motion Path

For the first motion path, you need to drag your text message from the center of the inner scene (where it is now) until it is completely outside of the right end of the inner scene:

1. With your text actor still selected, click the Record Motion tool.

2. Click and hold the mouse on the left end of your text message. Pull it in as straight a path as you can manage to the right, until the text message is completely outside of the right end of the inner scene. Lift off the mouse button to stop recording the motion path.

3. On the Timing toolbar, uncheck the Hold End check box.

 NOTE You might not succeed recording a fairly straight motion path on your first or second try. If you've noticed that your motion path has noticeably drifted up or down while drawing it (something hard to avoid when drawing a line with the mouse), just delete the crooked motion path and try again.

Recording the Second Motion Path

For the second motion path, you need to drag your text message from the center of the inner scene (where it is now) until it is completely outside of the left end of the inner scene:

1. Click the Record Motion tool. You'll be prompted that you're creating overlapping behaviors. Just click OK (you'll reset the start time for the second motion path so it won't overlap the first motion path).

2. Click and hold the mouse on the right end of your text message. Pull it in as straight a path as you can manage to the left, until the text message is completely outside of the left end of the inner scene. Lift off the mouse button to stop recording the motion path.

3. Double-click the "Motion Path (2)" behavior you just added. Click the Timing tab and change the Start value to When Previous Ends.

4. Since this motion path will end up outside of the scene, there's no need to uncheck the Hold End check box.

Reversing the Direction of the First Motion Path

Now, the last thing you need to do to make this work is to reverse the direction of the first motion path:

1. Click the first "Motion Path" behavior you added to select it.

2. Click the Play Backward arrow on the Timing toolbar to reverse the direction in which the motion path will play.

If you play the animation now, you'll see your text message scroll seamlessly from outside the right end to outside the left end of the inner scene.

Creating the Second Marquee Message

You'll now create a second marquee message that'll scroll through the marquee window following the first marquee message. The easiest way to do this is simply to copy and paste your first text actor (although you'll have to make one minor temporary change to your first text actor to make it easier to position your second text actor, the copy, in the inner scene window):

◆◆◆

For the examples in this book, text actor names inserted in the structure view were automatically created by Liquid Motion as "Text," "Text (2)," "Text (3)," and so on. Liquid Motion may behave differently on some computers, using the start of the text message you type in as the text actor name. When inserting a text actor, if you get a different text actor name from that shown in the book, you'll need to mentally substitute the text actor name Liquid Motion creates on your computer for the text actor name shown here. Just remember that "Text (2)" refers to the second text actor (marked with the "A" icon) listed in the structure view tree.

◆◆◆

1. Click the first "Motion Path" behavior under the "Text" actor in the structure view. Click the Play Forward arrow on the Timing toolbar. (This repositions the text actor in the middle of the inner scene, at the start of the first motion path. Doing this first, before copying and pasting the actor, will make it much easier to position the second text actor, the copy, in the inner scene window.)

2. Click the "Text" actor again to select it, and then press Ctrl+C to copy it and its behaviors.

3. Press Ctrl+V to paste a copy of the first actor in the inner scene.

4. You should now see a "Text (2)" actor added to the structure view below the "Text" actor. In the workspace view, you should see the text of the second actor superimposed over the text of the first actor, but offset slightly lower to the right.

Positioning the Second Marquee Message within the Inner Scene

For an actor in an inner scene, after you paste it in, you can't just click on it and grab it with the mouse to move it—its inner scene will get selected instead (if you accidentally grab and move the inner scene, just press Ctrl+Z to undo the move). Instead, bring your second text actor to the foreground before repositioning it:

1. Click the "Text (2)" actor in the structure view to select it.

2. Press Ctrl+F to bring it to the foreground (or select <u>E</u>dit, Show in <u>F</u>ront, from the menu bar).

3. Click and hold the mouse on the second (superimposed) text message in the structure view (see Figure 4.12). Drag the second text message so that it is positioned exactly over the first text message. Lift off the mouse button when you've got it positioned where you want it.

Figure 4.12

The second text message is brought to the foreground (Ctrl+F) and grabbed by the mouse, so it can be dragged to reposition in the middle of the inner scene.

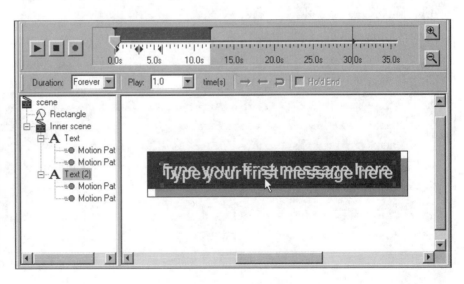

COPYING OR MOVING ACTORS

Copying and pasting actors (together with their behaviors) can be a great time saver. You need to be aware, however, that copies of actors get pasted in offset down and to the right from their originals. You'll need to reposition the copy to where you want it to appear in the scene. (If you paste within an inner scene, you may need to click on the new actor and press Ctrl+F to bring it to the foreground, before you'll be able to select it with your mouse and drag it to a new position, or edit any of its properties.)

You can also use cutting (Ctrl+X) and pasting (Ctrl+V) to move an actor to a higher or lower position in the structure view tree. Just click the actor you want to move and press Ctrl+X to cut it. Next, click the actor below which you want to paste in the cut actor and press Ctrl+V to paste it into its new position on the tree. As with copying and pasting an actor, you'll need to reposition your actor after you've pasted it in, since it will be pasted in offset down and to the right from its original position in the workspace view. (If you move an actor from the bottom of the structure view tree to a higher position, you need to press Ctrl+F to bring it to the foreground before you can select it with your mouse and drag it to a new position or edit any of its properties.)

To copy or move an actor from a higher position to the bottom of the structure view tree, first copy or cut the actor you want to paste, then click the "scene" actor and press Ctrl+V to paste it in at the bottom of the tree list.

This works fine for copying or moving an actor to any position except the top position in the structure view tree. To do this, copy or cut the actor you want to position at the top of the structure view tree, click the top actor, and press Ctrl+V to paste your actor in as the second actor in the tree. Next, cut the first actor in the tree, then click the mouse on the second actor and then paste in (Ctrl+V) the first actor so that it follows the second actor on the tree list. You'll need to reposition both actors, since they'll both be offset from their original positions in the workspace view.

You can also drag and drop actors to move them up or down the structure tree list. This is more of a hit or miss method than cutting and pasting, since it can be more difficult to get your actor to drop exactly where you want it to.

Changing the Timing Toolbar Settings

You need to change the first motion path for each of your text actors so that they'll be set again to play backward, instead of forward. While you're at it, you might as well reset the Duration value for your two text actors, so you can later set the second text actor to play after the first:

1. Click the "Text" actor in the structure view to select it. In the Duration box on the Timing toolbar, type **6.0** as its new value. (Add up the total time for the two motion paths, which are each three seconds long, to get this value.)

2. Under the "Text" actor, click its first "Motion Path" behavior. Click the Play Backward arrow on the Timing toolbar to reverse the direction of the motion path.

3. Click the "Text (2)" actor in the structure view to select it. In the Duration box on the Timing toolbar, type **6.0** as its new value.

4. Under the "Text (2)" actor, click its first "Motion Path" behavior. Click the Play Backward arrow on the Timing toolbar to reverse the direction of the motion path.

Both text actors have their durations reset to six seconds and have moved to outside of the right end of the inner scene. You'll be able to see the line for the shared motion path, and the text actor border for both text actors outside of the inner scene, but you'll no longer be able to see the text (since it is out of the inner scene).

Editing the Text for the Second Message

Next, edit the "Text (2)" actor's text message:

1. Double-click the "Text (2)" actor in the structure view.

2. Change the message in the text box to another message (if you can't think of a message, just type **Type your second message here**).

Setting the Start Time for the Second Message

1. Click the Timing tab and change the Start value to When Previous Ends. (This will cause the second text message to start playing after the first text message stops playing.)

2. Type **-2.5** as the Offset value. Click the Close button.

Because the first text actor has a duration of six seconds, the negative Offset value for the second text actor will cause it to start playing three and a half seconds after the first text actor starts playing (6.0 - 2.5 = 3.5). You can adjust the time between when the two text actors play by adjusting this Offset value up or down.

Now, if you play the animation from the start (click the Stop tool, then click the Play tool), you'll see the first text message scroll through the marquee window, followed closely by the second message (see Figure 4.13). Click the Stop tool to stop playing the animation.

Setting the Animation to Repeat

Right now, the two text messages each just scroll once through the marquee window. To have the two text messages loop indefinitely, you

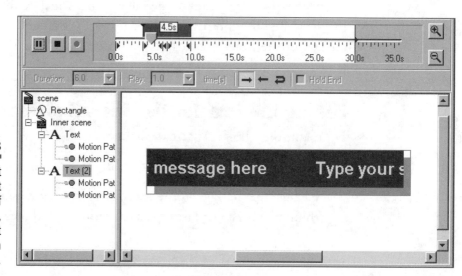

Figure 4.13

While the first text message scrolls out of the left end of the marquee, the second text message scrolls in from the right end.

need to reset the Timing toolbar values for both the scene and the inner scene:

1. Click the "scene" actor at the top of the structure view to select it.

2. Select Forever as the Duration value for the scene.

3. Click the "inner scene" actor in the structure view to select it.

4. Select **10.0** as the Duration value for the inner scene. Select Forever as the number of Play times.

Depending on the length of your second text message, you may need to increase the duration for the inner scene to keep the second text message's second motion path from getting clipped. When you play the animation, you'll see your two text messages scroll repeatedly through the marquee window.

Adding More Text Messages

You can add as many text messages as you want. Just copy and paste the last text actor (make sure you turn the first motion path back to Play Forward first, however). Use the steps detailed above to position the new text actor in the center of the inner scene, then edit its properties to insert a new text message. Since you've already set the Start, Offset, and Duration values for the text actor, you won't need to reset them for the new text actor.

Depending on how many additional text messages you add, you'll need to reset the Duration value for the "Inner scene" actor to allow for the additional messages. Taking into the negative Offset overlap between the messages, you should allocate five seconds for each text actor. Thus, if you include a total of six text messages in the inner scene, you'll need to reset the inner scene's Duration value to at least 30.0.

Now, go ahead and preview your animation in your Web browser:

1. Click the Preview in Browser tool.

2. Type **ScrollingMarquee** as the file name for your animation. Click Save.

3. At the Publish Wizard, leave Local Disk selected. Click Finish. (Your animation will be published to C:\Program Files\Microsoft Liquid Motion\publish\ScrollingMarquee\ScrollingMarquee.html.) Your animation should play in your browser pretty much as it plays in Liquid Motion (see Figure 4.14).

More Options with the Scrolling Marquee Animation

Feel free to play around with the colors for the inner scene background and the text and drop shadow colors. Insert some different messages in the first two text actors (but try to keep them about the same length, not more than four or five words.) If you want, you can try spanning a single message (say, ten words long) across both text actors, with the first part in

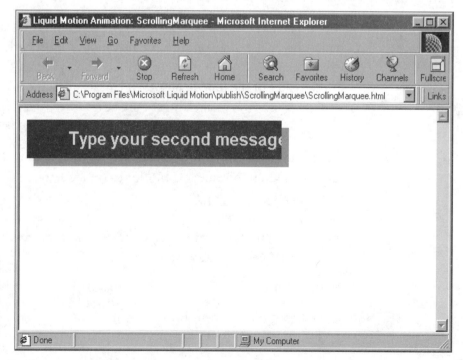

Figure 4.14

The second text message scrolls into the marquee window in Internet Explorer.

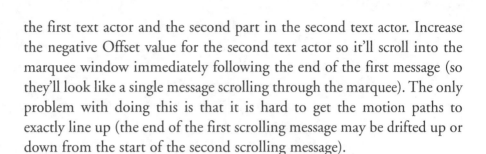
the first text actor and the second part in the second text actor. Increase the negative Offset value for the second text actor so it'll scroll into the marquee window immediately following the end of the first message (so they'll look like a single message scrolling through the marquee). The only problem with doing this is that it is hard to get the motion paths to exactly line up (the end of the first scrolling message may be drifted up or down from the start of the second scrolling message).

If you have some distance between the two messages, any small difference in their vertical positioning in the scene is much less noticeable. You can also space out the different parts of a single message, putting a period at the end of the concluding part, sort of like a series of Burma Shave signs (for those old enough to know what a series of Burma Shave signs looks like).

NOTE For those of you too young to understand the previous reference, back in the days (a long time ago) when most highways in the United States were two-lane blacktops, a kid could wile away a long trip reading the Burma Shave signs posted along the side of the road. They contained rather pithy messages, often rhymed, and broken up into five or six separate signs arrayed down the side of the road.

As detailed in the "Adding More Text Messages" section, it is fairly easy for you to add as many messages as you want to the ScrollingMarquee animation. Even if you want to add 50 or more scrolling text messages, go ahead. Just make sure that you reset the Duration value for the inner scene to allow for the additional messages.

Using the ScrollingMarquee Animation in Other Web Pages

This would be a great animation to paste at the top of the front page of a Web site where you want to post a series of scrolling messages that you can then easily update on a weekly basis. For instance, if you sell widgets, you could post your weekly specials.

Right now the ScrollingMarquee animation, like all Liquid Motion animations after you publish them, plays in the upper-left corner of the browser window. To center it in a Web page, you just need to bracket the animation code within a CENTER tag. You could also specify a background image for the Web page, which would be a great way to set off the marquee's drop shadow (it'll display transparently against the background). I give you a detailed rundown on how to apply both of these features in the Sunday Evening session, "Using Liquid Motion Animations in Web Pages."

Wrapping Up

Many of the effects used in tonight's session were also covered in the Saturday Afternoon session, when you created your first animations. In addition to using text, 2-D shapes, and images, as well as creating growing, shrinking, and motion paths, tonight you learned how to:

- Add a Sparkles AutoEffect and animate its Glow and Gleam colors.
- Include Liquid Motion animations in other Web pages.
- Insert .au sound clips that play in any Java-enabled browser.
- Create different color animation effects, including fading to or from white, black, or gray.
- Make running updates to an animation displayed in a Web browser, even if it is displayed in another Web page into which you've pasted the animation code.
- Include an inner scene in an animation's root scene and add actors and behaviors to it.
- Create two-part motion paths that will scroll in one end and out the other end of a scene or inner scene.
- Set a negative starting offset to cause a following actor to start playing a certain amount of time before the end of a preceding actor.
- Copy or move actors up or down in the structure view tree list.

If you want to save any of the example animations you created in this session, just resave any animation you want to play around with under a new name (such as ColorBar2, for instance). A lot of the fun of working with Liquid Motion is just messing around, trying to see what it will do. So feel free, if you still have the time, to just play around with the program, trying out many of the different effects covered so far. But don't stay up too late! You need a good night's sleep if you want to get up bright and early.

Creating Interactive Web Animations

- ✿ Creating Interactive Growing, Shrinking, Flipping, and Other Movement Effects.
- ✿ Creating Interactive Roll-Over Buttons
- ✿ Using a Single Trigger to Start More Than One Interactive Effect
- ✿ Creating a Panning Background

Good morning! You had a big day yesterday, learning to edit the Easy-Authoring Templates and creating your first Web animations. Well, I've got lots more scheduled for you today, so if you haven't had breakfast yet, you might want to have a bowl of cereal (or pop a couple of waffles in the toaster) before getting started.

I present the simplest and easiest examples at the start of this session. Because of this, it is probably best (although not absolutely necessary) to stick to doing the examples in the order that they are presented—learn to float in the shallow end of the pool before diving off the high dive, in other words.

In this session, you'll learn how to create interactive Web animations. This means that specific actors and behaviors can be triggered by user actions, such as passing the mouse over or off an animation or actor within an animation; or clicking, pressing, or releasing the mouse button on an actor in the animation. Whole sequences within an animation can be keyed to a particular trigger. Anyway, the best way to learn is simply by doing, so get started!

Creating a "Click Me!" Animation

This example uses many of the effects from previous examples in this book, along with a number of interactive effects. For example, clicking the mouse on the animation scene will activate a URL link (jumping to a specified Web address). Additionally, moving the mouse over or off the animation scene controls many of the effects included in the animation.

To get started, you need to run Liquid Motion and create a new animation. If you need to refresh your memory to start an animation, see "Starting a New Animation" in the Saturday Afternoon session.

Using a Background Image

You learned in the previous sessions how to include a background color in your animations, but you haven't used a background image yet. To add a background image to the scene:

1. Double-click the "scene" actor in the structure view (or just double-click within the animation scene).

2. Click the Use Background Image check box so that it is checked.

3. Click the Browse button, scroll to and double-click tile_marble1.gif to open it.

4. Click the Tile Image check box so that it is checked. (Don't close yet.)

NOTE   When you tile a background image, the image will be displayed multiple times at its actual size to fill up the background space. If you don't tile the background image, the entire image is resized to fill the background space.

Setting the Scene Dimensions

Set the scene dimensions to 300 x 200 pixels:

1. While still in the Edit window for the scene, click the Details tab.

2. Under Size, change the width (w:) to **300** and the height (h:) to **200.** Click the Close button (see Figure 5.1).

Adding a URL Link

The easiest way to add interactivity to a Liquid Motion animation is to add a URL link. If a URL link is associated with the scene of an animation, when the mouse is clicked on the scene, the link to the specified URL will be activated. (You can associate a URL link with any actor, not just with the scene.)

 ◄

A URL (or Universal Resource Locator) is another term for a Web address, such as **http://www.microsoft.com/**. A URL, however, can also be the address of a local Web page or other file, such as another Web page located in the same folder as your animation's Web page—this is sometimes called a "partial" or "relative" URL.

◄ ◄

Add the URL link now:

1. Click the URL Link tool on the Behavior toolbar.

2. For this animation, leave the default URL link (a link to Microsoft's Liquid Motion home page). (For some additional pointers on using the URL Link edit window, see the "Tips for Creating URL Links" sidebar.)

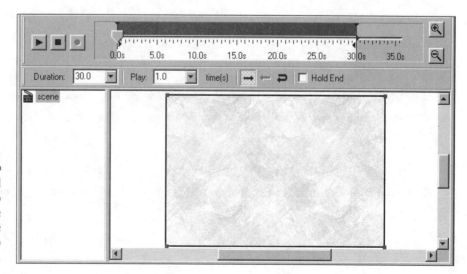

Figure 5.1

A background image is added to the scene, and the dimensions of the scene are reset to 300x200 pixels.

TIPS FOR CREATING URL LINKS

You can use the Browse button in the Edit window for the URL Link behavior to specify a local HTML file as your URL link. However, you should be aware that the link won't work after you've transferred your animation up onto your Web server on the Web. This is due to the fact that it still points to your local HTML file using the absolute path on your hard drive. To have your link work both on your local drive and on your Web server, you should use a "relative URL" here that works in both places. Examples of relative URLs are (you need to substitute the actual folder and file names you want to use for "myfolder" and "mypage"):

mypage.html—links to a file in your animation's publish folder.

myfolder/mypage.html—links to a file in a subfolder (a child folder) of your |animation's publish folder.

../mypage.html—links to a file in the parent folder of your animation's publish folder.

../myfolder/mypage.html—links to a file in a subfolder (child folder) of the parent folder of your animation's publish folder.

../../myfolder/mypage.html—links to a file in a subfolder (child folder) of the parent folder of the parent folder of your animation's publish folder.

You need to transfer any files you link to in this way separately using an FTP program, being careful to preserve the same relative locations (to your animation file) on your Web server that they have on your local drive.

Although Internet Explorer lets you get away with using DOS/Windows slashes ("\") in URLs, Netscape Navigator and most other Web browsers don't recognize a URL that doesn't use Unix slashes ("/").

The Frame list box options and the Name box (grayed out right now) in the Add New URL Link properties box are only relevant if you use your animations in a Web site with HTML frames.

3. Click the Close button. If you play the animation in your Web browser, when you click the animation scene, Microsoft's Liquid Motion home page will be linked to and displayed in your browser (if you're connected to the Internet or the Liquid Motion page is in your cache).

CAUTION

If you don't know any HTML, I recommend that you stick to using the first kind of relative URL shown in the sidebar on the previous page. If you place any files you want to link to in the same folder as your animation's HTML file (your animation's publish folder), you only need to type the file name (mypage.html, for instance) in the URL box of your URL Link behavior to link to that file.

After you get some experience with HTML, feel free to come back and experiment with the other kinds of relative links mentioned in the sidebar, especially if you want to link from your animations to other files within a multi-folder Web site (and not just to files in the same folder as your animation's HTML file).

BUZZ WORD

In the sidebar on the previous page, *parent folder* means the folder up one level on the directory tree from the current folder. For instance, if your animation is published as c:\mypages\animation\myanim\myanim.html, then a URL link of "../mypage.html" in your animation would link back up one level to c:\mypages\animation\mypage.html.

Adding a Polygon Shape

You'll now create a seven-sided polygon that is triggered when a user passes the mouse over the animation. To do this, you need to first select a hexagon (six-sided) shape and then increase the number of sides by one:

1. Click the Insert 2-D pull-down handle and select the hexagon shape (fifth one over in the second row).

2. Double-click the "Hexagon" actor in the structure view.

3. Click the Fill button and select a fill color for the 2-D shape. Try the purple-blue color (third down in the sixth column). Click OK.

4. In the spin box, change the <u>N</u>umber of Sides to 7. (Don't click the Close button yet.)

Setting the Polygon to Start When Triggered

To set the polygon to start only when triggered:

1. Still in the Edit window for the polygon, click the Timing tab.

2. For the Start value, select When Triggered. Click the Close button.

Creating the Trigger for the Polygon

Now create the actual trigger for the action:

1. Click the "scene" actor at the top of the structure view.

2. Click the Trigger tool on the Behavior toolbar.

3. For the Action value, select Mouse Moves Over.

4. Leave the Result value as it is (Turn On).

5. For the Target value, select scene.Septagon and close.

When you play the animation, the polygon will not appear in the animation scene until you pass the mouse over it. (Click the Stop button to stop playing the animation.)

Growing the Polygon

A plain polygon shape isn't very snazzy. Make it fill the whole scene:

1. Click the "Septagon" actor in the structure view.

2. Click the Grow tool on the Behavior toolbar.

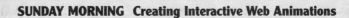

3. Double-click the "Grow" behavior in the structure view.

4. Change the Initial value to 25.0.

5. Change the Final value to 400.0.

6. Click the Close button.

When the animation is played and you pass the mouse over the scene, the polygon, starting from 25 percent, will grow to 400 percent of its original size, filling the whole scene, as shown in Figure 5.2.

Spinning the Polygon

To add even more movement to your animation, apply a spin behavior to your polygon shape:

1. If you played the animation after adding the grow behavior, reclick the mouse on the "Septagon" actor in the structure view to highlight it. (If the "Grow" behavior is still highlighted, you don't have to reclick the "Septagon" actor to add another behavior.)

2. Click the Spin tool on the Behavior toolbar.

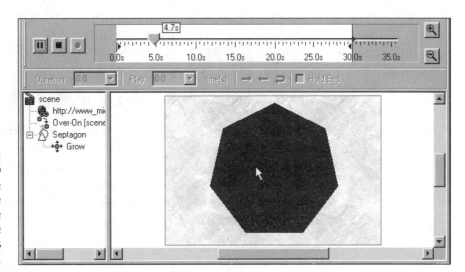

Figure 5.2

When the mouse passes over the animation, the polygon shape grows until it fills the whole scene.

Now if you play the animation again, the polygon shape will not only grow to fill the scene, but it will spin while it grows when you pass the mouse over the scene. (Click the Stop tool to stop playing the animation.)

Animating the Polygon's Colors

All that expanding purple color is a bit much. Add a color animation behavior to the polygon shape:

1. Click the mouse back on the "Septagon" actor to highlight it.

2. Click the Animate Color tool on the Behavior toolbar.

3. Change the number of Play times to Forever.

If you play the animation now, the colors of the spinning polygon will be animated as it grows to fill the scene. (Click the Stop tool to stop playing the animation.)

Adding the "Click Me!" Text

Next, create the "Click Me!" text message:

1. Click the Insert Text tool on the Object toolbar.

2. Type **Click Me!** as the text message.

3. Select Dialog as the Font, Bold as the Style, and 38 as the Size.

4. Click the Color button to select a color for the text. (Try the blue color (second down in the sixth column). Click OK.

5. To add a drop shadow behind the text and select its color, click the Drop shadow button. Select a color for the drop shadow. (Try the orange color (second down in the second column). Click OK.

6. Beneath the Drop shadow button, increase the values for both the horizontal (Horiz:) and vertical (Vert:) Offsets to 4. Click the Close button (see Figure 5.3).

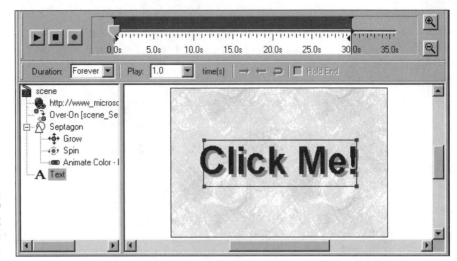

Figure 5.3

A "Click Me!" text message is added to the animation.

◆◆◆

CAUTION As noted in the last two sessions, Liquid Motion's behavior in creating text actor names is a bit quirky. The text actor names I've consistently used in this book ("Text," "Text (2)," "Text (3)," and so on) are those automatically created by Liquid Motion. Liquid Motion may behave differently on some computers, using the first words of the text message as the basis for creating text actor names.

◆◆◆

Rather than let the "Click Me!" text just sit there idly, add a two-way shrink behavior that'll cause the text to shrink and regrow. To add in some more interactivity, set the behavior to be triggered when the mouse passes over the animation scene. To add these effects, do the following

1. Click the Shrink tool on the Behavior toolbar.

2. Double-click the "Shrink" behavior in the structure view. Leave the Initial and Final values as they are (100.0 and 50.0).

3. Click the Timing tab and change the Start value to When Triggered. Click the Close button.

4. To turn this into a two-way shrink behavior (that'll both shrink and regrow), click the Play Forward then Backward arrow on the

Timing toolbar. (You'll notice that the Duration value on the Timing toolbar doubled, from 3.0 to 6.0, when you clicked the Play Forward then Backward arrow.)

5. Change the Play value to Forever on the Timing toolbar.

Triggering the Shrink Behavior

To have the text shrink when the mouse moves over the scene, you need to set a trigger under the "scene" actor:

1. Click the "scene" actor at the top of the structure view.

2. Click the Trigger tool on the Behavior toolbar.

3. For the Action value, select Mouse Moves Over.

4. Leave the Result value as it is (Turn On).

5. For the Target value, select scene.Text.shrink. (If Liquid Motion has named your text actor "Click Me!," instead of "Text," select scene.Click Me!.shrink.)

6. Click the Timing tab and make sure that the Offset value is 0.0. Click the Close button.

If you play the animation, when you pass the mouse over the animation scene, the text shrinks and the spinning polygon grows back out of the scene (see Figure 5.4).

Animating the Text's Color

Animate the color of the text:

1. Click the "Text" actor in the structure view (may be the "Click Me!" actor on some computers).

2. Click the Animate Color tool on the Behavior toolbar.

3. Change the number of Play times to Forever on the Timing toolbar.

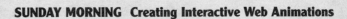

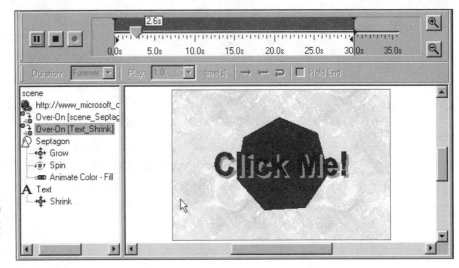

Figure 5.4

A "Click Me!" text message is added to the animation.

4. Double-click the "Animate Color" actor in the structure view.

5. Click the Timing tab, and then change the Start value to When Triggered. Click the Close button.

Triggering the Color Animation

Since you set the Color Animate behavior to start when triggered, you now need to create the trigger that'll cause the behavior to play:

1. Click the "scene" actor at the top of the structure view.

2. Click the Trigger tool on the Behavior toolbar.

3. For the Action value, select Mouse Moves Over.

4. Leave the Result value as it is (Turn On).

5. For the Target value, select scene.Text.Animate Color-Text. (If Liquid Motion has named your text actor "Click Me!," instead of "Text," select scene.Click Me!.Animate Color-Text.)

6. Click the Timing tab and make sure that the Offset value is 0.0. Click the Close button.

Now, if you play the animation, when you pass the mouse over the scene, you'll see that the colors of both the growing polygon and the shrinking "Click Me!" text are animated.

Adding Interactive Sound Effects

In the Saturday Evening bonus session, you included some sound effects in your animations. Now you'll add some interactive sound effects. The first sound effect is a "double-click" sound triggered when the scene is clicked on. The second sound effect is a "boing" sound triggered when the mouse is passed over the scene.

Add the two sound effects, the "double-click" and "boing" sounds, and then set them to start when triggered. Start by adding the "double-click" sound:

1. Click the Insert Audio tool on the Object toolbar.

2. Double-click the click7.au sound file to insert it into the animation.

3. Change the number of play times to 2.0 on the Timing toolbar (this will create a "double" click).

4. Double-click the "click7" actor in the structure view.

5. Select the Timing tab, and then change the Start value to When Triggered. Click the Close button.

Now, add the "boing" sound to the animation and set it to start when triggered:

1. Click the Insert Audio tool on the Object toolbar.

2. Double-click the boing1.au sound file to insert it into the animation.

3. For this sound effect, leave the number of play times at 1.0

4. Double-click the "boing1" actor in the structure view.

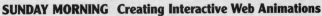

5. Select the Timing tab, and then change the Start value to When Triggered. Click the Close button.

Triggering the Sound Effects

You still need to create the triggers that cause your sound effects to play. First create the trigger for the "double-click" sound, which will cause it to play when the mouse is clicked on the animation scene:

1. Click the "scene" actor at the top of the structure view.

2. Click the Trigger tool on the Behavior toolbar.

3. Leave Mouse Click selected as the Action.

4. Leave the Result value as it is (Turn On).

5. For the Target value, select scene.click7.

Next, create the trigger that will cause the "boing" sound to play when the mouse moves over the animation scene:

1. With the previous trigger you just added still selected, click the Trigger tool on the Behavior toolbar.

2. For the Action value, select Mouse Moves Over.

3. Leave the Result value as it is (Turn On).

4. For the Target value, select scene.boing1. Click the Close button.

If you now play the animation, passing the mouse over the animation will also cause a "boing" sound to be played. Clicking on the animation scene will cause a "double-click" sound to be played (Liquid Motion can have a bit of a stutter sometimes, so you may hear three, even four clicks play, even though the sound effect is a single click that is set to play only twice.) Click the Stop button to stop playing the animation.

Setting the Animation to Play Forever

Right now, your animation is set to play only 30 seconds, after which it will simply stop playing and go blank. If you want the animation to remain visible beyond 30 seconds and continue to respond to mouse actions, you'll need to set it to keep on playing. Change the Duration value for the animation's scene to Forever:

1. Click the "scene" actor at the top of the structure view.

2. Change the Duration value to Forever on the Timing toolbar.

Turning Off the Color Animation Behaviors

Right now, the color animation behaviors for the "Septagon" and "Text" actors will also keep on playing forever. Runaway color animation behaviors can be a little irritating. To add even more interactivity into the animation, set two more triggers that will be activated by moving the mouse off of the animation scene. Set the first trigger to turn off the "Septagon" actor's color animation, and the second trigger to turn off the "Text" actor's color animation:

1. Click the mouse on the "scene" actor at the top of the structure view.

2. Click the Trigger tool on the Behavior toolbar. Select Mouse Moves Off as the Action. Select Turn Off as the Result. For the Target, select scene.Septagon.Animate Color - Fill. Click the Close button.

3. Click the Trigger tool again. Select Mouse Moves Off as the Action. Select Turn Off as the Result. For the Target, select scene.Text.Animate Color - Text (or, select scene.Click Me!.Animate Color Text, if that's how it's listed). Click the Close button.

Now, if you play the animation, moving the mouse off of the animation scene will turn off both of the color animation behaviors. Click the Stop tool to stop playing the animation.

Previewing Your Animation in Your Browser

Now preview your animation in your Web browser:

1. Click the Preview in Browser tool on the Standard toolbar.

2. Type **ClickMe** as the file name for your animation. Click Save.

3. At the Publish Wizard, leave Local Disk selected. To accept all of
    the default settings, click Finish. (Your animation will be published
    to C:\Program Files\Microsoft Liquid Motion\publish\ClickMe
    \ClickMe.html.

When your animation is displayed in your browser, experiment passing
the mouse over and off of the animation to check out the different trigger
effects (see Figure 5.5). If you connect to the Internet, clicking on the animation scene will jump to Microsoft's Liquid Motion home page.

NOTE Often, when running an animation from your hard disk, you won't be able to hear the
sound effect triggered by a mouse click if you've also set a URL link that is activated by
the same mouse click. Once you've transferred the animation up onto the Web, you'll be
able to hear the mouse click sound effect.

TIP If you want to check out this animation's URL link while connected to the Internet, after
clicking on the animation, don't be surprised if you get an "HTTP Error 404" message.
That can happen fairly frequently at Microsoft's Web site—just click your browser's
Refresh (or Reload) button to try again.

More Fun with the ClickMe Animation

Feel free to experiment further with the ClickMe animation. You might
try changing the text message to something other than "Click Me!" Since
the current URL is set to Microsoft's Liquid Motion site, you might

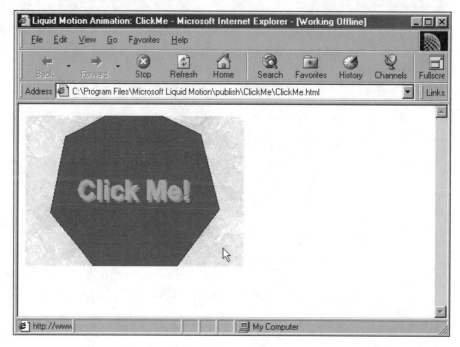

Figure 5.5

The ClickMe
animation plays in
Internet Explorer.

change the text message to "Liquid Motion." Or you could change the
URL to a different location, such as your own personal home page, if
you've got one. Experiment with different text messages, replacing "Click
Me!" with "Enter Here!" or "Welcome!" Play around with the text and
drop shadow colors. You could add a motion path to the text actor and
then trigger it to turn on when the mouse moves over or off the animation. Or you might add one or more AutoEffects, triggered or not.

Using the ClickMe Animation in Other Web Pages

Use the ClickMe animation anywhere you want a hot button that'll jump
to another Web page. You can easily change the text message and insert a
different URL. You can also use the animation on a "welcome" page, with
the ClickMe animation working as a hot button that jumps to the actual
front page of your site. In the Sunday Evening session, "Using Liquid
Motion Animations in Web Pages," you'll learn how to copy and paste
Liquid Motion animations into another Web page, as well as how to use

HTML to control how your animation is displayed in a browser, such as centering your animation on a Web page, displaying a background image behind an animation, flowing text and other elements around an animation, and so on.

Creating a Flipping Navigation Bar

A great way to add real pizazz to your Web site is to add an interactive animated navigation bar. This example uses three buttons, including two buttons that link to the previous and next Web pages in a series of pages, and a third button that links back to the home page.

This animation is probably best used at the bottom or top of a subpage in a series of pages, like the chapters in a book. You would want to publish a separate rendition for each subpage, but the only change you'd have to make would be to the URL links for the the BACK and NEXT buttons. The HOME button URL link would remain the same. First, start a new animation.

Setting the Scene Dimensions

You'll need to reset the scene dimensions. To provide some room above and below the animation, set the scene dimensions to 400 x 125:

1. Double-click the "scene" actor in the structure view (or double-click within the scene itself).

2. Click the Details tab. Under Size, change the width to 400 and the height to 125.

Creating the Back Bar

For this animation, create a "back bar" that will be displayed behind and connect the "BACK," "HOME," and "NEXT" buttons:

1. Click the pull-down handle for the Insert 2-D button, and then select the rectangle shape (third over in the first row).

2. Double-click the "Rectangle" actor in the structure view (or double-click inside the rectangle shape in the scene.

3. Click the Fill button, and then select dark gray (third over in the fifth row) as the color. Click OK.

4. Click the Details tab, and then under Size, change the width to 400 and the height to 25 and close. As shown in Figure 5.6, a dark gray rectangle horizontally bisects the scene.

Creating the Buttons for the Bar

Create the first button for the navigation bar. To add the first button:

1. Click the pull-down handle for the Insert 2-D button, and then select the rounded rectangle shape (fifth over in the first row).

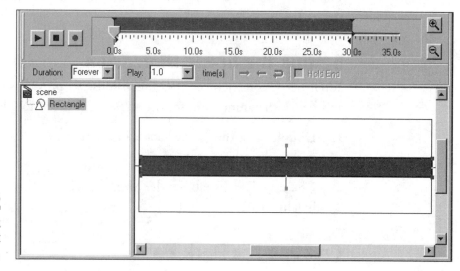

Figure 5.6

A dark gray "back bar" is the first object added to the scene.

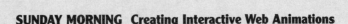

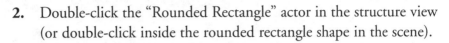

2. Double-click the "Rounded Rectangle" actor in the structure view (or double-click inside the rounded rectangle shape in the scene).

3. Click the Fill button, and then select a lighter gray (try the fifth over in the fifth row) as the color. Click OK.

4. To round off the corners of your shape even more, change the Rounding radius spin control to 15 and close. As shown in Figure 5.7, a rounded rectangle is added to the center of the scene.

Instead of creating two more button shapes from scratch, you can just copy and paste your first button shape to create the other buttons. Just click the mouse on the "Rounded Rectangle" actor in the structure view and press Ctrl+C to copy it, and then press Ctrl+V to paste in the copy. In the workspace, position the first copy at the left end of the back bar, as shown in Figure 5.8. Repeat to create the third button shape, positioning it at the right end of the back bar, as shown in Figure 5.9.

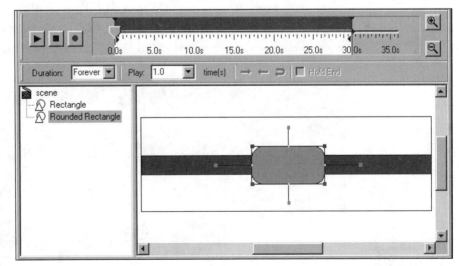

Figure 5.7

A lighter gray button is added to the middle of the back bar.

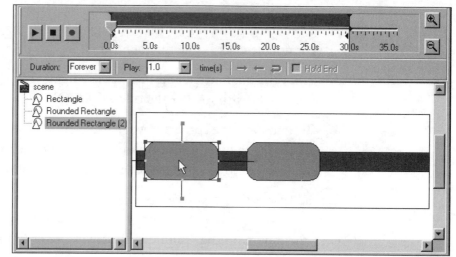

Figure 5.8

A second lighter gray button is added and positioned at the left end of the back bar.

Creating the Text for the HOME Button

Next, you need to create some text that'll be displayed on top of your buttons, "HOME," "BACK," and "NEXT," so viewers will know which ones to click on. To create the "HOME" text for the middle button:

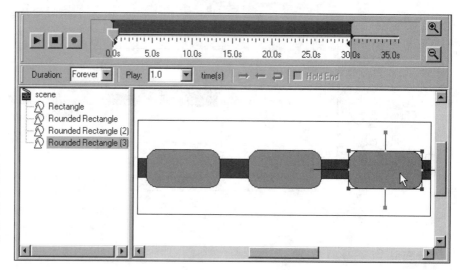

Figure 5.9

A third lighter gray button is added and positioned at the right end of the back bar.

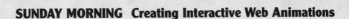

1. Click the Insert Text tool. Type **HOME** as your text.

2. Select Dialog, Bold, and 20 as the Font, Style, and Size.

3. Click the Color button, and then select the white color (seventh over on the fifth row). Click OK.

4. Click the Drop Shadow button, and then select the black color (first in the fifth row). Click OK.

5. Change both of the Offsets spin controls to 3 to increase the horizontal and vertical offsets for the drop shadow and close. As shown in Figure 5.10, the word "HOME," colored white with a black drop shadow, is added on top of the middle button.

Creating the Text for the "BACK" Button

Repeat the same steps shown for creating the "HOME" text, but substitute "BACK" as the text. When you finish adding the text, you'll need to click and drag it so that it is positioned on top of the button on the left end of the bar, as shown in Figure 5.11.

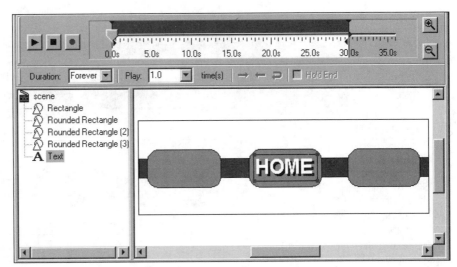

Figure 5.10

The "HOME" text, with its fill set to white and the drop shadow set to black, is added.

NOTE You can also copy and paste your first text actor to create your other two text actors, then edit their properties to change the text message from "HOME" to "NEXT" and "BACK," respectively.

Creating the Text for the "NEXT" Button

Repeat the steps shown for creating the "HOME" text, but substitute "NEXT" as the text. When you finish adding the text, you'll need to click and drag it so that it is positioned on top of the button on the right end of the bar, as shown in Figure 5.12. Don't worry about getting this positioned exactly right—you can always adjust it later.

Following the Mouse with the Sparkles Effect

For a nice touch, add a Sparkles AutoEffect that follows any movement of the mouse:

1. Click the pull-down handle for the Insert AutoEffect tool, and then select the Sparkles effect.

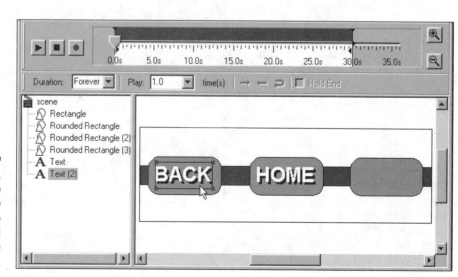

Figure 5.11

The "BACK" text, with its fill set to white and the drop shadow set to black, is added and positioned over the left button.

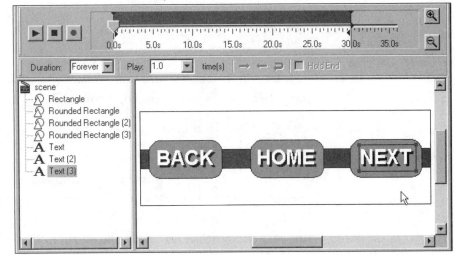

Figure 5.12

The "NEXT" text, with its fill set to white and the drop shadow set to black, is added and positioned over the right button.

2. Grab one of the corners of the Sparkles effect with the mouse and resize the effect so that it fills most of the scene, as shown in Figure 5.13.

3. Double-click the "Sparkles" actor in the structure view.

4. Change the Cause value to Mouse Moves.

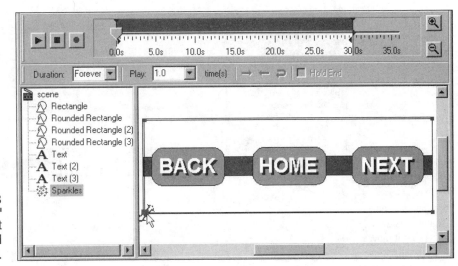

Figure 5.13

The Sparkles effect is resized to fill most of the scene.

5. Click the Glow button, and then change the color to violet-pink (last color in the second row). Click OK.

6. Click the Gleam button, and then change the color to bright orange (second color in the second row). Click OK.

7. Move the Lifespan slider to the right, so that it is centered between Shorter and Longer.

8. Move the Size slider a bit to the right to cause the Sparkles to be larger (rather than smaller). Click the Close button. Now when you play the animation, you'll notice that the Sparkles effect follows the mouse whenever it moves within the scene, as shown in Figure 5.14.

Adding a "Boing" Sound

Now add the last actor, a "boing" sound, and set it so that it will play when triggered:

1. Click the Insert Audio tool.

2. Double-click boing1.au to open it.

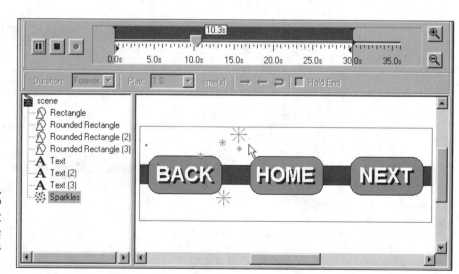

Figure 5.14

The Sparkles effect follows the mouse whenever it moves within the scene.

3. Double-click the "boing1" actor in the structure view.

4. Click the Timing tab, and then change the Start value to When Triggered. Click the Close button.

 NOTE You won't create the trigger for the "boing1" sound yet because you'll set multiple triggers, one for each of the rectangle buttons. I'll have you set them all at one time later.

Color Animating the Back Bar

For this part of the example, add a color animation behavior to the back bar shape, and then create some triggers that will turn the color animation on when the mouse moves over the scene and turn it off when the mouse moves off the scene.

Animating the Back Bar's Colors

First, you need to add a color animation behavior to the back bar shape:

1. Click the "Rectangle" actor in the structure view.

2. Click the Animate Color tool.

3. Double-click the "Animate Color" behavior in the structure view.

4. Click the Initial button, and then select any color you want as your initial color (if you're at a loss, try the blue color, second down in the sixth column). Click OK.

5. Click the Final button, and then select the same color you picked as the initial color. Click OK.

6. Click the Timing tab. Change the Start value to When Triggered. Click the Close button.

7. On the Timing toolbar, change the number of Play times to Forever.

Triggering the Back Bar's Color Animation

Since you set the color animation behavior to start only when triggered, you need to create the trigger that will cause it to play:

1. Click the "scene" actor at the top of the structure view.

2. Click the Trigger tool on the Behavior toolbar.

3. Change the Action value to Mouse Moves Over.

4. Leave the Result value as it is (Turn On).

5. Change the Target value to scene.Rectangle.Animate Color - Fill. Click the Close button. Now when you play the animation, the back bar changes colors when the mouse is moved over the animation scene.

Turning the Back Bar's Color Animation Off

The trigger you just created turns on the back bar's color animation, but it doesn't turn it off. Add another trigger that will turn the color animation off when the mouse moves off the animation scene:

1. With the last trigger still selected, click the Trigger tool again.

2. Change the Action value to Mouse Moves Off.

3. Change the Result value to Turn Off.

4. Change the Target value to scene.Rectangle.Animate Color - Fill. Click the Close button.

Now when playing the animation, the color animation not only is turned on when the mouse moves over the scene, but is also turned off when the mouse moves off the scene. (Click the Stop tool to stop playing the animation.)

Creating the HOME Button's Behaviors and Triggers

For the HOME button, assign color animation and a spin as the behaviors and then trigger them to turn on or off when the mouse moves over or off the button.

Animating the HOME Button's Colors

First, add color animation to the HOME button and set it to start when triggered:

1. Click the "Rounded Rectangle" actor in the structure view.

2. Click the Animate Color tool.

3. Double-click the "Animate Color" behavior you just added to the structure view.

4. Click the Initial button, and then select any color you want as your initial color (if you're at a loss, try the bright green color, second down in the fourth column). Click OK.

5. Click the Final button, and then select the same color you picked as the initial color. Click OK.

6. Click the Timing tab. Change the Start value to When Triggered. Click the Close button.

7. On the Timing toolbar, change the number of Play times to Forever.

Triggering the HOME Button's Color Animation

Since you set the HOME button's color animation behavior to start only when triggered, you need to create the trigger that will cause it to play. This time, set the trigger so it'll turn on the HOME button's color animation when you move the mouse over the HOME button (actually, over the 2-D rectangle shape):

1. Click the Trigger tool.

2. Change the Action value to Mouse Moves Over.

3. Leave the Result value as it is (Turn On).

4. Change the Target value to scene.Rounded Rectangle.Animate Color - Fill. Click the Close button.

Now if you play the animation, the HOME button's color animation is turned on when the mouse moves over it. (Click the Stop tool to stop playing the animation.)

Turning Off the HOME Button's Color Animation

For a bit of a twist, create a trigger that'll turn off the HOME button's color animation when the mouse moves off the scene (and not when it moves off the button):

1. Click the "scene" actor at the top of the structure view.

2. Click the Trigger tool.

3. Change the Action value to Mouse Moves Off.

4. Change the Result value to Turn Off.

5. Change the Target value to scene.Rounded Rectangle.Animate Color - Fill. Click the Close button.

Now when you play the animation, the HOME button's color animation turns on when you pass the mouse over the button, but it doesn't turn off until the mouse moves off the scene.

Flipping the HOME button

Set the HOME button to flip once (do a half-spin) when it is triggered:

1. Click the "Rounded Rectangle" actor in the structure view.

2. Click the Spin tool.

3. Double-click the "Spin" behavior in the structure view.

4. Click the Timing tab, and then change the Start value to When Triggered. Click the Close button.

5. On the Timing toolbar, change the Duration to 1.0 and the number of Play times to 0.5.

Triggering the HOME Button's Flip

Now set the trigger that'll cause the HOME button to flip when the mouse passes over the button:

1. With the HOME button's "Spin" behavior still selected, click the Trigger tool.

2. For the Action value, select Mouse Moves Over.

3. Leave the Result value as it is (Turn On).

4. For the Target value, select scene.Rounded Rectangle.Spin. Click the Close button.

Play the animation now and pass the mouse over the HOME button. You'll see the button's color animation turn on and the button will do a flip (half a spin). You may also notice that, if you leave the mouse in the right position (the upper-right corner, for instance), the button will continually flip (as the mouse cursor keeps getting "kicked" by the flipping button).

Triggering the "Boing" Sound

To cause the boing1.au sound actor to play when the mouse moves over the HOME button, you'll need to create a trigger:

1. With the trigger you just created (under the "Rounded Rectangle" actor) still selected in the structure view, click the Trigger tool again.

2. For the Action value, select Mouse Moves Over.

3. Leave the Result value as it is (Turn On).

4. For the Target value, select scene.boing1. Click Close. Play the animation now and you'll hear a pronounced "boing" sound when the mouse moves over the HOME button.

Creating the "HOME" Text's Behaviors and Triggers

Now create some behaviors and triggers for the "HOME" text. First, set some color animation and make it trigger when the mouse passes over the text. Then, set the text to grow when the mouse passes over it and shrink when it passes off it.

Animating the "HOME" Text's Color

To set color animation for the "HOME" text and set it to start when triggered:

1. Click the "Text" actor in the structure view. (Or click the "HOME" text actor, if that's how your first text actor is named.)

2. Click the Animate Color tool.

3. Double-click the "Animate Color" actor you just added.

4. Click the Initial button and select whatever color you want as the initial color. But make it a bright color—try the orange (second down in the second column), for instance. Click OK.

 NOTE The reason you want to pick a bright color is that the color animation will then cycle only through bright colors, which is what you want for your button text.

5. Click the Final button and select the same color you selected for the initial color. Click OK.

6. Click the Timing tab, and then change the Start value to When Triggered. Click the Close button.

7. On the Timing toolbar, change the number of Play times to Forever.

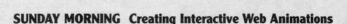

Triggering the "HOME" Text's Color Animation

Add a trigger that'll cause the color animation of the "HOME" text to start when the mouse moves over the "HOME" text:

1. The "Text" actor (or the "HOME" actor, if that's how your first text actor is named) should still be selected in the structure view.

2. Click the Trigger tool.

3. For the Action value, select Mouse Moves Over.

4. Leave the Result value as it is (Turn On).

5. For the Target value, select scene.Text.Animate Color - Text. (Or, select scene.HOME.Animate Color - Text, if that's how it's displayed.) Click the Close button.

Turning the Color Animation Off

Next, set the trigger that will turn off the "HOME" text's color animation. For a bit of a change, set it to be turned off when the mouse moves off the scene (instead of when the mouse moves off the text):

1. Click the "scene" actor at the top of the structure view to select it.

2. Click the Trigger tool.

3. For the Action value, select Mouse Moves Off.

4. For the Result value, select Turn Off.

5. For the Target value, select scene.Text.Animate Color - Text. (Or, select scene.HOME.Animate Color - Text, if that's how it's displayed.) Click the Close button.

Play the animation now and you'll see that the "HOME" text's color animation will turn on when the mouse moves over the text but won't turn off until the mouse moves off the scene.

Growing and Shrinking the "HOME" Text

For the next effect, cause the "HOME" text to grow (and then reshrink) when the mouse moves over the text:

1. Click the "Text" actor in the structure view again (or the "HOME" actor, if that's how your first text actor is named).

 2. Click the Grow tool.

3. Double-click the "Grow" behavior you just added to the structure view.

4. Leave the Initial value as it is (100.0).

5. Change the Final value to 125.0.

6. Click the Timing tab and select When Triggered as the start value. Click the Close button.

 7. On the Timing toolbar, change the Duration to 1.0. Click the Play Forward then Backward arrow to cause the text to both grow and shrink.

Triggering the Grow Behavior

To trigger the Grow behavior to start when the mouse moves over the "HOME" text:

1. The "Text" actor (or "HOME" text actor, if that's how your first text actor is named) should still be selected in the structure view.

2. Click the Trigger tool.

3. For the Action value, select Mouse Moves Over.

4. Leave the Result value as it is (Turn On).

5. For the Target value, select scene.Text.Grow. (Or, select scene.HOME.Grow, if that's how it's displayed.) Click the Close button.

Creating the "BACK" Button Behaviors and Triggers

Now create the same behaviors and triggers for the "BACK" button that you just created for the "HOME" button:

1. Click the "Rounded Rectangle (2)" actor in the structure view.

2. Click the Animate Color tool. Double-click the "Animate Color" behavior and select a color for both the initial and final colors. (Make this a different color than the HOME button, but try to also choose a bright color.) Under the Timing tab, set the Start value as When Triggered. On the Timing toolbar, select Forever as the number of Play times.

3. Click the Spin tool. Double-click the "Spin" behavior and set the Start value as When Triggered. On the Timing toolbar, change the Duration to 1.0 and the number of Play times to 0.5.

Now add the following triggers:

1. Turn on the Animate Color behavior: Click the Trigger tool and set the Action as Mouse Moves Over and the Target as scene.Rounded Rectangle (2).Animate Color - Fill.

2. Turn off the Animate Color behavior: Click the "scene" actor, and then click the Trigger tool. Set the properties as Mouse Moves Off (Action), Turn Off (Result), and scene.Rounded Rectangle (2).Animate Color - Fill (Target).

3. Turn on the Spin behavior: Click the "Rounded Rectangle (2)" actor, and then click the Trigger tool. Set the properties as Mouse Moves Over (Action), Turn On (Result), and scene.Rounded Rectangle (2).Spin (Target).

4. Turn on the Audio actor: Click the Trigger tool, and then set the properties as Mouse Moves Over (Action), Turn On (Result), and scene.boing1 (Target).

Creating the "BACK" Text's Behaviors and Triggers

Now create the same behaviors and triggers for the "BACK" text that you just created for the "HOME" text:

1. Click the "Text (2)" actor (or the "BACK" actor, if that's how your second text actor is named) in the structure view.

2. Click the Animate Color tool and select a color for both the initial and final colors (try to make it a bright color, but a different color from what you've selected before). Under the Timing tab, set the Start value as When Triggered. On the Timing toolbar, select Forever as the number of Play times.

3. Click the Grow tool. Double-click the "Grow" behavior and set 125.0 as the final size. Under the Timing tab, set When Triggered as the Start value. On the Timing toolbar, set 1.0 as the Duration. Click the Play Forward then Backward arrow to cause the text to both grow and shrink.

Now add the following triggers:

1. Turn on the Animate Color behavior: Click the Trigger tool and set the Action as Mouse Moves Over and the Target as scene.Text (2).Animate Color - Text (or scene.BACK.Animate Color - Text, if that's how it's displayed).

2. Turn off the Animate Color behavior: Click the "scene" actor, and then click the Trigger tool. Set the properties as Mouse Moves Off (Action), Turn Off (Result), and scene.Text (2).Animate Color - Text (or scene.BACK.Animate Color - Text, if that's how it's displayed). This will cause the "BACK" text's color animation to be turned off when the mouse moves off the scene.

3. Turn on the Grow behavior: Click back on the "Text (2)" actor (or "BACK" actor, if that's how your second text actor is named), and then click the Trigger tool. Set the properties as Mouse Moves Over (Action), Turn On (Result), and scene.Text (2).Grow (or scene.BACK.grow, if that's how it's displayed).

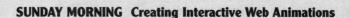

Now when you play the animation, both the HOME and BACK buttons and text should jump to life when the mouse passes over them. Figure 5.15 shows the BACK button in mid-flip.

Creating the NEXT Button's Behaviors and Triggers

Create the same behaviors and triggers for the "NEXT" button that you just created for the "HOME" and "BACK" buttons:

1. Click the "Rounded Rectangle (3)" actor in the structure view.

2. Click the Animate Color tool. Double-click the "Animate Color" behavior and select a color for both the initial and final colors (but a different color than you've used before). Under the Timing tab, set the Start value as When Triggered. On the Timing toolbar, select Forever as the number of Play times.

3. Click the Spin tool. Double-click the "Spin" behavior and set the Start value as When Triggered. On the Timing toolbar, change the Duration to 1.0 and the number of Play times to 0.5.

Figure 5.15

The BACK button in mid-flip (after the mouse moves over it)

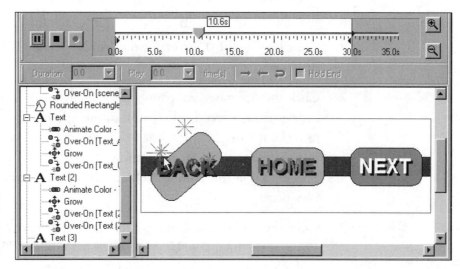

Now add the following triggers:

1. Turn on the Animate Color behavior: Click the Trigger tool and set the Action as Mouse Moves Over and the Target as scene.Rounded Rectangle (3).Animate Color - Fill.

2. Turn off the Animate Color behavior: Click the "scene" actor, and then click the Trigger tool. Set the properties as Mouse Moves Off (Action), Turn Off (Result), and scene.Rounded Rectangle (3).Animate Color - Fill (Target).

3. Turn on the Spin behavior: Click the "Rounded Rectangle (3)" actor, and then click the Trigger tool. Set the properties as Mouse Moves Over (Action), Turn On (Result), and scene.Rounded Rectangle (3).Spin (Target).

4. Turn on the Audio actor: Click the Trigger tool, and then set the properties as Mouse Moves Over (Action), Turn On (Result), and scene.boing1 (Target).

Creating the "NEXT" Text's Behaviors and Triggers

Create the same behaviors and triggers for the "NEXT" text that you just got through creating for the "HOME" and "BACK" text:

1. Click the "Text (3)" actor (or the "NEXT" actor, if that's how your third text actor is named) in the structure view.

2. Click the Animate Color tool. Double-click the "Animate Color" behavior and select a color for both the initial and final colors (try to make it a bright color, but a different color from what you've selected before). Under the Timing tab, set the Start value as When Triggered. On the Timing toolbar, select Forever as the number of Play times.

3. Click the Grow tool. Double-click the "Grow" behavior and set 125.0 as the final size. Under the Timing tab, set When Triggered as the Start value. On the Timing toolbar, set 1.0 as the Duration.

Click the Play Forward then Backward arrow to cause the text to both grow and shrink.

Now add the following triggers:

1. Turn on the Animate Color behavior: Click the Trigger tool and set the Action as Mouse Moves Over and the Target as scene.Text (3).Animate Color - Text (or scene.NEXT.Animate Color - Text, if that's how it's displayed).

2. Turn off the Animate Color behavior: Click the "scene" actor, and then click the Trigger tool. Set the properties as Mouse Moves Off (Action), Turn Off (Result), and scene.Text (3).Animate Color - Text (or scene.NEXT.Animate Color - Text, if that's how it's displayed). This will cause the "NEXT" text's color animation to be turned off when the mouse moves off the scene.

3. Turn on the Grow behavior: Click back on the "Text (3)" actor (or the "NEXT" actor, if that's how your third text actor is named), and then click the Trigger tool. Set the properties as Mouse Moves Over (Action), Turn On (Result), and scene.Text (3).Grow (or scene.NEXT.Grow, if that's how it's displayed).

Now when you play the animation, all three buttons should jump to life when the mouse passes over them. Figure 5.16 shows the NEXT button in mid-flip.

Adding the URL Links

A button bar, flipping or not, isn't much good if it doesn't go anywhere. Go ahead now and add the URL links for your three buttons:

1. Add the HOME button URL link: Click the "Rounded Rectangle" actor, and then click the URL Link tool. In the URL box, type **home.html.** Click the Close button.

2. Add the BACK button URL link: Click the "Rounded Rectangle (2)" actor, and then click the URL Link tool. In the URL box, type **back.html.** Click the Close button.

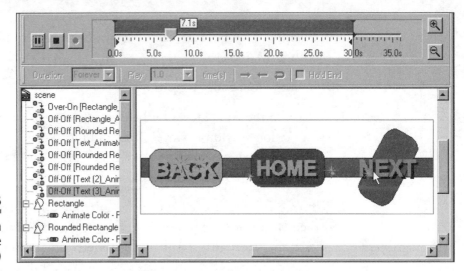

Figure 5.16

The NEXT button in mid-flip (after the mouse moved over it)

3. Add the NEXT button URL link: Click the "Rounded Rectangle (3)" actor, and then click the URL Link tool. In the URL box, type **next.html.** Click the Close button.

NOTE The three Web page file names given here, home.html, back.html, and next.html, are "dummy" file names. If you published this animation multiple times for different pages in a series of pages, the "home" page would be the same for all of the pages, but the "back" and "next" pages would differ for each one (instead of back.html, for instance, you might need to link to page3.html, and instead of next.html, you might need to link to page5.html, and so on).

Setting the Animation to Run Forever

Finally, set the animation so that it won't run out after 30 seconds, as it does now:

1. Click the "scene" actor at the top of the structure view.

2. Change the Duration value to Forever.

Previewing Your Animation in Your Browser

Now preview your animation in your Web browser:

1. Click the Preview in Browser tool on the Standard toolbar.

2. Type **FlippingBar** as the file name for your animation. Click Save.

3. At the Publish Wizard, click Finish to accept all of the default publish settings. (Your animation will be published as C:\Program Files\Microsoft Liquid Motion\publish\FlippingBar\FlippingBar.html.)

In your browser, pass the mouse in and out of the scene, and then pass the mouse over and off the different objects in the scene, including the back bar, the button shapes, and the text for the different buttons. Figure 5.17 shows the HOME button flipping in Internet Explorer.

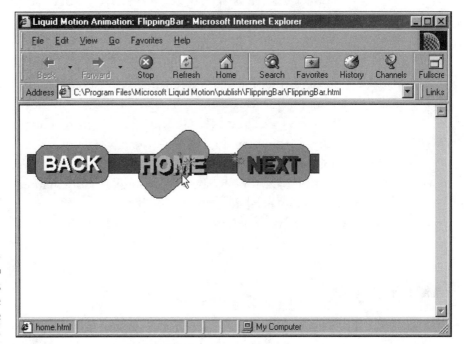

Figure 5.17

As the mouse is passed over the HOME button, the button flips.

Working with the FlippingBar Animation

If you want to use the FlippingBar animation as a menu on the front page of a Web site, you just need to edit the text and URLs for the buttons to match the site you want to use it for. Of course, as designed, it is limited to linking to only three subpages. However, by decreasing the size of the rounded rectangle shapes and the text, you can easily add additional buttons.

Feel free to play around with the colors and color animation used in the animation. For instance, you might want the starting animation to be colored rather than grayed. You could try using some darker colors for the rounded rectangles, for instance.

You could also add a second audio effect, triggered to play when the mouse moves off any of the rounded rectangles or the scene.

Using the FlippingBar Animation in Other Web Pages

The FlippingBar animation, as currently designed, is best used as a navigation bar at the top or bottom of the subpages of a Web site where the subpages function like the chapters in a book. Thus, for a FlippingBar animation placed on the Chapter 5 page, the Back button would go to Chapter 4 and the Next button would go to Chapter 6, whereas the Home button would go back to the table of contents. You would need to publish a separate animation for each page on which you wanted to use it (FlippingBar1 for Chapter 1, FlippingBar2 for Chapter 2, and so on). You would also need to change the "Back" and "Next" URL links in each version of your animation so they'd link to the right Web pages in your sequence of pages.

Take a Break?

If you feel you need a break, get up and stretch a bit, do your morning exercises, or stare at the horizon to relax your eyes. I'll see you back in 10

minutes or so for the last two bonus examples in this session. If the morning is pushing noontime, feel free to break for lunch and then skip ahead to the next session.

Creating a Sidebar Menu Using Roll-Over Buttons

This example shows you how easy it is to create menus, a sidebar menu in this case, using roll-over buttons. A roll-over button is a button that changes its colors when the mouse moves over it, but reverts to its original appearance after the mouse moves off of it.

Setting the Scene Dimensions

Go ahead and start a new animation and reset the scene dimensions. Since this will be a vertical sidebar menu, set the scene dimensions to 100 x 150 (to allow for three buttons sized 100 x 50 pixels):

1. Double-click the "scene" actor in the structure view (or double-click within the scene itself).

2. Click the Details tab. Under Size, change the width to 100 and the height to 150.

3. This is an animation you'll want to play forever: On the Timing toolbar, change the Duration value to Forever.

Creating the Buttons

You'll need to insert and position three 2-D shapes that'll be your buttons:

1. Click the pull-down handle for the Insert 2-D tool and select the rounded rectangle shape (fifth shape over in the first row).

2. Click and hold the mouse on the rounded rectangle in the workspace view and drag it to the top of the scene (see Figure 5.18).

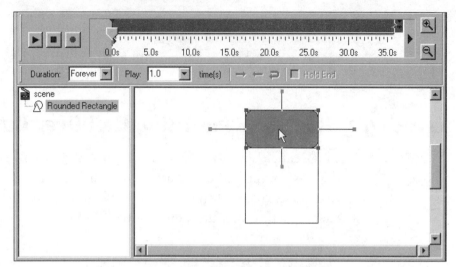

Figure 5.18

The first button is dragged and positioned at the top of the scene.

3. With the rounded rectangle still selected, press Ctrl+C to copy it, then Ctrl+V to paste in a copy. Click and hold the mouse on the second rounded rectangle and drag it below the first rounded rectangle.

4. Press Ctrl+V to paste in another copy of the rounded rectangle. Click and hold the mouse on the third rounded rectangle and drag it to the bottom of the scene (see Figure 5.19).

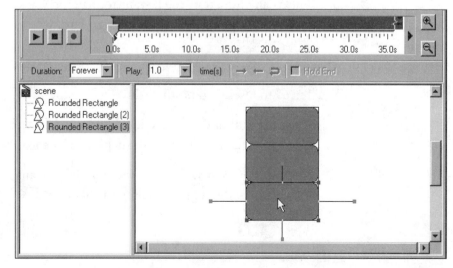

Figure 5.19

The third button is dragged and positioned at the bottom of the scene.

Increasing the Scene Dimensions

You set the initial scene dimensions to make it easier to vertically line up the button shapes. If you leave the dimensions as they are, however, you may have trouble getting triggers to work that are activated by moving the mouse off of a button. That's because the mouse cursor might not be able to get off of the actor (the button, in this case) before it leaves the scene. Therefore, it's always a good idea to add a bit of a margin in the scene around any actor with which you want to associate effects triggered by moving the mouse off of the actor. Go ahead and increase the scene dimensions to 120 x 170:

1. Double-click the "scene" actor at the top of the structure view.

2. Click the Details tab and change the width to 120 and the height to 170. Click the Close button (see Figure 5.20).

Setting the Color of the Buttons and Scene

You need to set the starting colors for your buttons and the scene. Follow these steps to do that now:

1. Double-click the "Rounded Rectangle" actor in the structure view

Figure 5.20

The scene dimensions are increased to create a margin around the buttons (so mouse over and off triggers will work on the buttons).

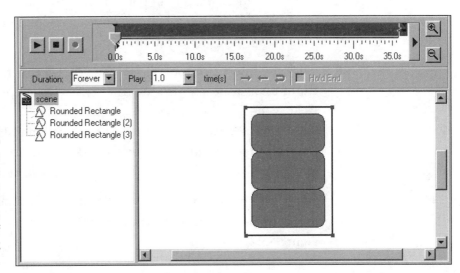

(or double-click the top rectangle shape in the workspace view). Click the Fill button and select a color (try the bright red color, second down in the first column, but feel free to select another color, if you want). Click OK, then click the Close button.

2. Repeat for the other two buttons (the "Rounded Rectangle (2)" and "Rounded Rectangle (3)" actors), selecting a different fill color for each one. For the second button, try bright blue, second down in the sixth column; for the third button, try the green color, third down in the fourth column. Feel free to select different colors if you want—just make sure they're different than the color you selected for the first button.

3. Double-click the "scene" actor again and click the Fill Color button. To contrast this with the brighter colors you selected for the buttons, select a darker color (try dark purple, fourth down in the sixth column). Click OK and then click the Close button (see Figure 5.21).

Adding the Text for the Buttons

Next, you need to add the text for your buttons. For this example, I'll use "Products," "Orders," and "Support" as the text labels for the buttons (you can use different text labels, if you want). Go ahead and add these three text actors to your animation:

1. Click the Insert Text tool. Delete the "Your text here" text and type **Products** as your new text message. Select DialogInput as the Font, Bold as the Style, and 16 as the Size. Click the Color button and select light yellow (first color in the third column). Click OK. Click the Drop shadow button and select dark purple (fourth color down in the sixth column). Click OK. Click the Close button.

2. Click and hold the mouse on the "Products" text you just added to the scene and drag it so it's positioned on top of the top button (see Figure 5.22).

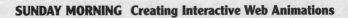

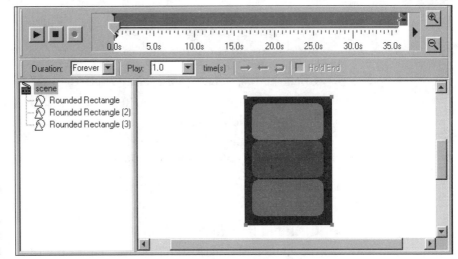

Figure 5.21

Colors are added to the three buttons and the scene background.

3. Click the Insert Text tool again. Delete the "Your text here" text and type **Orders** as your new text message. Select DialogInput as the Font, Bold as the Style, and 16 as the Size. Click the Color button and select light yellow (first color in the third column). Click OK and click the Drop shadow button and select dark purple (fourth color down in the sixth column). Click OK and the Close button.

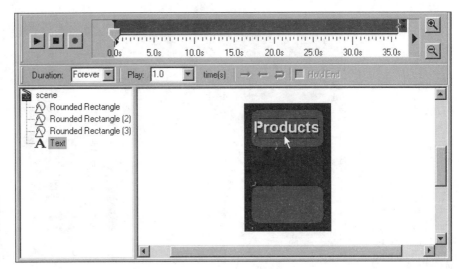

Figure 5.22

The "Products" text is positioned on top of the top button.

4. The "Orders" text should already be positioned over the middle button, so you shouldn't have to reposition it.

5. Click the Insert Text tool again. Delete the "Your text here" text and type **Support** as your new text message. Select DialogInput as the Font, Bold as the Style, and 16 as the Size. Click the Color button and select light yellow (first color in the third column). Click OK. Click the Drop shadow button and select dark purple (fourth color down in the sixth column). Click OK and the Close button.

6. Click and hold the mouse on the "Support" text you just added to the scene and drag it so it's positioned on top of the bottom button (see Figure 5.23).

Creating the Roll-Over Effects

To create the roll-over effects for your buttons, you need to add color animation behaviors for each of the buttons that'll be set to display only one color. You'll then add triggers for each button that'll turn the color animation on and off when the mouse moves over and off the button.

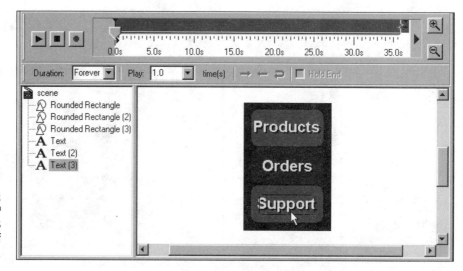

Figure 5.23

The "Support" text is positioned on top of the bottom button.

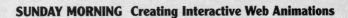

Follow these steps to add the color animation behavior and triggers for the first button:

1. Click the "Rounded Rectangle" actor in the structure view, and then click the Animate Color tool.

2. Double-click the "Animate Color - Fill" behavior you just added. Click the Initial button and select a color for your roll-over effect (try the bright orange color, second down in the second column. Click OK. Click the Final button and select the same color you selected for the Initial color. Click OK.

3. Select the <u>N</u>o Change radio button. (This will cause only the color selected as both your Initial and Final color to be displayed when the color animation is turned on.)

4. Click the Timing tab and change the Start value to When Triggered. Click the Close button.

5. Click the Trigger tool. For the Action, select Mouse Moves Over. Leave the Result as it is (Turn On). For the Target, select scene.Rounded Rectangle.Animate Color - Fill. Click the Close button.

6. Click the Trigger tool again. For the Action, select Mouse Moves Off. For the Result, select Turn Off. For the Target, select scene.Rounded Rectangle.Animate Color - Fill. Click the Close button.

Now, if you play the animation, when you move the mouse over the top button, the button's color changes to orange. When you move the mouse off the button, the button's color changes back to red. Click the Stop tool to stop playing the animation.

To create the roll-over effects for the other buttons, you follow the same steps as for the first button, except you need to substitute "Rounded Rectangle (2)" and "Rounded Rectangle (3)," respectively, for "Rounded Rectangle."

1. Click the "Rounded Rectangle (2)" actor and then click the Animate Color tool. Double-click the "Animate Color - Fill" behavior you just added. Select the same color for both the Initial and Final color (try violet pink, second color down in the eighth column). Select the No Change radio button. Click the Timing tab and change the Start value to When Triggered. Click the Close button.

2. Click the Trigger tool. For the Action, select Mouse Moves Over. Leave the Result as it is (Turn On). For the Target, select scene.Rounded Rectangle (2).Animate Color - Fill. Click the Close button.

3. Click the Trigger tool again. For the Action, select Mouse Moves Off. For the Result, select Turn Off. For the Target, select scene.Rounded Rectangle (2).Animate Color - Fill. Click the Close button.

4. Click the "Rounded Rectangle (3)" actor and then click the Animate Color tool. Double-click the "Animate Color - Fill" behavior you just added. Select the same color for both the Initial and Final color (try the blue violet color, first color in the sixth column). Select the No Change radio button. Click the Timing tab and change the Start value to When Triggered. Click the Close button.

5. Click the Trigger tool. For the Action, select Mouse Moves Over. Leave the Result as it is (Turn On). For the Target, select scene.Rounded Rectangle (3).Animate Color - Fill. Click the Close button.

6. Click the Trigger tool again. For the Action, select Mouse Moves Off. For the Result, select Turn Off. For the Target, select scene.Rounded Rectangle (3).Animate Color - Fill. Click the Close button.

Try playing the animation now. When you move the mouse over the buttons, their colors will change to the colors you set in the color animation behaviors. When you move the mouse off of the buttons, they revert back to their original colors. Click the Stop button to stop playing the animation.

 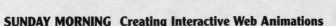

Adding Some Interactive Sound Effects

For the final touch, add some interactive sound effects that'll play when you move the mouse over the buttons:

 The following steps use one of the audio files included with the Book Examples on the CD-ROM. If you've installed the Book Examples from the CD-ROM, you'll find a selection of additional audio files you can use in your animations in the C:\Program Files\Microsoft Liquid Motion\Prima Examples\Audio folder. If you haven't installed the Book Examples yet, feel free to substitute one of the .au format audio files from Liquid Motion's Audio folder.

1. Click the Insert Audio tool. From Liquid Motion's Audio folder, click the Up One Level button (to the right of the Look in box) twice to go to the Microsoft Liquid Motion folder. Double-click the Prima Examples folder, and then double-click the Book Sounds folder.

2. Double-click pogo.au to insert it into your animation. Double-click the "pogo" actor in the structure view, select the Timing tab, and change the Start value to When Triggered. Click the Close button.

3. Click the "Rounded Rectangle" actor and click the Trigger tool. Select Mouse Moves Over as the Action. Leave the Result as it is (Turn On). Select scene.pogo as the Target. Click the Close button.

4. Click the "Rounded Rectangle (2)" actor and click the Trigger tool. Select Mouse Moves Over as the Action. Leave the Result as it is (Turn On). Select scene.pogo as the Target. Click the Close button.

5. Click the "Rounded Rectangle (3)" actor and click the Trigger tool. Select Mouse Moves Over as the Action. Leave the Result as it is (Turn On). Select scene.pogo as the Target. Click the Close button.

TIP

A good way to save time when the triggers you add have the same action, result, and target, is to copy and paste triggers from one actor to another. That way you won't have to re-edit the trigger's properties for the second actor.

Now, when you play the animation, you'll hear the pogo.au sound file play when you move the mouse over any of the buttons. Click the Stop tool to stop playing the animation.

NOTE

All of the .au format sound files included in the Prima Examples\Book Sounds folder are compatible with Netscape Navigator and other Java-capable Web browsers. You should be aware, however, that not just any old .au file will do. It has to be an 8-bit, mono, 8000Hz, mu-Law .au file. For information on using CoolEdit 96, a shareware sound editor included on the CD-ROM, to create 8-bit, mono, 8000Hz mu-Law .au files, see the HonkingCar example in the Friday Evening session.

Adding Some URL Links

Right now, the buttons in your sidebar menu don't do anything but change colors and make noises. Fun, but not very functional. Go ahead and add some URL links to your buttons:

1. Click the "Rounded Rectangle" actor and then click the URL Link tool. In the URL box, type **products.html** as the URL. Click the Close button.

2. Click the "Rounded Rectangle (2)" actor and then click the URL Link tool. In the URL box, type **orders.html** as the URL. Click the Close button.

3. Click the "Rounded Rectangle (3)" actor and then click the URL Link tool. In the URL box, type **support.html** as the URL. Click the Close button.

NOTE These are fake URLs. If you wanted to check them out, you'd need to create and save the specified HTML files in the same folder where your animation is published.

Previewing Your Animation in Your Browser

Feel free to preview your sidebar roll-over menu in your browser:

1. Click the Preview in Browser tool and type **RollOverMenu** as the file name for your animation. Click Save.

2. At the Publish Wizard, click Finish to accept all of the default publish settings. (Your animation will be published as C:\Program Files\Microsoft Liquid Motion\publish\RollOverMenu\RollOver-Menu.html.) In your browser, move the mouse over and off the buttons to which you've added roll-over effects (see Figure 5.24).

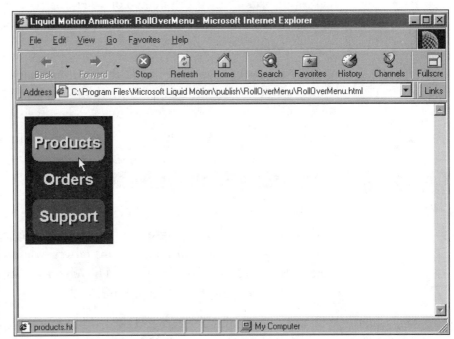

Figure 5.24

In Internet Explorer, the mouse moves over the top button, turning its color to orange.

Working With the RollOverMenu Animation

This is just a sample three-button menu. For a real Web page, you might want to create a sidebar menu using six, seven, or more buttons. To expand the current menu to more buttons, you'd have to resize the scene, and then reposition your buttons and text. If you wanted to expand your sidebar menu to five buttons, for instance, you could resize the scene to 100 x 250 pixels, then reposition your old buttons and text. Next, you'd need to add two more rounded rectangle 2-D shapes and two more text actors for the button labels, positioning them in the scene. When you've got all your buttons lined up in their new positions, increase the size of the scene to 120 x 270 pixels to form a margin around your buttons. Then you'd need to repeat the steps given previously for adding color animation behaviors and triggers to your rounded rectangle actors ("Rounded Rectangle (4)" and "Rounded Rectangle (5)").

You could also create roll-over effects for the text actors, so the color of the text would change when you moved the mouse over the text actors, then revert back to their original color when the mouse moves off of the text actors. You could also create a roll-over effect for the scene.

The RollOverMenu is not an animation you'd play on its own. It's an animation you'd want to include in a Web page, inserting it in a table cell or a frame window. For guidance on how you might use the RollOverMenu animation in other Web pages, see the Sunday Evening session, "Using Liquid Motion Animations in Web Pages."

Creating the Running Man Animation

A classic animation technique used in almost every cartoon is the panning background. A panning background occurs when the scene in the background (trees, buildings, hills, and so on) moves, while a character in the foreground walks or runs in place. The character in the foreground appears to move against the background.

You'll create a panning background by dividing the scene into three image strip panels. Each image strip contains the whole scene, but the second

image strip starts one-third into the image, whereas the third image strip starts two-thirds into the image. By setting each image strip horizontally with three frames across the scene, you give the appearance of a single image. Because they are image strips, they each individually progress through one-third of the scene for each frame. You have a continuously moving (although repeating) background.

Inserting the Panels of the Panning Background

This technique involves creating a panning background that makes use of three images strips. They are actually three images, but each jogged over one-third.

NOTE An image strip, also called an image sequence, is an ordinary image, a GIF or JPG file, that is displayed as a series of frames. The image strips for the panning background, for instance, will be displayed in three frames, each comprising a third of the image (the left, middle, and right third). Later in the example, you'll add another image strip, the running man. That image strip will have two frames, each separate images of the running man, which when played give the impression that he's running in place.

Start out by creating a new animation and inserting the first of the three image strips that will form the panning background:

1. Click the Insert Image tool. From Liquid Motion's Images folder, click the Up One Level button (to the right of the Look in box) twice to go up to the Microsoft Liquid Motion folder. Double-click the Prima Examples folder, then double-click the Book Images folder. Double-click movback1.jpg to insert it into your animation.

2. Double-click the "scene" actor and then click the Resize to Contents button. Click the Close button.

3. Double-click the "movback1" actor in the structure view. For the File Structure, select Horizontal Strip. For the Number of Frames, select 3. Change the Frames per second to 3.0. Click the Close button.

4. Use the mouse to drag and position the image strip so that it is positioned at the left end of the scene, as shown in Figure 5.25. (If you haven't resized the Liquid Motion window, you may need to use the bottom scroll bar to see the left end of the scene.)

Now insert and position the image strip that will form the second of the three panels:

1. Click the Insert Image tool. (The Book Images folder should automatically be displayed.) Double-click movback2.jpg to insert it into the animation.

2. Double-click the "movback2" actor in the structure view. For the File Structure, select Horizontal Strip. For the Number of Frames, select 3. Change the Frames per Second to 3.0. Click the Close button.

3. This image strip will be automatically positioned in the middle of the scene, as shown in Figure 5.26, so you don't have to drag it with the mouse to reposition it.

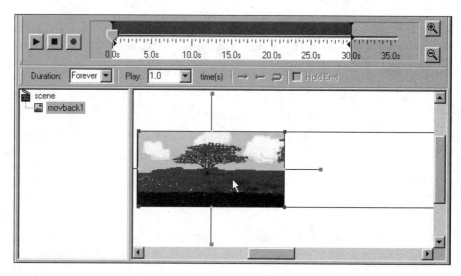

Figure 5.25

The first panel of the panning background is positioned at the left end of the scene.

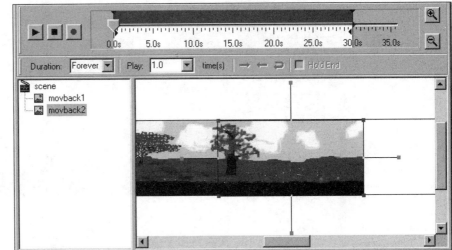

Figure 5.26

The second panel of the panning background is automatically inserted at the middle of the scene.

Insert and position the third image strip:

1. Click the Insert Image tool. (The Book Images folder should automatically be displayed.) Double-click movback3.jpg to insert it into your animation.

2. Double-click the "movback3" actor in the structure view. For the File Structure, select Horizontal Strip. For the Number of Frames, select 3. Change the Frames per Second to 3.0 and close.

3. Use the mouse to drag and position the image so that it is positioned at the right end of the scene, as shown in Figure 5.27. (If you haven't resized the Liquid Motion window, you may need to use the bottom scroll bar to see the right end of the scene.)

TIP The position of an actor in a scene is shown on the status bar at the bottom of the Liquid Motion window. For instance, "x: 300 y: 50" would indicate that the center of the image is positioned 300 pixels in from the left side of the scene and 50 pixels down from the top of the scene. You can use this position indicator to position actors (shapes, images, and text) exactly where you want them in the scene.

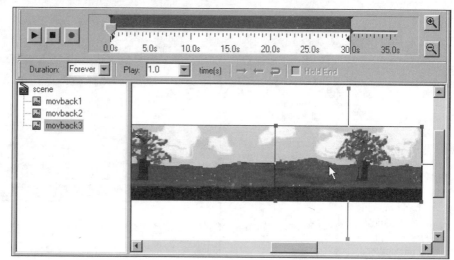

Figure 5.27

The third panel of the panning background is positioned at the right end of the scene.

Now when you play the animation, the three panels look like a single image moving from the right to the left. Figure 5.28 shows all three panels (I've widened the Liquid Motion window to 640 pixels and turned off the structure view) of the background, with the second frame displayed in each panel.

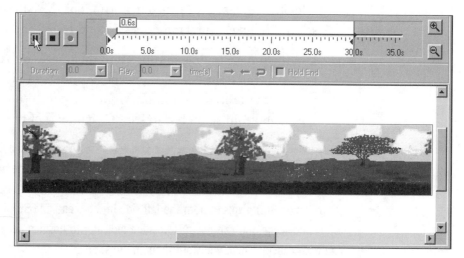

Figure 5.28

The full panning background plays (the second frame in each panel is displayed).

Inserting the Running Man Image Strip

Now that you've created your panning background, you need to add a figure to it. To do this, you'll use another image strip, this time comprising two frames which include different images of a "running man" (thus the name of the example animation). When played as an image strip, the figure in the image appears to run in place (or maybe skip in place).

Now, go ahead and insert the image strip for your "running man" into the animation:

1. Click the Insert Image tool. (The Book Images folder should be automatically displayed.) Double-click running_man.gif to insert it into the animation.

2. Double-click the "running_man" actor. For the File Structure, select Horizontal Strip. For the Number of Frames, select 2. Change the Frames per Second to 3.0. Click the Close button.

The image strip is automatically positioned at the middle of the scene, so you don't need to reposition it. Figure 5.29 shows the running man image strip positioned at the middle of the scene. Now when you play the animation, the man appears to run against the panning background.

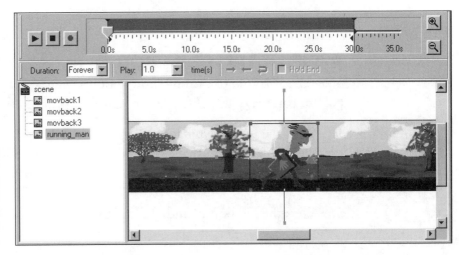

Figure 5.29

The full panning background plays (the second frame in each panel is displayed).

THE RUNNING MAN IMAGE STRIP

To create the running_man.gif image strip, I pulled the man_running.gif file into Paint Shop Pro 5 (included on the CD-ROM) from Liquid Motion's Clip Art\Images folder. I flipped the image horizontally and turned the background transparent. I then made a copy of the image and played around with Paint Shop Pro 5's paint tools to alter the positions of the legs, arms, and briefcase. Next, I created a new blank image, twice as wide as the running_man.gif image. Finally, I copied and pasted both my original running_man.gif image and my altered copy of that image into my new blank image, positioning them side-by-side in the new image. I then resaved my new image as running_man.gif.

If you want, you could experiment with adding extra frames to the running_man.gif image, to have the figure look more like he is really running (instead of skipping). You could, for instance, pull running_man.gif into any photo-paint program (such as Paint Shop Pro 5 or Adobe Photoshop). You could then make a copy of the image and alter the copy, so you'd have two more frames of the running man figure, but in different positions from those in the original image. Then, you could copy and paste both your original and your copy into a new image (twice the width of your original or your copy), positioning them side-by-side. (You should make sure the background of your new image is set to be transparent. You could then resave your image (as really_running_man.gif, for instance) and use it in your animation (specifying four frames rather than two for the horizontal strip).

Adding a Speech Balloon

Since this is a kind of cartoon, how about adding a speech balloon that'll pop up part way through the scene? Go ahead and do that now:

1. Click the pull-down handle of the Insert 2-D tool, and then click the speech balloon shape (third over in the third row).

2. Double-click the "Speech Balloon" actor in the structure view.

3. Click the Fill button and change the color to white. Click OK.

4. Click the Timing tab and change the Offset value to 5.0. Click the Close button.

5. On the Timing toolbar, change the Duration to 5.0. (Leave the number of Play times set as 1.0.)

6. To make the speech balloon visible again, move the Timeline Slider to the right (5 seconds) until the speech balloon appears in the scene. Grab and drag one of the red corner handles of the speech balloon to make it smaller, and then drag it in front (to the right) of the running man.

7. Also, grab one of the green side handles and rotate the speech balloon a bit clockwise, as shown in Figure 5.30.

Adding the Text for the Speech Balloon

Add the first word of the speech balloon message:

1. Click the Insert Text tool. Type **Click** as the text.

2. Select Italic as the Style and 18 as the Size.

Figure 5.30

The speech balloon is resized and positioned in front of the running man.

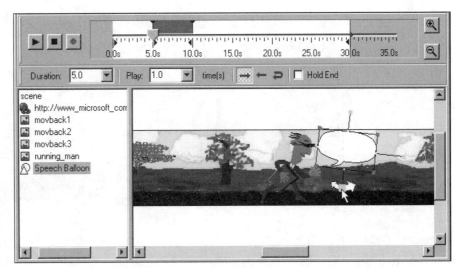

3. Click the Timing tab, and then change the Start value to When Previous Starts. Change the Offset value to 0.0. Click the Close button.

4. On the Timing toolbar, change the Duration to 2.5 (you'll need to type it into the box). (Leave the number of Play times set to 1.0.)

5. Click and drag the text so that it is positioned inside the speech balloon, as shown in Figure 5.31.

6. Click the Insert Text tool. Type **Me!** as the text. Select Italic as the Style and 18 as the Size.

7. Click the Timing tab, and then change the Start value to When Previous Ends. Leave the Offset value at 0.0. Click the Close button.

NOTE By selecting When Previous Ends as the Start value for the "Me!" text, it'll automatically play immediately following the "Click" text. That way, if you want to shorten the durations for the two text actors and the speech balloon, you won't have to reset the start offset for the "Me!" text.

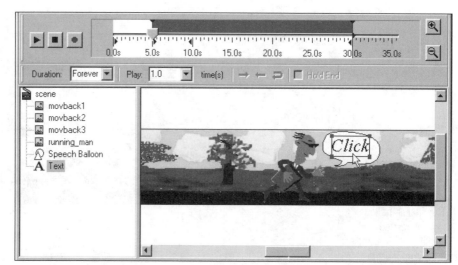

Figure 5.31

The text, "Click," is positioned inside the speech balloon.

8. On the Timing toolbar, change the Duration to 2.5 (you'll need to type it into the box). (Leave the number of Play times set to 1.0.)

9. Click and drag the text so that it is positioned inside the speech balloon. (You'll be able to see the borders of the text actor, but you'll have to move the Timeline slider to the right if you want to make the text visible.)

Now if you play the animation from the beginning (click the Stop tool, and then the Play tool), you'll see the speech balloon and text appear five seconds into the animation. The word "Click" will be displayed for 2.5 seconds, and then the word "Me!" will be displayed for another 2.5 seconds, after which both the speech balloon and the text will disappear.

Adding Some Traffic

Right now, the running man seems a bit lonely, just running along down a country road. I've included an image of a taxi cab in the Book Images folder you can use to add some traffic. For this example, you'll draw a motion path with the taxi cab, causing it to come zooming along the road, entering the left end of the scene and exiting out of the right end. Go ahead and add the image for the taxi cab and draw its motion path:

NOTE For this part of the animation, you'll create a motion path that'll run the full length of the scene. To do this in one fell swoop, you should turn off the structure view and widen Liquid Motion's window so that you can see the whole scene.

1. Click the Insert Image tool. (The Book Images folder should be automatically displayed.) Double-click taxi.gif to insert it in your animation.

2. Drag the taxi image so that the front of the taxi is just visible inside of left end of the scene. You'll also want to lower the taxi so that its wheels are on the road, as shown in Figure 5.32.

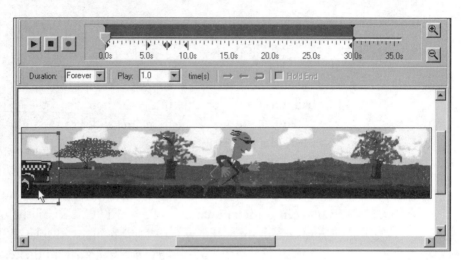

Figure 5.32

The taxi is positioned at the left end of the scene, prior to recording a motion path that will take it to the other end of the scene.

3. Click the Record tool on the Player toolbar, and then grab and drag the taxi image to the other end of the scene. (You want to try to get the taxi as far out of the right end of the scene as you can, but if the back bumper is still showing, that's okay.) Lift up the mouse to stop recording the motion path. A preview of the animation will play, in which the taxi careens (hopefully) down the road as it passes the running man and exits out the other end of the scene.

Triggering the Taxi Cab's Motion Path

To add some interactivity to this animation, set the taxi to drive down the road only when triggered by the viewer of the animation clicking on the running man (now you see the reason for the speech balloon message):

1. Double-click the "taxi" actor in the structure view.

2. Click the Timing tab and change the Start value to When Triggered. Click the Close button.

3. Click the "running_man" actor in the structure view, and then click the Trigger tool.

4. Leave the Action and Result values as they are. For the Target value, select scene.taxi. Click the Close button. Now, when you play the

CREATING A TWO-PART MOTION PATH

You want your motion path to be as straight as you can manage it, but it doesn't have to be perfectly straight. If you did the scrolling marquee animation example in the Saturday Evening session, you might want to try using the two-part motion path technique you learned for that one.

To review, the technique used involves creating two motion paths for the object, each starting at the center of the scene. The first motion path runs out of the left end of the scene and the second motion path runs out of the right end of the scene. You then reverse the direction of the first motion path, causing it to run from outside the left end to the center of the scene and set the Start value of the second motion path as When Previous Ends. The result is one continuous motion, running in from one end of the scene and out of the other end, even though it is actually two separate motion paths. If you try this technique for this example, you'll need to decrease the motion path durations to 1.5 seconds, so the two motion paths will run for a total of 3.0 seconds.

animation and click the running man, the taxi comes careening down the road, as shown in Figure 5.33.

Honking the Taxi's Horn

Remember the car honk sound you used in the HonkingCar animation? Why not use it here to add an apt sound effect to your animation? Add it now:

1. Click the Insert Audio tool.

2. If you did the roll-over menu animation example earlier in this session, you loaded an image from the Book Sounds Folder. That folder will be displayed here, instead of Liquid Motion's Audio folder. To get to Liquid Motion's Audio folder, click the Up One Level button (just to the right of the Look in box) to go to the Microsoft Liquid Motion folder, then double-click the Clip Art folder, then the Audio folder. (If you didn't do the roll-over menu

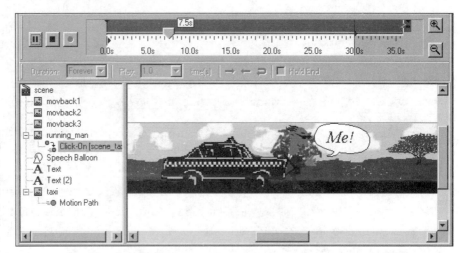

Figure 5.33

When you click on
the running man,
the taxi cab comes
zooming down the
road from the left
end of the scene.

example or used an audio file from Liquid Motion's Audio folder
for that example, you should already be in Liquid Motion's Audio
folder.)

3.   Double-click carhonk.au to insert it in your animation.

4.   Double-click the "carhonk" actor in the structure view and then
click the Timing tab. Change the Start value to When Triggered.
Click the Close button.

5.   Click the "running_man" actor, and then click the Trigger tool.
Leave the Action and Result values as they are. For the Target value,
select scene.carhonk. Click the Close button.

Now when playing the animation, if you click the running man, the taxi
will honk its horn just as it enters the scene.

Bumping the Running Man into the Air

For one final touch, add a motion path and sound effect that will make it
look (and sound) like the taxi actually runs into the running man and
bumps him up into the air. First, create the motion path:

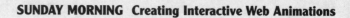
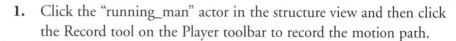

1. Click the "running_man" actor in the structure view and then click the Record tool on the Player toolbar to record the motion path.

2. Grab the running man with the mouse and lift him up so that only his feet are visible at the top of the scene, and then lower him back down to where he was. Lift up the mouse button to stop recording the motion path.

3. Double-click the "Motion Path" behavior that is under the "running_man" actor in the structure view. Click the Timing tab and change the Start value to When Triggered. Change the Offset value to 1.0 (you may want to adjust this later to get the timing just right). Click the Close button.

4. Click the "taxi" actor in the structure view. Click the Trigger tool. For the Action, select Starting. Leave the Action set as it is (Turn On). For the Target, select scene.running_man.Motion Path. Click the Close button.

When the careening taxi bumps the running man into the air, you must have a sound effect, right? Do the following to add a "boing" sound effect that'll play when the running man gets bumped into the air:

1. Click the Insert Audio tool, and then double-click boing1.au (in Liquid Motion's Audio folder) to insert it into your animation.

2. Double-click the "boing1" actor in the structure view. Click the Timing tab. For the Start value, select When Triggered. Change the Offset value to 1.0 (as with the Motion Path offset, you may need to adjust this later). Click the Close button.

3. Click the "taxi" actor again in the structure view, and then click the Trigger tool. For the Action, select Starting. Leave the Action set as it is (Turn On). For the Target, select scene.boing1. Click the Close button.

Now when playing the animation, if you click the running man, the taxi will honk its horn just before careening down the road. But instead of passing the running man, the taxi bumps him up into the air (and with an audible "boing!" at that).

Setting the Animation Duration

This may not be an animation you want to play forever (the running man might get a little tired, after all, not to mention the patience of the viewer). If you want to, however, just click the "scene" actor and change the Duration to Forever. On the other hand, you might consider setting the Duration to something like 60 seconds.

If you set the duration for this animation to less than Forever, it's a good idea to select the Hold End check box for the scene to cause the final image of the animation to remain visible after after the animation finishes playing. Otherwise, the viewer will just be left with an empty space where the animation was.

Another neat touch would be to add a pop-up message ("Again?") at the end of the animation that the viewer could click to restart the animation, but I'll leave that for you to figure out—you should have enough experience now with using interactive triggers to figure out how to do that on your own.

Previewing Your Animation in Your Browser

Now preview your animation in your Web browser:

1. Click the Preview in Browser tool.

2. Type **RunningMan** as the file name for your animation. Click Save.

3. At the Publish Wizard, leave Local Disk selected. Click Finish to accept all of the Publish Wizard's default settings. (Your animation will be published to C:\Program Files\Microsoft Liquid Motion\publish\RunningMan\RunningMan.html.)

Wait for the speech balloon to appear, prompting you to click the running man, then after clicking him, watch the taxi cab come zoom down the road and bump him into the air (see Figure 5.34). Click him again. And again.

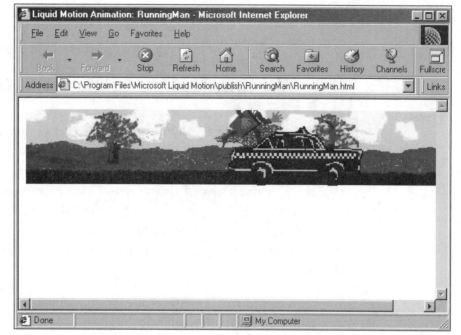

Figure 5.34

The running man right after being bumped into the air by the careening taxi cab

Working with the RunningMan Animation

You can do a lot more to further gussy up the RunningMan animation. You could add more traffic, for one thing! I've included another taxi image, taxi2.gif, in the Book Images folder, that you can use. It is the same image as in taxi.gif, but I've turned it around to go the other way. Also, look on the Web site for this book (**http://www.callihan.com/liquidmotion/**) for additional Web art images you can use.

If you want to add some more sound effects, you might start by adding the sound of a car engine that plays while the taxi careens down the road. Just trigger it to start when the taxi starts, that is, when the running man is clicked, and then trigger it to stop when the taxi's motion path ends.

You can also add some more speech balloon messages. You could use a speech balloon message at the end of the animation that the viewer could click to restart the animation.

If you feel comfortable working with a paint program, you could also edit the panning background image strips. Add an extra tree (remember, you'll need to include it in all three panning background image strips). Or place a house off in the distance.

Using the RunningMan Animation in Other Web Pages

This animation doesn't really do anything, other than play. It's a fun animation, however, and can easily stand on its own. If you want to link the animation to another page, all you have to do is insert a URL link under the "scene" actor. Then when the viewer clicks the mouse on the scene, the Web page specified by the URL link is displayed. Clicking on the running man, however, won't activate the URL link, since the running man is in the foreground in relation to the scene and has a couple mouse click triggers.

You can also edit the HTML file for the animation and insert a hypertext link underneath the animation that a viewer can click to move on to the next page. Just insert the following line (substituting the actual name of the page you want to link to) beneath the animation codes, but above the `</BODY>` code:

```
<P ALIGN="center"><A HREF="linkpage.html">Go to Next
    Page</A>.
```

In the Sunday Evening session, I'll show you how to set a Web page to automatically cause a link to be activated after a set period of time, although you'll need to make allowance for the amount of time it takes the animation to download. That way, you can create an animation that is 60 seconds long, for instance, and then have the Web page automatically jump to another Web page after two minutes.

Wrapping Up

Many of the effects you used in this morning's session were also covered in the Saturday Afternoon and Evening sessions. In addition to using text, 2-D shapes, and images, as well as using growing effects, shrinking effects, and motion paths, you also learned how to:

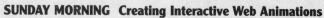

✿ Add a background image to a scene.

✿ Add a URL link to a scene or an actor.

✿ Add varying polygon 2-D shapes, such as a seven-sided polygon, as well as a speech balloon shape.

✿ Set actors and behaviors to be triggered by mouse actions.

✿ Create triggers that cause actors and behaviors to play (or stop playing).

✿ Cause an AutoEffect (such as Sparkles) to follow the mouse.

✿ Create roll-over menu buttons using triggers to turn one-color animation behaviors off and on.

✿ Use image strips to create a panning background.

If you want to experiment further with any of the examples presented in this session, go ahead. Also, you might want to try your hand at creating some animations from scratch, using any of the techniques and effects covered in this and the previous two sessions.

The next session covers creating 3-D animations, as well as using filters and transitions. These are effects that are viewable only in Internet Explorer 4.0 or greater. If you are using an earlier version of Internet Explorer, Netscape Navigator, or another browser as your default browser, you may want to skip doing the next session until you've downloaded and installed the latest version of Internet Explorer. Feel free to continue to experiment with the techniques and effects covered in the previous three sessions, or skip ahead to the Sunday Evening session, "Using Liquid Motion Animations in Web Pages."

If you do have Internet Explorer 4.0 installed as your default browser (meaning that it comes up when you preview your animations), take a break and grab some lunch. Water the plants. Read the funnies. I'll see you back in a bit to learn how to create 3-D and other Internet Explorer 4.0-specific animations.

Creating 3-D and Other Internet Explorer Animations

- ✪ Creating Complex 3-D Motion Paths with 3-D Images
- ✪ Using Filters and Transitions
- ✪ Rotating 3-D Shapes and Controlling Light Sources
- ✪ Applying Surface Textures to 3-D Shapes
- ✪ Using WAV Audio Effects

In this session, I'll cover 3-D and other animation effects that are specific to Internet Explorer Version 4.0 or greater. These include inserting, manipulating, and rotating 3-D objects, using surface textures and light sources, and including filters and transitions in your Web animations. All of the main effects covered in this session will not display in Java-capable Web browsers such as Netscape Navigator or versions of Internet Explorer prior to version 4.0.

If you are not using Internet Explorer 4.0 (or greater) as your Web browser, and don't want to take the time right now to download and install it on your computer, you should skip this session and go on to the Sunday Evening session, "Using Liquid Motion Animations in Web Pages."

If you are using Netscape Navigator as your Web browser and would also like to install the latest version of Internet Explorer, see Appendix A, "Installing Liquid Motion," for pointers on how to run both Navigator and Internet Explorer 4.0+ in Windows 95/98.

Even if you're using Internet Explorer 4.0+ as your Web browser, you need to realize that many potential visitors to your Web pages will use other Web browsers. In the next session, "Using Liquid Motion Animations in Web Pages," I'll show you some ways that you can use the effects covered

in this session without inconveniencing visitors using browsers other than Internet Explorer 4.0+.

Only in Internet Explorer 4.0+

The following are the features included in Liquid Motion that will only work in Internet Explorer 4.0 (or greater), both as a preparation for doing the examples in this session and as a later reminder of exactly what features will not work in all Java-capable browsers:

- Spinning images and text (you can spin 2-D shapes in Navigator, however)
- 3-D shapes
- Rotating 3-D shapes
- Filters (Drop Shadow, Glow, Gray, Negative, Transparency, and Wave)
- Transitions (Dissolve, Fade, Blinds, Box, Checkerboard, Circle, Strips, Split, Wipe)
- Audio formats (WAV, MID, MPG) other than 8-bit 8000 Hz mono mu-Law .AU (or .AUZ) format sound files
- Audio panning
- Transparent backgrounds
- External triggers and script triggers

Creating a Swimming 3-D Fish Animation

In this example, you'll combine 3-D shapes, rotating, growing and shrinking, and motion paths to create the illusion of 3-D fish actually swimming within a 3-D space (the deep blue sea). This is not anywhere near as difficult as it might sound, and is a great way to truly astound your friends, family, or associates (they'll *definitely* think you're an absolute Web animation guru!).

Setting the Scene Dimensions

To start out, create a new animation and set your scene dimensions to 400 x 200 pixels:

1. Double-click the "scene" actor in the structure view.

2. Click the Details tab and set the width to 400 and the height to 200. Click the Close button.

You'll add a background image later to give the background the look of the deep blue sea. For right now, however, primarily so the motion paths you make will show up in the figures, just leave the background as it is.

Creating the First Swimming 3-D Fish

The first effect you'll create is the 3-D fish swimming in a counterclockwise 3-D circle. Go ahead and add the first fish:

1. Click the pull-down handle of the Insert 3-D tool, and then click the last button (the cone superimposed over the sphere). If you haven't turned it off yet, just click OK at the Information message telling you this is an Internet Explorer 4.0+-only effect.

2. Double-click Fish1.x to open it into the scene.

Right now, the 3-D fish is turned at an angle from the plane of the scene and is positioned in the middle of the scene. First, use the green handles to reorient the 3-D fish so that it is turned to the right, perpendicular to the scene. Then, use the mouse to drag the fish so it is positioned at the bottom of the scene. See Figure 6.1 for the orientation and position you need to achieve with your fish.

Recording the First Fish's Motion Path

Now record an oval, counterclockwise motion path with your fish. It is not terribly important that your motion path be perfectly oval, but you want to try to make your starting and ending points coincide (otherwise,

your fish will appear to jump at that point when swimming repeatedly around in the circle). To record the motion path:

1. With your fish still selected, click the Record Motion tool.

2. Click and hold the mouse button in the center of the 3-D fish, and then drag it in a rough oval, counterclockwise. When finished drawing the motion path, lift off the mouse button to stop recording the motion path.

NOTE   See Figure 6.2 to get a feel for what your motion path should look like. If you have trouble getting the starting and ending points of your motion paths to coincide at least fairly closely, just delete your motion path and try it again.

3. Change the Duration of the motion path to 6.0 and the number of Play times to Forever.

Adding Some Color to the First 3-D Fish

Right now, the fish is a bit hard to see against the white background. Add some color to it:

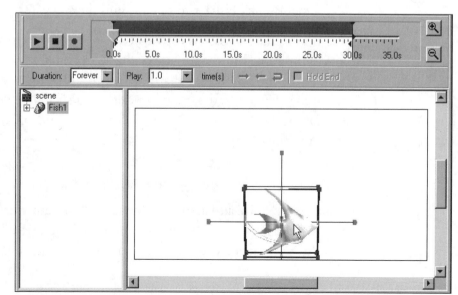

Figure 6.1

The first 3-D fish is oriented perpendicular to and positioned at the bottom of the scene.

1. Double-click the "Fish1" actor in the structure view.

2. Select the <u>C</u>olor radio button, and then click the button next to the <u>C</u>olor radio button to select a color for your fish.

3. Select a bright color for your fish (try the bright pink color in the upper-right corner). Click OK. Click the Close button.

Rotating the First 3-D Fish

Right now, your fish just traverses a 2-D oval path in the scene without rotating in the space. Follow these steps to rotate the 3-D fish so that it turns in a circle while following the motion path you just drew:

1. Click the Rotate 3-D tool.

2. Double-click the "Rotate 3-D" actor in the structure view.

3. Leave the Counterclockwise radio button selected. Click the Y button to rotate the fish around the y-axis. Click the Close button.

4. To make it match the motion path, change the Duration of the rotation to 6.0. (Leave the number of Play times set at Forever.)

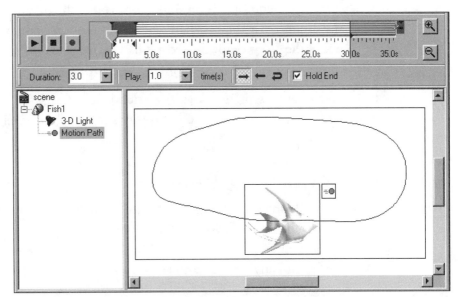

Figure 6.2

A rough oval motion path is drawn for the 3-D fish.

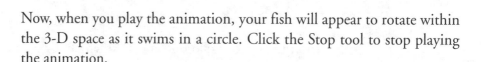

Now, when you play the animation, your fish will appear to rotate within the 3-D space as it swims in a circle. Click the Stop tool to stop playing the animation.

Adding a Two-Way Shrink Behavior to the First 3-D Fish

To make your animation look more realistic, your fish needs to appear to recede into and emerge from the background while it swims in its circle. To easily add this effect to your animation, assign a two-way shrinking behavior to your fish:

1. With the "Fish1" actor still selected, click the Shrink tool.

2. Double-click the "Shrink" actor in the structure view. Leave the Initial value as it is (100.0). Change the Final value to 25.0. Click the Close button.

3. Click the Play Forward then Backward arrow on the Timing toolbar so that the fish will shrink and regrow.

4. Leave the Duration set at 6.0. Change the number of Play times to Forever.

Now when you play your animation, your fish will appear to recede into the distance for the first half of the oval motion path and then reemerge out of the distance for the second half (see Figure 6.3). Click the Stop tool to stop playing the animation.

Hey, that was pretty easy! The trick here, of course, is just having the motion path, rotation, and two-way shrink behavior all set to the same Duration (6.0) and Play (Forever) values.

Adding Some Bubbles

You'll add the water background (the "deep blue sea") later, but why not add some bubbles right now with the Bubbles AutoEffect. Adding the bubbles at this point will insure that they appear in front of the first fish you add, but behind any subsequent fish you add to the scene (you can always add

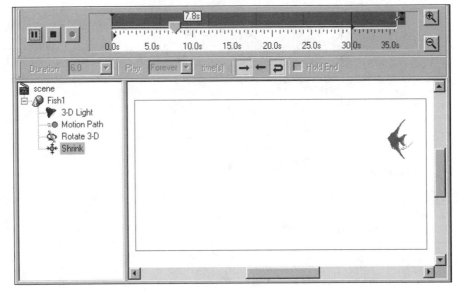

Figure 6.3

As the fish follows the motion path, it appears to recede back into the background.

more bubbles later, if you want bubbles to appear in front of your other fish as well). Add a Bubbles AutoEffect to your scene at this point:

1. Click the pull-down handle of the Insert AutoEffect tool, and then select Bubbles.

2. Double-click the "Bubbles" actor in the structure view.

3. Click the <u>G</u>low button and select a color for the bubbles' glow color. Try the bright blue color (second color down in the sixth column). Click OK.

4. Click the Glea<u>m</u> button and select a color for the bubbles' gleam color. Try the bright yellow color (second color down in the third column). Click OK.

5. Nudge the Size slider a bit to the left (toward "Smaller"). Nudge the Rate slider a bit to the right (toward "Quicker"). Nudge the Wind slider a bit to the right.

6. Click the Details tab and change the width to 400 and the height to 200. Click the Close button.

Now if you play the animation, you'll see the blue and yellow bubbles float up and slightly to the right in the scene (see Figure 6.4). Click the Stop tool to stop playing the animation.

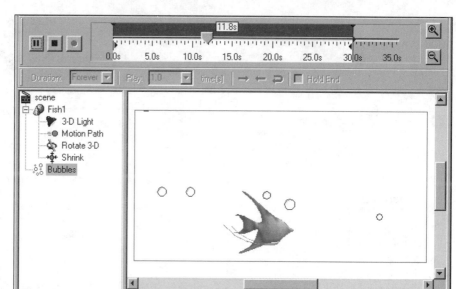

Figure 6.4

Rising bubbles are a good way to add some more movement and realism to the animation.

Creating the Second Swimming 3-D Fish

If you want to add another 3-D fish, you need to come up with a new motion path. For this fish, you'll have it swim in a clockwise circle, starting at the back of the scene. First, add the 3-D fish and position it at the top of the scene:

1. Click the Insert 3-D tool. If you haven't turned it off yet, just click OK at the Information message.

For both the Insert 2-D and Insert 3-D tools, your previous selection remains active from the last time you used the tool—the tool's icon changes to reflect the last chosen selection (the cone superimposed over the sphere, in this case). This is true as long as you haven't exited and rerun Liquid Motion.

2. Double-click Fish1.x to open it again into the scene.

3. Using the green handles, turn the fish so that it faces to the right, perpendicular to the scene. (The second fish faces the same direction

as the first fish.)

4. Drag the fish with the mouse and position it at the top of the scene, with the top of the fish overlapping the border of the scene (see Figure 6.5).

It's okay for the fish to overlap the top border of the scene because you'll add a two-way grow behavior a bit later, with the fish starting out at 25 percent of its full-size.

Recording the Second Fish's Motion Path

Now record a motion path for the second 3-D fish. As with the first 3-D fish, this should be an oval symmetrically inscribed in the scene, except you need to draw it in a clockwise direction. As with the first motion path you drew, the oval doesn't need to be perfect, but the start and end points should be fairly close to each other. When you draw the oval motion path, also make sure the 3-D fish doesn't overlap the bottom of the scene. To record the motion path:

Figure 6.5

The second 3-D fish is perpendicular to the scene and overlaps the top of the scene.

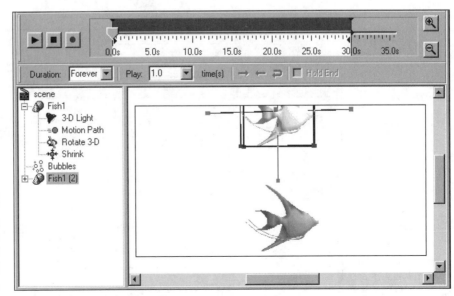

1. Click the Record Motion tool on the Player toolbar.

2. Click and hold the mouse in the center of the 3-D fish, then drag it in a rough oval, clockwise. When finished drawing the motion path, lift off the mouse button to stop recording the motion path (see Figure 6.6).

NOTE Once again, it is okay if your oval is a little irregular. You want to make sure that your motion path starts and ends as close to the same spot as you can manage. If you don't like your result, just delete the motion path and try again.

3. To have this fish swim at a different rate than the first fish, change the Duration of the motion path to 5.0. Set the number of Play times to Forever.

Adding Some Color to the Second 3-D Fish

Right now, the fish is a bit hard to see against the white background. Add some color to it:

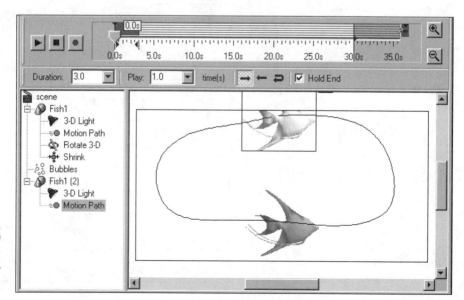

Figure 6.6

A rough oval motion path is drawn for the 3-D fish.

1. Right-click the "Fish1 (2)" actor and select Properties from the shortcut menu.

2. Click the Color radio button so that it is checked. Click the button next to the Color radio button to select a color.

3. Select a color for your fish (try the light green color, the first color in the fourth column). Click OK. Click the Close button.

Rotating the Second 3-D Fish

You now need to rotate the second 3-D fish, but in a clockwise direction:

1. Click the Rotate 3-D tool.

2. Double-click the "Rotate 3-D" actor in the structure view.

3. Select the Clockwise radio button. Click the Y button to rotate the fish around the y-axis. Click the Close button.

4. To make it match the duration of the motion path, change the Duration of the rotation to 5.0. (Leave the number of Play times set at Forever.)

Adding a Two-Way Grow Behavior to the Second 3-D Fish

To have this fish first swim out of, then back into, the background, you need to assign a two-way grow behavior to the fish:

1. Click the Grow tool.

2. Double-click the "Grow" actor in the structure view.

3. Change the Initial value to 25.0. Change the Final value to 100.0. Click the Close button.

4. Click the Play Forward then Backward arrow on the Timing toolbar so that the fish will grow and reshrink.

5. Change the Duration to 5.0. Change the number of Play times to Forever.

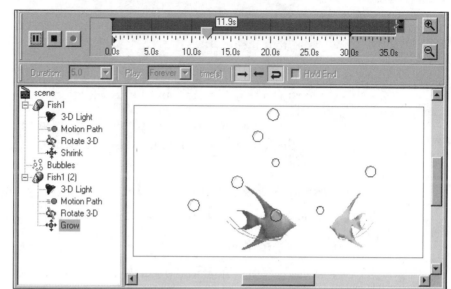

Figure 6.7

Two 3-D fish
swim in opposite
3-D circles.

Now if you play the animation, both fish appear to swim in opposite circles from each other (see Figure 6.7). Click the Stop tool to stop playing the animation.

Creating the Third Swimming 3-D Fish

You could add more fish swimming in circles, but I think the traffic lanes might get a little crowded. Instead of making this fish swim in another circle, like the first two 3-D fish, try something different. Draw the motion path so that it runs diagonally from the upper-right to the lower-left corner of the scene and apply a grow behavior so it'll also appear to emerge out of the background. Add the 3-D fish, then orient and position it where the motion path will start:

1. Click the Insert 3-D tool. If you haven't turned it off yet, just click OK at the Information message.

2. Double-click Fish1.x to open it again into the scene.

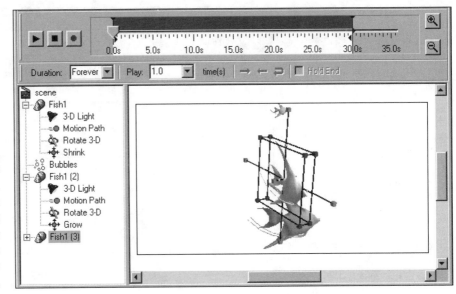

Figure 6.8

The third 3-D fish, although still at an angle relative to the scene, is oriented so that it points between the two corners of the scene.

3. You only need to change the orientation of the fish a little bit. Grab the green handle in front of the fish's head and pull it slightly up, so that it points in the direction of the lower-right corner of the scene (see Figure 6.8).

Recording the Third Fish's Motion Path

For this fish, you'll draw a motion path that will run from beyond the top-left corner to beyond the bottom-right corner of the scene:

1. Drag the fish to just beyond the upper-left corner of the scene.

NOTE To complete the motion path for your third 3-D fish, you may need to get yourself some maneuvering room in the workspace window. You need enough room to pull your fish from outside of the upper-left corner to outside of the lower-left corner. Feel free to resize Liquid Motion's window to get more room. You can also temporarily turn off the structure view, or drag its border to the left.

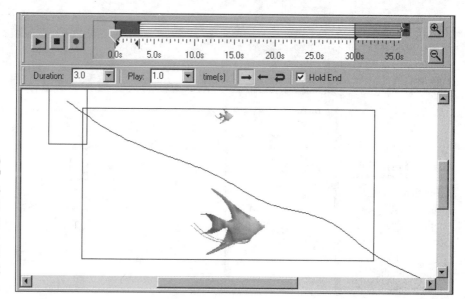

Figure 6.9

A motion path is drawn for the third 3-D fish, running from beyond the top-left corner to beyond the bottom-right corner of the scene.

2. Click the Record Motion tool and then drag the fish from beyond the upper-left corner until it is all the way beyond the bottom-right corner. Lift off the mouse button to stop recording the motion (see Figure 6.9).

NOTE As with the other motion paths, the path doesn't need to be perfect. In fact, it'll look more realistic if the path meanders just a bit.

3. Change the Duration of the motion path to 7.0. Set the number of Play times to 1.0. If you turned the structure view off, click the Structure View tool to turn it back on.

Adding Color to the Third 3-D Fish

Choose a color for this fish that's different than the colors you selected for the other two fish:

1. Double-click the "Fish1 (3)" actor in the structure view.

2. Click the Color radio button, then click the button next to it and

choose a color (try the bright yellow color, second color down in the third column). Click OK and click the Close button.

Adding a Grow Behavior to the Third 3-D Fish

Now add a grow behavior that makes the fish look as if it is emerging out of the distance while it swims diagonally across the scene:

1. Click the Grow tool.

2. Double-click the "Grow" actor in the structure view. Change the Initial value to 15.0. Change the Final value to 125.0. Click the Close button.

3. Change the Duration to 7.0. Leave the number of Play times to 1.0.

Now if you play the animation, the third 3-D fish will appear to swim out of the background from the upper left to the lower right. Click the Stop tool to stop playing the animation.

Accelerating the Third 3-D Fish

You can accelerate the motion of the fish as it swims out of the background to give it a more realistic appearance. To get the full-effect of this, you need to accelerate the 3-D fish, its motion path, and its grow behavior:

1. Double-click the "Fish1 (3)" actor in the structure view. Click the TimeEffects tab and change the Accelerate value to 100.0. Click the Close button.

2. Double-click the "Motion Path" behavior. Click the TimeEffects tab and change the Accelerate value to 100.0. Click the Close button.

3. Double-click the "Grow" behavior. Click the TimeEffects tab and change the Accelerate value to 100.0. Click the Close button.

Adding Wiggles to the Third 3-D Fish

It would be nice to add some wiggles to the movement of the third 3-D fish. This is a bit of a trick! What you do is create a series of partial two-

way 3-D rotations, but with their number of Play times set to only 0.1, alternating between counterclockwise and clockwise. Their durations vary from 1.0 to 1.9. If their start offsets are then staggered to allow some time between each rotation, the final result looks as if the 3-D fish is wiggling while swimming. Anyway, talk is cheap, so do it:

1. Click the "Fish1 (3)" actor, then click the Rotate 3-D tool. Change the number of Play times to 0.1, then click the Play Forward then Backward arrow. Change the Duration to 1.0. Click the Hold End check box so that it is unchecked.

2. Double-click the "Rotate 3-D" actor you just added. Leave the Counterclockwise radio button selected. Click the Y button to have the fish rotate around the y-axis. Click the Timing tab and change the Offset value to 1.5. Click the Close button.

3. With the "Rotate 3-D" actor still selected, press Ctrl+C to copy it, and then press Ctrl+V to paste in a copy. For the "Rotate 3-D (2)" actor, increase the Duration to 1.4.

4. Double-click the "Rotate 3-D (2)" actor. Select the Clockwise radio button. Click the Timing tab and change the Offset value to 3.2. Click the Close button.

5. Press Ctrl+V to paste in another copy. For the "Rotate 3-D (3)" actor, increase the Duration to 1.9. Double-click the "Rotate 3-D (3)" actor. Leave the Counterclockwise radio button selected. Click the Timing tab and change the Offset value to 4.5. Click Close.

Adding the Final Touches for the Third 3-D Fish

For the final touches for the 3-D fish, set it to play forever and set its start offset so it first swims into the scene one and a half seconds after the start of the animation:

1. Click the "Fish1 (3)" actor in the structure view. Change the Duration to 10.0. Change the number of Play times to Forever.

2. Double-click the "Fish1 (3)" actor. Click the Timing tab and change the Offset value to 1.5. Click Close.

NOTE Because you've set the duration of the third 3-D fish to be longer than its motion path, there'll be some extra time before the fish swims into the scene again. To increase the interval between swims, increase the duration of the third 3-D fish. You don't want to increase it too much though, or you're liable to lose some of the effect of the acceleration.

Creating the Fourth Swimming 3-D Fish

Now add the fourth of your 3-D fish. You'll have it emerge out of the background from the top of the scene, swimming in a swerving "S" pattern. As an added feature for this 3-D fish, you'll also set it so it will swim into the scene only when the mouse is moved over the scene. First, add another 3-D fish to your animation:

1. Click the Insert 3-D tool. If you haven't turned it off yet, just click OK at the Information message.

2. Double-click Fish1.x to open it again into the scene.

Recording the Motion Path for the Fourth 3-D Fish

You don't need to reorient the fourth 3-D fish before drawing its motion path. You'll draw the motion path from the top of the scene to the bottom. To create the motion path:

1. Reposition the fourth 3-D fish just above the top of the scene.

2. Click the Record Motion tool.

3. Drag the fish with the mouse from the top to the bottom of the scene, but in a swerving reversed "S" pattern (see Figure 6.10). When the motion path is beyond the bottom of the scene, lift off the mouse button to stop recording the motion path.

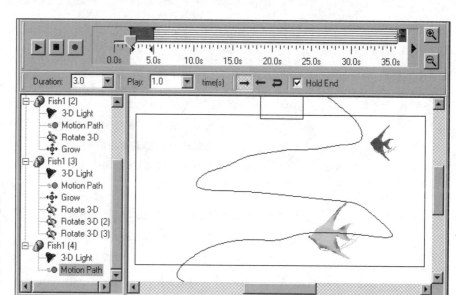

Figure 6.10

A swerving reversed "S" motion path is drawn from the top to the bottom of the scene.

Your motion path doesn't need to match exactly the motion path shown in Figure 6.10, but it should roughly approximate it. You may need to make a few attempts before you get it right (just delete the motion path, then start over). The main thing is that you have four turns in your swerve, progressively widening towards the bottom. The last turn can be mostly or even completely below the bottom of the scene (you'll use a Grow behavior, so the top of the fish should still be visible in the scene, even if the last part of the motion path isn't).

4. Change the Duration of the motion path to 6.0.

5. Double-click the "Motion Path" behavior you just added to the structure view. Click the Timing tab and make sure the Offset is set to 0.0. Click Close.

When you play the animation, you may notice that the swerving fish doesn't get entirely out of the scene. This is because motion path for the third 3-D fish doesn't go far enough out of the bottom of the scene to allow for the grow behavior's final value (125%). If it is just the tip of the fish's top fin that sticks up, you can cause it to disappear at the end of the motion path by unselecting the motion path's Hold End check box. If more of the fish than that is sticking up, you should try redrawing the motion path so it extends further beyond the bottom of the scene.

Setting the Fourth 3-D Fish's Properties

Go ahead and set the properties for the fourth 3-D fish. To make it more visible, you'll color it. To add some interactivity to the animation, you'll need to also set the fourth 3-D fish to appear only when triggered (you'll add the trigger later). Go ahead and do this now:

1. Click the "Fish1 (4)" actor. Change the Duration to 15.0. Change the number of Play times to Forever.

2. Double-click the "Fish1 (4)" actor. Select the Color radio button, then click the button next to it. Choose a color for the fish (try the salmon pink color in the upper-left corner). Click OK.

3. Click the Timing tab and select When Triggered as the Start value. The Offset value should be 0.0. Click the Close button.

Adding the Trigger for the Fourth 3-D Fish

Now before you forget to do it, add the trigger so that the fourth 3-D fish appears when the mouse is moved over the scene:

1. Click the "scene" actor at the top of the structure view.

2. Click the Trigger tool. Select Mouse Moves Over as the Action. Leave the Result set as it is (Turn On). Select scene.Fish1 (4) as the Target. Click the Close button. Now while the animation plays and the mouse is moved over the animation scene, the fourth 3-D fish appears.

Adding the Grow Behavior for the Fourth 3-D Fish

Now add a Grow behavior, so the fish will appear to emerge out of the distance in the scene:

1. Click the "Fish1 (4)" actor in the structure view.

2. Click the Grow tool.

3. Change the Duration to 6.0.

4. Double-click the "Grow" behavior you just added to the structure view. Change the Initial value to 25.0. Change the Final value to 150.0.

5. Click the Timing tab and make sure the Offset value is set to 0.0. Click the Close button.

Adding the Rotate Behaviors

Now you'll add a series of four rotate behaviors that will reorient the fish at each of the turns in your motion path:

1. Click the Rotate 3-D tool. (Click OK at the Information message, if you haven't turned it off.) Change the Duration to 1.5. Change the number of Play times to 0.2. Leave the Hold End check box checked.

2. Double-click the "Rotate 3-D" behavior you just added to the structure view. Select the Clockwise radio button and click the Y button. Click the Timing tab and change the Offset value to 0.5. Click Close.

3. Press Ctrl+C to copy the rotate behavior and then Ctrl+V to paste in a copy. Change the Duration for the second rotate behavior to 2.2. Change the number of Play times to 0.3. Leave the Hold End check box checked.

4. Double-click the "Rotate 3-D (2)" behavior you just added to the structure view. Select the Counterclockwise radio button and click the Y button. Click the Timing tab and change the Offset value to 1.7. Click the Close button.

5. Press Ctrl+V to paste in another copy of the rotate behavior. Change the Duration for the third rotate behavior to 2.5. Change the number of Play times to 0.3. Leave the Hold End check box checked.

6. Double-click the "Rotate 3-D (3)" behavior you just added to the structure view. Select the Clockwise radio button and click the Y

button. Click the Timing tab and change the Offset value to 2.5. Click the Close button.

7. Press Ctrl+V to paste in another copy of the rotate behavior. Change the Duration for the third rotate behavior to 2.5. Change the number of Play times to 0.4. Leave the Hold End check box checked.

8. Double-click the "Rotate 3-D (4)" behavior you just added to the structure view. Select the Counterclockwise radio button and click the Y button. Click the Timing tab and change the Offset value to 4.5. Click Close.

Now if you play the animation, you should see the fourth 3-D fish appear to meander from the back to the front of the scene. If your rotation turns don't quite match the swerves in the motion path, go back and adjust the Offset values of the rotate behaviors up or down a notch to synchronize them with the swerves.

Adding the Background Image

Since no more motion paths need to be displayed in the figures, go ahead and add the background image (the "deep blue sea") now:

This section uses a background image installed from the CD-ROM if you installed the Book Examples. You'll find it in the \Prima Examples\Book Images folder inside of the Liquid Motion folder (C:\Program Files\Microsoft Liquid Motion). If you haven't installed the book examples, you can do so now, or you can substitute a dark blue background color instead.

1. Double-click the "scene" actor at the top of the structure view.

2. Select the Use Background Image check box and then click the Browse button.

3. In the Book Images folder in the Microsoft Liquid Motion folder, double-click dark-water.gif. In this case, leave the Tile Image check box unchecked. Click the Close button.

Setting the 3-D Light Color

For one last touch, assign a color for each fish's "3-D Light" behavior:

1. Under the "Fish1" actor, double-click the "3-D Light" behavior. Click the Light Color button and select a color for the 3-D light source. Choose a bright color (try the bright yellow color, second down in the third column). Click OK. Click Close.

2. Repeat for each of the other fish actors ("Fish1 (2)," "Fish1 (3)," and "Fish1 (4)").

The animation only plays for 30 seconds. Set it so that it will play forever: With the "scene" actor still selected, change the Duration to Forever.

Now if you play the animation, you'll see the first three 3-D fish moving repeatedly against the dark blue water background image. When you move the mouse over the animation scene, the fourth 3-D fish will also appear, as shown in Figure 6.11.

Figure 6.11

The fourth 3-D fish swerves through the scene.

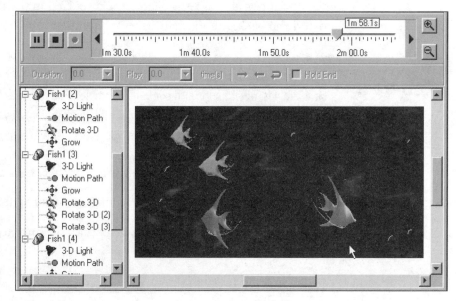

Adding a "Bubbles" Sound Effect

Right now your animation is completely mute. Add a sound effect that sounds like "bubbling." To keep it from being too irritating (this animation is set to play forever, after all), set it to be turned on when the mouse moves over the animation scene and turned off when the mouse moves off the animation scene. Do it:

1. Click the Insert Audio tool.

2. Go to the \Prima Examples\Book Sounds folder (in the Liquid Motion folder) and double-click bubbles.wav to insert it in the animation. If you haven't turned it off already, at the Information message, click OK.

3. Double-click the "bubbles" actor in the structure view. Click the Timing tab and select When Triggered as the Start value. Click the Close button.

4. Change the number of Play times to Forever.

Setting the Sound Effect Triggers

Now set the triggers that turn the sound effect on and off:

1. Click the "scene" actor at the top of the structure view.

2. Click the Trigger tool. Select Mouse Moves Over as the Action. Leave the Result set as it is (Turn On). Select scene.bubbles as the Target (way down at the bottom of the list). Click Close.

3. Click the Trigger tool again. Select Mouse Moves Off as the Action. Select Turn Off as the Result. Select scene.bubbles as the Target. Click Close.

Now if you play the animation, when you move the mouse over the animation scene, the "bubbles" sound effect plays. When you move the mouse off the scene, the sound effect stops playing.

Previewing the Animation in Internet Explorer

Go ahead now and preview your animation in Internet Explorer:

1. Click the Preview in Browser tool.

2. Type **Swimming3DFish** as the name of the animation. Click the Save button.

3. At the Publish Wizard, click the Finish button to accept all the default settings. (Your animation will be published as C:\Program Files\Microsoft Liquid Motion\Publish\Swimming3DFish\Swimming3DFish.html.)

 ◆◆

CAUTION   You should always start the names of your animation files with a letter. You might be tempted to name your animation file 3DFish. However, if you save an animation file that begins with a number, you won't be able to publish it.

◆◆

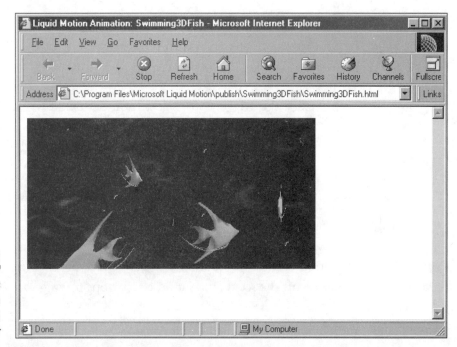

Figure 6.12

The Swimming3DFish animation in action in Internet Explorer

The animation should play in Internet Explorer. When you move the mouse over the scene, the third 3-D fish appears from the left-rear of the scene and the "bubbles" sound effect starts playing. When you move the mouse off the scene, the "bubbles" sound effect stops playing. Figure 6.12 shows the Swimming3DFish animation playing in Internet Explorer.

Working with the Swimming3DFish Animation

You can do a lot more with this animation. You can add more swimming fish, for one thing. You might add a fish swimming from the front to the back of the scene, or a fish swimming across the scene from left to right.

You can also experiment with different colors for the fish and their 3-D light sources. You can use the Animate Color tool to animate the colors of the fish.

You can add some additional interactivity. For instance, you might set the 3-D fish that swims diagonally across the scene to be triggered only when the mouse moves off the scene.

Right now, this animation doesn't lead anywhere. It just plays. If you wanted to use it as a lead-in for other Web pages, one neat trick would be to attach URL links to the 3-D fish actors, then set text messages to pop up when the viewer moves the mouse over any of the fish. The messages could say something like "Click to go to my home page," or "Click to go to my resume,"—stuff like that. You can also add a delayed message set to pop up after three minutes, for instance, that would say something like "Pass the mouse over one of the fish, you dummy!"

Using the Swimming3DFish Animation in Other Web Pages

Because the Swimming3DFish animation, except for the background image, contains 3-D shapes that are only visible in Internet Explorer 4.0+, you should probably link to it from another Web page, rather than use it on the front page of a Web site. That way, you can warn visitors that the animation can only be viewed using Internet Explorer 4.0+.

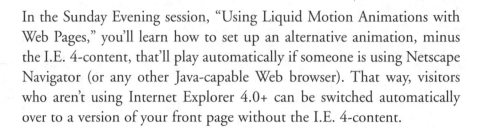

In the Sunday Evening session, "Using Liquid Motion Animations with Web Pages," you'll learn how to set up an alternative animation, minus the I.E. 4-content, that'll play automatically if someone is using Netscape Navigator (or any other Java-capable Web browser). That way, visitors who aren't using Internet Explorer 4.0+ can be switched automatically over to a version of your front page without the I.E. 4-content.

Take a Break?

Hey, you've come a long way! You deserve a break! Pry your fingers loose from that mouse, go look out the window, or water your plants if you've neglected them all weekend. If the kids are squawking because they haven't seen you since Friday evening, try bribing them with a treat to shut them up.

If you've already spent most of the day creating interactive and 3-D Web animations, feel free to skip the rest of this session and do it later. If, however, you've got time and energy left over, or you just want to have some more fun creating 3-D animations, I'll see you back in ten minutes or so.

Using Filters

Because filters are specific to Microsoft's rendition of Dynamic HTML, they can only be viewed in Internet Explorer 4.0+. Filters can only be applied to the root scene of an animation and, as their name implies, affect the entire scene (they can't be resized). They affect any actors included in the scene, as well as a background image if one is used.

◄ ◄

Dynamic HTML generally refers to the capability integrated in recent Microsoft and Netscape browsers to provide dynamic Web content that is interactively responsive to user actions. Microsoft's version, however, is quite different from Netscape's version. Thus, the "Dynamic HTML" features incorporated into Liquid Motion, such as filters and transitions, will only play in Internet Explorer 4.0+.

◄ ◄

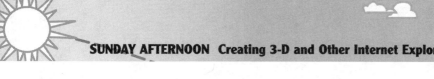
The filters that can be set are: Drop Shadow, Glow, Gray, Negative, Transparency, and Wave.

You should be aware of a few points when using filters:

- Filters can only be inserted in the root scene of an animation, but they can affect subsequent inner scenes that fall within their duration.

- You can offset the start time of filters so that they start part way through the animation, as well as set any of the Start values (When Previous Starts, When Previous Ends, and When Triggered). By doing this, you can time your filters to coincide with specific actors and events, or have them triggered by other events.

- The Drop Shadow and Glow filter effects will not be visible if you use a nontransparent background image or a background color in your animation. If you use a transparent background image, these filter effects are only visible against the transparent areas of the background image.

- The Gray, Negative, Transparency, and Wave filter effects are applied only to nontransparent areas in an animation. If you use a nontransparent background image or a background color, these effects are applied to the entire animation scene.

The following section contains a demonstration of what these filters do and how to use them. By timing filters, you can apply them to any actor at any time in your animation (but they still affect the whole scene). For the demonstration, use the image strip of the running man you used in the last example for the last session.

Applying the Drop Shadow Filter

Filters can only be applied to the root scene of an animation. To apply the Drop Shadow filter to the root scene of your animation, start a new animation and do the following:

1. Select Effects from the menu bar, and then select Filters and Drop Shadow.

2. If you haven't already turned it off, at the message telling you the effect can only be viewed in Internet Explorer 4.0+, click OK.

Inserting the Running Man Image Strip

Next, insert the image strip of the running man:

1. Click the Insert Image tool.

2. If you are not already at the \Prima Examples\Book Images folder, you'll need to change to it—you'll find it in the Liquid Motion folder (C:\Program Files\Microsoft Liquid Motion).

3. Double-click running_man.gif to open it into your animation.

4. Double-click the "running_man" actor in the structure view.

5. Select Horizontal Strip as the File Structure. Select 2 as the Number of Frames. Type 3.0 as the Frames per second. Click the Close button.

Setting the Scene Dimensions

You've probably still got the scene dimensions left over from the previous animation example. Go ahead and reset the scene dimensions to 125 x 125 pixels:

1. Double-click the "scene" actor in the structure view.

2. Click the Details tab and change the width to 125 and the height to 125. Click the Close button.

 NOTE You didn't use the Resize to Contents button in the scene properties here because that would result in a cropped drop shadow when the animation is viewed in Internet Explorer 4.0+.

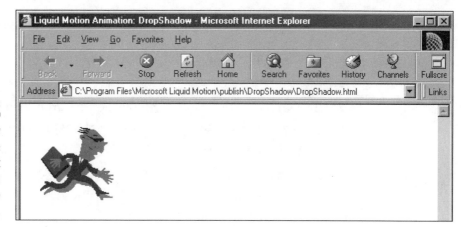

Figure 6.13

The DropShadow animation must be played in Internet Explorer before you can see the Drop Shadow filter.

Previewing Your Animation in Your Browser

You can't see the effect of filters inside of Liquid Motion. To see what a filter is doing, you have to preview your animation in Internet Explorer 4.0+. To check out what the Drop Shadow filter has done, preview your animation:

1. Click the Preview in Browser tool.

2. Type **DropShadow** as the file name for your animation. Click Save.

3. At the Publish Wizard, click Finish to accept all of the default settings (your animation will be published as C:\Program Files \Microsoft Liquid Motion\publish\DropShadow\DropShadow.html).

Besides the running man figure, you should also see a drop shadow behind the running man figure (see Figure 6.13).

Setting the Drop Shadow Properties

You can change the appearance of the Drop Shadow filter by editing its properties. To change the Drop Shadow properties, return to Liquid Motion, and then follow these steps:

1. Double-click the "Drop Shadow" actor in the structure view.

2. If you want to change the color of the drop shadow, click the Color box.

3. To increase or decrease the amount of the drop shadow offsets, change the values up or down in the Horiz or Vert boxes. (Click the Close button to close the window.)

If you've changed the color or offset properties for the "Drop Shadow" actor, go ahead and click the Preview in Browser tool again to see the changes in Internet Explorer.

Setting Filter Durations

Right now, the Drop Shadow filter is set to run forever (or until the end of the animation). Set another filter, the Transparency filter, but set it to run for only the first five seconds of the animation.

1. Select Effects, Filters, Transparency.

2. Select 25% Opaque as the degree of transparency. Click OK at the message window (if you haven't turned it off).

3. Change the Duration value to 5.0.

Now when you preview the animation in Internet Explorer, the running man appears faded out for the first five seconds (see Figure 6.14).

Running Filters in Sequence

By staggering the start times for filters, you can run filters in sequence. Add another filter, the Wave filter, but set it to start only after the Transparency filter stops running:

1. Select Effects, Filters, Wave. Click OK at the message window (if you haven't turned it off).

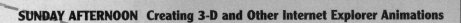

Figure 6.14

For the first five seconds of the animation, the running man figure is transparently displayed against the background.

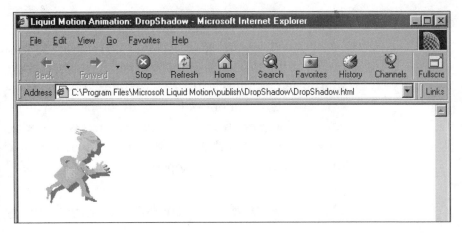

2. Double-click the "Wave" actor in the structure view. Click the Timing tab. Change the Offset value to 5.0. Click the Close button.

3. Change the number of Play times from Forever to 2.0.

NOTE Instead of offsetting the second filter's start time to coincide with the end of the first filter's duration, you could alternatively change the Start value to When Previous Ends.

Now if you preview your animation in Internet Explorer, you'll see the Wave filter effect start up when the Transparency filter ends (five seconds into the animation). It will continue for a total of six seconds (two cycles of three seconds each), after which the Drop Shadow filter alone will continue to be displayed until the end of the animation.

NOTE Although Filter effects can only be attached to the root scene, not to objects or even to inner scenes, the combination of the start offset and duration time can be used to time the points at which a filter will turn on and off in an animation.

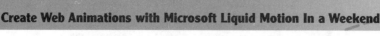

If you want, go ahead and apply some of the filters you haven't tried yet. For instance, you can attach a Glow filter to the scene, reset the number of Play times to 1 or 2, and then time it to start up after the Wave filter stops playing. Another filter you haven't tried yet is the Negative filter. You can also try out one or both of the other Transparency filters. I haven't covered changing the filter properties—feel free to experiment changing them around to see what they can do. Just double-click a filter actor in the structure view to edit its properties.

Working with the DropShadow Animation

The DropShadow animation is a demonstration, and not a full animation. If you want, however, you can take the current demonstration and expand it into a full animation. For right now, however, I recommend that you just use it as a platform for exploring what all the different filter options will do.

You can also apply filters to background images set in the scene properties. For the Drop Shadow and Glow filter effects to be visible, the background image must be a transparent GIF image. Some transparent GIF images work for this (you'll just have to check them out to see which

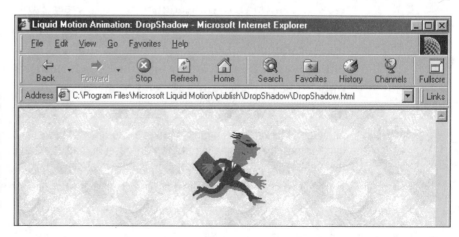

Figure 6.15

The Drop Shadow filter is displayed against a background image set in the animation's HTML file.

ones). The remainder of the filter effects can be used with both transparent and nontransparent images (including JPEG images).

The way to display a filter against a background image (or background color) is to set it in the HTML file, and not within the animation scene. Figure 6.15 shows an example of what the last part of the DropShadow animation (after the Transparency and Wave filters stop) looks like when displayed against a background image set in the HTML file's BODY tag. (I've also centered the animation in the HTML file).

Since you've made lots of changes to the DropShadow animation after you first published it, you need to save it so that your later changes will be included in your project file.

♦♦

CAUTION Any hand edits you make to DROPSHADOW.HTML come undone when you republish the animation by clicking on the Preview in Browser tool. For that reason, if you plan on making any extensive changes to your animation's HTML file, you should make the changes in a copy, rather than in the original file generated by Liquid Motion. Actually, if you don't make any changes to your animation's name or location, you won't have to repaste the animation's codes into your copy. Just open up the copy in your browser and click the Refresh (or Reload) button to see the updated changes to your animation.

♦♦

Using Transitions

Transitions are also Dynamic HTML effects that'll display only in Internet Explorer 4.0+. They are very similar to filters, the only real difference being their general function, which is to affect a "transition" within an animation. As with filters, transitions can only be applied to the root scene, but can be timed to coincide with actors and events at any point in the animation.

There are two classes of transition that you can create: Transition In and Transition Out. These are the same, except they display the transition in opposite fashions. For instance, selecting Transition Out and Dissolve

causes the affected part of the animation to gradually dissolve out of view, while selecting Transition In and Dissove causes the affected part of the animation to gradually dissolve, from nothing, into view.

You can apply the following transitions to the root scene of the animation: Dissolve, Fade, Random, Blinds, Box, Checkerboard, Circle, Random Bar, Split, Strips, and Wipe. Many of these transitions have additional options that further control how they will be displayed (for instance, you can set the Blinds to open or close vertically or horizontally, or you can set the Box or Circle to expand out or shrink back into the scene).

You'll combine the following example with the example for the next section on using 3-D shapes to create a full example animation.

Applying a Transition to a Background Image

Add a background image to the animation scene, then use a Dissolve transition to cause it to dissolve into the scene at the start of the animation. First, create a new animation and add the background image to your animation's root scene:

1. Double-click the "scene" actor in the structure view.

2. Select the Use Background Image check box. Click the Browse button to select the background image.

3. If you are not already at the \Prima Examples\Book Images folder, you'll need to change the current folder to it—you'll find it inside of Liquid Motion's folder (C:\Program Files\Microsoft Liquid Motion). Double-click 58.jpg to open it.

4. For this particular background image, make sure the Tile Image check box is unchecked.

5. While you're at it, set the scene dimensions. Click the Details tab. Change the width to 400 and the height to 200. Click the Close button. As shown in Figure 6.16, a blue and white "sky" image is the background image and the scene size is 400 **x** 200.

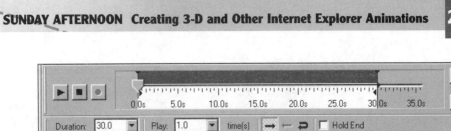

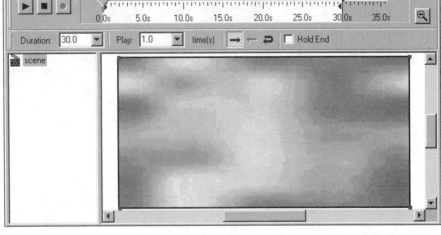

Figure 6.16

A background image of blue sky and white clouds is added to the scene.

Applying a Dissolve Transition

For your first transition, apply a Dissolve transition effect to the root scene:

1. Select Effects, Transition In, Dissolve.

2. At the Internet Explorer Only message (if you haven't turned it off by now), just click OK.

As with filters, you can't see the results of a transition inside of Liquid Motion. To see what the transition will look like, preview the animation in Internet Explorer:

1. Click the Preview in Browser tool.

2. Type **Transitions** as the file name and click Save.

3. At the Publish Wizard, click Finish to accept the default settings (your animation will be published as C:\Program Files\Microsoft Liquid Motion\publish\Transitions\Transitions.html).

Figure 6.17 shows the background "sky" image as it dissolves into the scene. (If you selected Transition Out instead of Transition In, then the "sky" image dissolves out of the scene.)

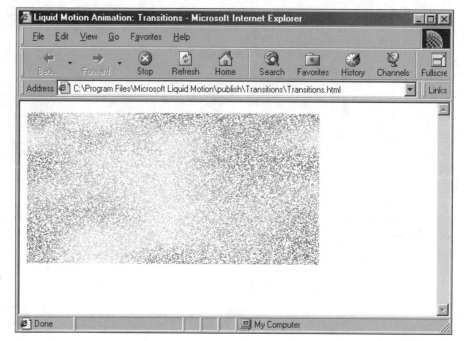

Figure 6.17

A "sky" background
image dissolves into
the scene.

Applying Mirrored Box Transitions

Combine a Transition Out and a Transition In transition to add some
impact to your transition. You'll first use a Transition Out/Box-In transition
to cause the background image to disappear within a shrinking box. Then,
you'll use a Transition Out/Box-Out transition to cause the background
image to reappear within an expanding box. Add the first transition:

1. Select Effects, Transition Out, Box, In.

2. If you haven't turned them off yet, just click OK at the message boxes.

3. Double-click the "TransOut [Box-In]" actor in the structure view.
    Click the Timing tab and change the Offset value to 4.0. Click the
    Close button.

The offset is set to 4.0 to cause the transition to start one second after the previous transition ends (it was set to run for three seconds). By starting this transition one second after the end of the previous transition, you allow the full background image to remain visible for one second after it dissolves. Add the second paired transition:

1. Select Effects, Transition In, Box, Out.

2. If you haven't turned them off yet, just click OK at the message boxes.

3. Double-click the "TransIn [Box-Out]" actor in the structure view. Click the Timing tab. Change the Offset value to 7.0. Click the Close button.

The offset is set to 7.0 here so that it follows immediately after the previous transition. If you include a one-second delay, as with the previous transition, the full background image pops back into view, which is not what you want.

Go ahead and click the Preview in Browser tool to check out what these two filters look like in Internet Explorer. Figure 6.18 shows the first Box transition in progress (although it could just as well show the second transition).

Applying Transitions to Inner Scenes

While you can only apply a transition to the root scene, you can time it to coincide with any inner scenes you want to add to your animation. That way, for instance, you can apply transitions to a series of background images, each set in a different inner scene.

Starting out, add an inner scene to the animation. You'll set it so that it is smaller than the root scene, has a different background image, and jumps around inside of the root scene. You'll also set the start offset so that the root scene starts at the same time as the second paired Box transition and first appears within the expanding box. Add the inner scene:

1. Select Insert, Inner Scene from the menu bar.

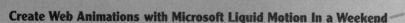

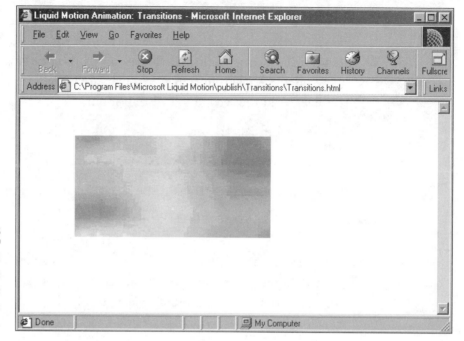

Figure 6.18

The background image makes the transition out of the scene as a shrinking box.

2. Double-click the "Inner Scene" actor in the structure view. Click the Select the Background Image check box, and then click Browse. In the Book Images folder, double-click Rdsand.gif. Select the Tile Image check box so the background image is tiled.

3. Click the Timing tab and set the Start offset to 7.0 so that it is the same as the preceding behavior.

4. Click the Details tab and change the width to 300 and the height to 125. Click the Close button.

 5. Click the Jump tool on the Behaviors toolbar.

6. Double-click the "Jump" behavior in the structure view. Change the jump rate to 0.3 jumps per second. Click the Close button.

7. On the Timing toolbar, change the Duration value to 5.0.

Now when you preview the animation in Internet Explorer, while the second Box transition runs, you'll see the inner scene background image jump around inside of the expanding Box transition (see Figure 6.19).

Adding a Checkerboard Transition

Next, add another transition, a Checkerboard transition, that runs immediately following the second Box transition:

1. Click the "scene" actor to apply the transition to the root scene.

2. Select Effects, Transition Out, Checkerboard, Across. If you haven't turned them off yet, just click OK at the message boxes.

3. Double-click the "TransOut [Checkerboard-Across]" actor in the structure view. Click the Timing tab and change the Offset value to 12.0. Click the Close button.

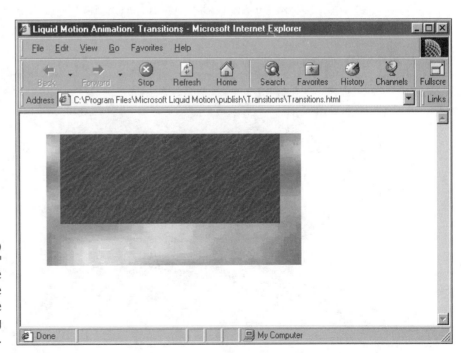

Figure 6.19

The inner scene background image jumps around inside of the expanding Box transition.

Now when you preview your animation in Internet Explorer, you'll see the Checkerboard transition in action immediately following the second Box transition (see Figure 6.20).

Adding Another Inner Scene

Now add a second inner scene that appears after the Checkboard transition has finished running. As with the first inner scene, assign a new background image. However, instead of having it jump around, create a motion path for it. First, add the inner scene and set the background image:

1. Click back on the "scene" actor at the top of the structure view.

2. Select Insert, Inner Scene from the menu bar.

3. Double-click the "Inner Scene (2)" actor in the structure view.

4. Select the Use Background Image check box. Click the Browse button. In the Book Images folder, double-click back_rock.jpg. Click the Tile Image folder so that it is checked.

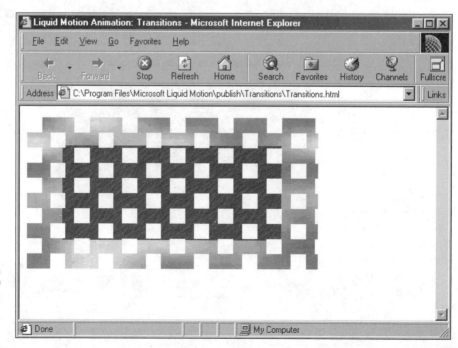

Figure 6.20

The Checkerboard transition in action in Internet Explorer.

5. Click the Timing tab. Change the Offset value to 15.0.

6. Click the Details tab. Change the width to 225 and the height to 75. Click Close.

Now add the motion path:

1. Click the Record Motion tool on the Player toolbar.

2. Click inside the borders of the scene you just added, drag the scene in a circle several times, then lift up off the mouse button to stop recording the motion path. An animation preview will play.

3. Click the Hold End check box so that it is not checked.

Adding an Expanding Circle Transition

Now add another transition, one that will cause the inner scene you just created to first appear inside of an expanding circle that grows to fill the animation scene:

1. Click the "scene" actor at the top of the structure view.

2. Select Effects, Transition In, Circle, Out. If you haven't turned them off yet, just click OK at the message boxes.

3. Double-click the "TransIn [Circle-Out]" actor in the structure view. Click the Timing tab and change the Offset value to 15.0. Click Close.

Now if you preview the animation in Internet Explorer, following the Checkerboard transition, you'll see the background image of the second inner scene moving in circles inside of the expanding Circle transition (see Figure 6.21).

Adding Sound Effects

Right now, the Transitions animation doesn't have any sound effects attached to it. Go ahead and add some sound, just to give it some additional dramatic flair:

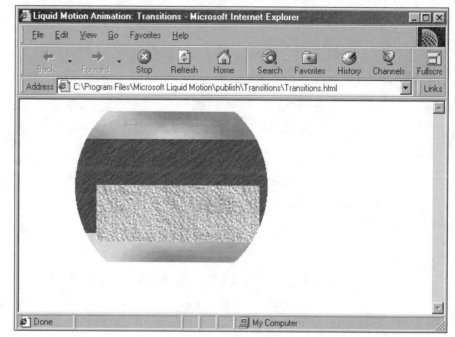

Figure 6.21

An expanding Circle transition reveals a second inner scene moving in circles.

1. Click the "scene" actor at the top of the structure view.

2. Click the Insert Audio tool. Go to the \Prima Examples\Book Sounds folder (inside of Liquid Motion's folder) and double-click Gong3.wav. At the Information window telling you that WAV files can only be heard in Internet Explorer 4.0+, just click OK.

3. Double-click the "Gong3" actor in the structure view. Click the Timing tab and change the Offset to 0.0 (you want this sound effect to play at the start of the animation).

4. Click the Insert Audio tool again. In the Book Sounds folder, double-click Affair.wav. At the Information window, just click OK (unless you've turned it off).

5. Double-click the "Affair" actor in the structure view. Click the Timing tab and change the Offset to 7.0. Click the Close button.

6. Click the Insert Audio tool one more time. In the Book Sounds folder, double-click Fanfare3.wav. Just click OK at the Information window (if you haven't turned it off already).

7. Right-click the "Fanfare3" actor in the structure view and select Properties from the shortcut menu. Click the Timing tab and change the Offset to 15.5. Click Close.

Now go ahead and preview your animation in Internet Explorer. You'll hear three different sound effects spaced out through the animation. If you want to adjust the points at which they play in the animation, just adjust their Offset values.

Setting Your Animation's End State

As it is now, the Transitions animation will shut off after 30 seconds, leaving a blank screen. To have the end of the scene stay onscreen at the end of the animation:

1. Click the "scene" actor in the structure view.

2. Click the Hold End check box so that it is checked.

Since you've made lots of changes to the Transitions animation after you first published it, you need to save it so that your later changes will be included in your project file. Go ahead and save the Transitions animation: Select <u>F</u>ile, <u>S</u>ave.

Working with the Transitions Animation

You'll use the Transitions animation as the basis for the next animation example, so if you want to experiment further with using transitions, you

should first save it under another name. Select File, Save As, and then save it under a different name (Transitions2, for instance).

If you want to play around some more creating transitions, go ahead and try adding some of the other Transition effects that you haven't used yet, such as the Fade, Split, or Wipe transitions, for instance. Just make sure you space them out (with the Offset start value) so that they don't overlap each other. Go ahead and add some additional inner scenes, if you want. (If you look in the \Prima Examples\Book Images folder, you'll find lots of background images you can use—they're the images with "back_" in their names.)

The animation is at this point a work in progress, a demonstration of how some of the Transition effects work. You can add some text objects to it so that a message unfolds as the animation is plays. The last text object could have a URL link associated with it so that clicking on it would hop to another Web page. You can also add some additional sound effects or substitute different sound effects for the ones already added.

Take a Break?

This is a long session (and it's been a long weekend), so take another break if you want. Do some deep breathing, stand up and touch your toes, do some eye exercises. I'll see you back in a bit when you'll learn how to add rotating textured 3-D shapes to your animations.

Using 3-D Objects

At the start of this session, you used a 3-D image of a fish to create a bunch of 3-D swimming fish. You also set the light source for your 3-D fish. In this example, I'll show you how to use some of the other 3-D shapes, as well as how to add some surface textures to them.

3-D shapes can be moved and rotated in space, their direct or ambient light sources can be controlled, and textures can be applied to their surfaces. 3-D shapes, like the other main effects covered in this session, are displayable only in Internet Explorer 4.0+.

NOTE This example builds on the previous example, so if you didn't do the previous example, "Using Transitions," you should return and do it first before continuing. If you still have the Transitions animation open in Liquid Motion and haven't saved it yet, you should save it now. If you've experimented and made additional changes to the Transitions animation since saving it, you should save it now under another name: Select File, Save As, and save it using a name other than Transitions.

To open the Transitions animation you saved previously, do this:

1. If you are still inside Liquid Motion, select File, Open. If you have exited Liquid Motion, just rerun Liquid Motion and select the Open an Existing Animation File radio button at the Getting Started window, and then click OK.

2. Double-click Transitions.jck to open it in Liquid Motion.

3. If the structure view is not turned on, click the Structure View tool.

Now, you need to resave the Transitions animation you just opened under another name. That way, you can reuse the Transitions animation as a base for further animations, if you want.

1. Click File, Save As.

2. Type **FlyingShapes** as the new name for the animation. Click Save.

For this particular animation, you want it to keep it running at the end (you'll see why at the end). Change the duration of the animation so that it will run forever:

1. Click the "scene" actor at the top of the structure view.

2. Change the Duration to Forever.

Adding Another Transition

Add another transition effect that will open the 3-D object section of the animation. You'll use a Split transition this time:

1. The "scene" actor should still be selected.

2. Select Effects, Transition In, Split, Horizontal In. Click OK at each of the Information windows (if you haven't previously turned them off).

3. Right-click the "TransIn [Split-Horizontal (In)]" actor in the structure view and select Properties from the shortcut menu.

4. Change the Offset value to 18.0 in the Timing tab. Click Close.

Adding Another Inner Scene

Go ahead and add another inner scene that will be used as the backdrop for the 3-D shapes you'll add. To give it a "spatial" look, you'll assign a background image that looks like a field of stars in the nighttime sky:

1. Select Insert, Inner Scene.

2. Right-click the "Inner scene (3)" actor in the structure view and choose Properties from the shortcut menu.

3. Click the Use Background Image check box so that it is checked. Click the Browse button and then double-click back_stars2.jpg in the Book Images folder. Select the Tile Image check box to tile the background image.

4. Click the Timing tab and change the Offset value to 18.0.

5. Click the Details tab and change the width to 375 and the height to 175. Click Close.

6. Change the Duration to Forever.

Inserting the 3-D Cube

Now insert a 3-D cube:

1. The "Inner scene (3)" actor should still be highlighted in gray. Click the pull-down handle of the Insert 3-D tool and click the "cube" shape to insert a 3-D cube.

2. Click OK at the Information window telling you 3-D shapes can be displayed only in Internet Explorer 4.0+.

Since you inserted the cube shape immediately after inserting the inner scene, the "Cube" actor should now be inserted underneath the "Inner scene (3)" actor (see Figure 6.22).

Applying a Surface Texture to the Cube

Edit the properties for the cube shape and apply a texture to its surface (and get rid of that icky split pea soup color):

1. Double-click the "Cube" actor in the structure view.

2. Select the Texture radio button (so that it is filled). Click the Browse button that is below the Texture radio button.

3. You'll need to go to the \Prima Examples\Book Images folder (inside of the Liquid Motion folder). Double-click bk.jpg in the Book Images folder. Click the Close button.

The cube shape now looks somewhat like a block of concrete (a big improvement over split pea soup, I think. See Figure 6.23).

Figure 6.22

A 3-D cube shape is inserted into an inner scene with a "starry" background image.

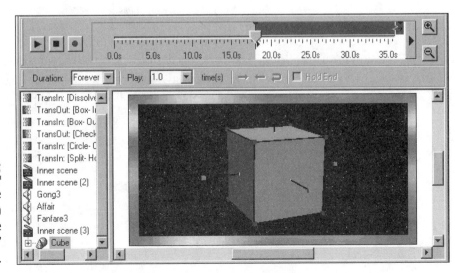

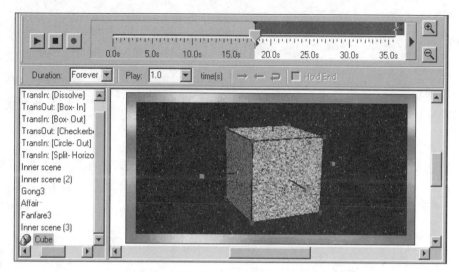

Figure 6.23

A surface texture, somewhat resembling concrete, is applied to the cube.

You can change the attitude of the cube by grabbing one of the green handles and then pulling it to change the dimensional position of the cube. Grab the front green handle and then pull it to the right (so that more of the shadow side of the cube is visible).

Rotating the Cube

Right now, the cube shape sits motionless. To cause it to rotate, click the Rotate 3-D tool.

You should see the cube rotate for one cycle (three seconds), after which the rotational axis, indicated by a yellow arrow, is displayed. You can change the direction of the rotational axis by grabbing the head of the yellow arrow with the mouse and dragging it to a new position. Try dragging it downward slightly (see Figure 6.24).

Adjusting the Light Source

You can also adjust the light source, changing its position and color, for instance:

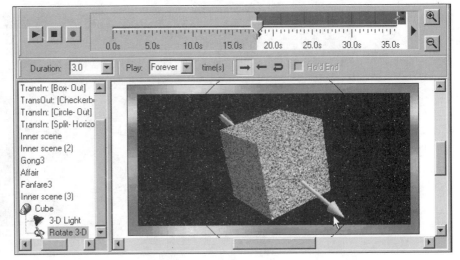

Figure 6.24

The rotational axis for the cube is moved slightly to the right.

1. Double-click the "3-D Light" behavior listed under the "Cube" actor.

2. Click the <u>L</u>ight Color box and then select a color for the light source. Try the salmon red color (first color in the first row). Click OK.

3. Click the lamp (above the upper-right corner of the cube) and pull it to adjust its position and angle. Feel free to try out more than one position and angle (see Figure 6.25).

Growing the Cube out of the Background

Finally, apply a Grow behavior to the cube so that it grows out of the background:

1. Click the Grow tool. Double-click the "Grow" behavior added under the "Cube" actor.

2. Change the Initial value to 0.0 and the Final value to 100.0. Click Close.

You'll notice that the cube disappears. That's because at the point you are at on the timeline, the grow size of the cube is zero.

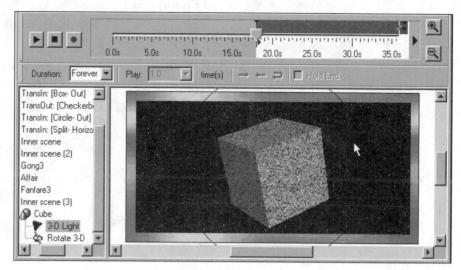

Figure 6.25

The lamp position and angle are adjusted.

Changing the Cube's Start Time and Duration

You want the cube to first become visible after the Split transition finishes playing. You also don't want it to play forever. Set the cube to start three seconds after the start of the inner scene and to run for a duration of six seconds:

1. Double-click the "Cube" actor and click the Timing tab.

2. Change the Offset value from 0.0 to 3.0 to cause it to first appear three seconds after the start of the inner scene. Click the Close button.

3. Change the Duration value to 6.0.

Previewing the Animation

To see the Split transition, inner scene, and rotating cube all working together in combination, click the Preview in Browser tool. Click the Finish button (the animation will be published as C:\Program Files\Microsoft Liquid Motion\publish\FlyingShapes\FlyingShapes.html). Figure 6.26 shows the flying cube shape while it rotates and grows out of the starry background.

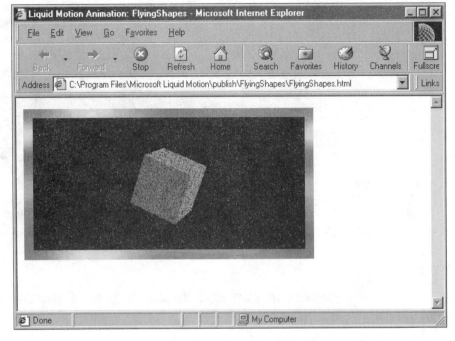

Figure 6.26

The cube shape grows out of the starry background.

Inserting the 3-D Cylinder

Next, insert a 3-D cylinder shape that grows out of the starry background once the rotating cube disappears. With the "Cube" actor still selected, follow these steps:

1. Click the pull-down handle of the Insert 3-D tool.

2. Click the "cylinder" shape (the fourth button) to insert a 3-D cylinder.

3. Click OK at the Information window telling you 3-D shapes can be displayed only in Internet Explorer 4.0+ (if you haven't already turned this off).

Since you inserted the cube shape immediately after inserting the inner scene, the "Cylinder" actor is also inserted underneath the "Inner scene (3)" actor (see Figure 6.27).

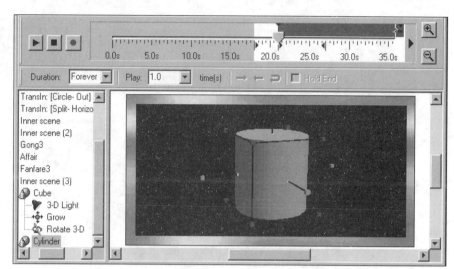

Figure 6.27

A 3-D cylinder shape is added to the scene.

Repositioning and Reshaping the Cylinder

Reposition the cylinder so that it inclines, and reshape it so that it looks more like a "pillar."

1. Use the cylinder's green handles to reorient it so it is inclined on its side (see Figure 6.28).

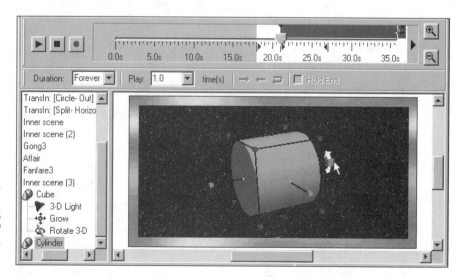

Figure 6.28

The cylinder turns on its side.

2. Grab one of the cylinder's red handles and pull it to reshape the cylinder into a pillar (see Figure 6.29).

You want to rotate the cylinder like the cube, but you'll change the rotational axis in another way:

1. Click the Rotate 3-D tool.

2. Doubgle-click the cylinder's "Rotate 3-D" behavior in the structure view.

3. Select the Clockwise radio button. Click the X button to have the cylinder rotate along the x-axis. Click the Close button.

Applying a Surface Texture to the Cylinder

To get rid of that icky split pea soup color, go ahead and apply a surface texture to the cylinder:

1. Double-click the "Cylinder" actor in the structure view.

2. Select the Texture radio button, then click its Browse button.

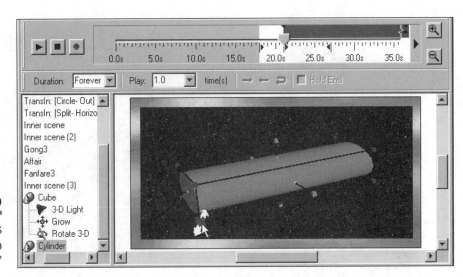

Figure 6.29

The cylinder is reshaped into a "pillar."

3. Double-click cf.jpg in the Book Images folder to open it. Click the Close button.

4. Double-click the "3-D Light" actor (under "Cylinder"). Click the Light Color button and select a color for the light source. Try the second light blue color (the second color down in the fifth row). Click OK. Click the Close button. The cylinder looks like it has a marbled dark green surface (see Figure 6.30).

Growing the Cylinder out of the Background

Just as with the cube, grow the cylinder out of the background:

1. Click the Grow tool.

2. Double-click the "Grow" behavior (under "Cylinder").

3. Change the Initial value to 0.0 and the Final value to 90.0. (You can adjust the Final value later, if you want.) Click the Close button.

You'll notice that the cylinder disappeared. That's because at the point you are at on the timeline, the grow size of the cube is zero.

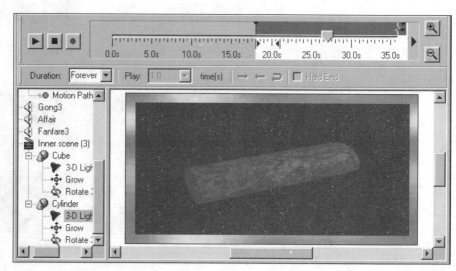

Figure 6.30

A dark marbled surface texture is applied to the cylinder.

Changing the Cylinder's Start Time

The cylinder has the same start time as the cube. Change its start time so that it appears after the Cube disappears:

1. Double-click the "Cylinder" actor in the structure view.

2. Click the Timing tab and change the Offset value to 9.0. Click Close.

Now if you preview the animation, after the cube disappears, the cylinder revolves out of the starry background (see Figure 6.31).

Inserting the 3-D Skeleton Key

Besides the standard 3-D shapes included with the minimum installation or evaluation version of Liquid Motion, some more specific 3-D shapes are also included (you already used one, the 3-D fish). For this example animation, you'll add a 3-D skeleton key and set it to rotate in front of the rotating cylinder. Finally, you'll attach a URL link to the 3-D skeleton

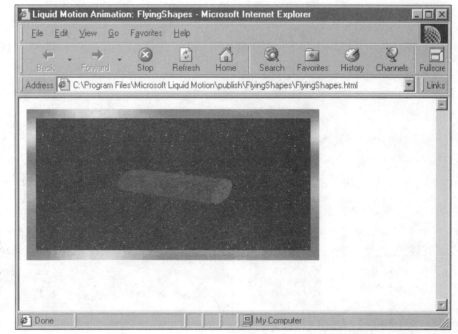

Figure 6.31

The dark green marbled cylinder grows out of the background in Internet Explorer.

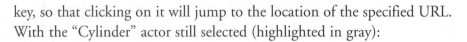

key, so that clicking on it will jump to the location of the specified URL. With the "Cylinder" actor still selected (highlighted in gray):

1. Click the pull-down handle of the Insert 3-D tool.

2. Click the last button (the one with a cone and a sphere). At the Information message, click OK (if you didn't previously turn it off).

3. Double-click SkeletonKey.x to insert it into the scene.

4. By grabbing and pulling the green and red handles, reposition and increase the size of the skeleton key (see Figure 6.32).

Rotating the 3-D Skeleton Key

Now rotate the 3-D skeleton key. You'll leave it rotating counterclockwise so that it will rotate the opposite direction of the cylinder's rotation. Go ahead and rotate the 3-D skeleton key now:

1. Click the Rotate 3-D tool.

2. Double-click the "Rotate 3D" behavior (under "SkeletonKey"). Click the X button to specify the x-axis as the rotational axis. Click Close (see Figure 6.33).

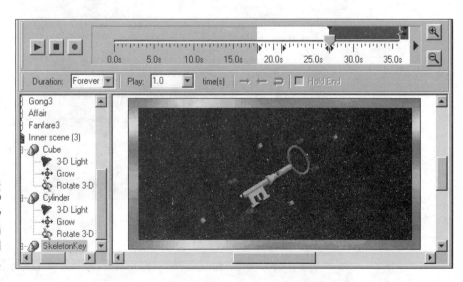

Figure 6.32

A 3-D skeleton key is inserted, then repositioned and resized.

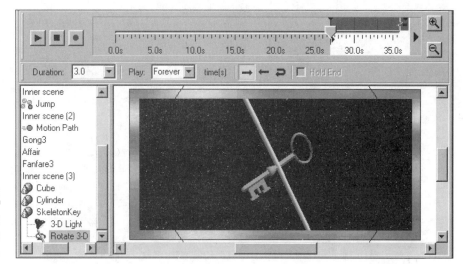

Figure 6.33

The 3-D skeleton key is set to rotate around the x-axis.

You may want to experiment with repositioning the yellow rotational axis arrow to get just the right rotation. Grab and pull it anywhere along its shaft. Click the Play tool on the Player toolbar to check out the new rotation, and then click the Stop tool to stop the animation from playing. Click again on the "Rotate 3D" actor under the "SkeletonKey" actor and then repeat to check out different positions and angles (you can also manually slide the Slider Button until the 3-D skeleton key becomes visible).

Setting the 3-D Skeleton Key's Start Time

Set the Offset value for the 3-D skeleton key so that it starts after the rotating cylinder emerges out of the starry background. Follow these steps:

1. Double-click the "SkeletonKey" actor.

2. Click the Timing tab and change the Offset value to 14.0. Click the Close button.

Now when you preview the animation in Internet Explorer, you'll see the rotating 3-D skeleton key appear five seconds after the rotating cylinder emerges out of the background (see Figure 6.34).

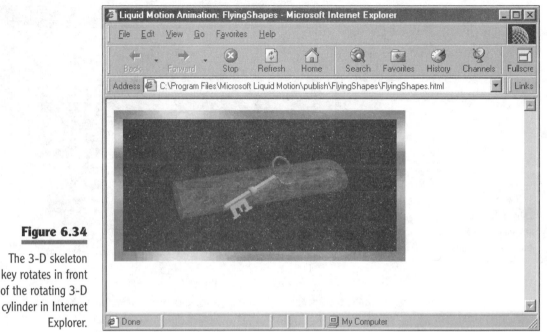

Figure 6.34

The 3-D skeleton key rotates in front of the rotating 3-D cylinder in Internet Explorer.

Adding Some More Sound Effects

How about some sound to jazz up your animation? Add sound effects that are synchronized to the appearance of the cube, cylinder, and skeleton key shapes:

1. Click the "Cube" actor in the structure view, and then click the Insert Audio tool. In the Book Sounds folder, double-click ominous.wav to add it to the scene. Click OK at the Information message (if you haven't already turned it off).

TIP   By first selecting the "Cube" actor and then inserting the ominous.wav sound file, the start offset of the sound file will be automatically set to coincide with the "Cube" actor.

2. Click the "Cylinder" actor, and then click the Insert Audio tool. In the Book Sounds folder, double-click ominous.wav again to add it

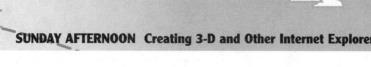

once more to the scene. Click OK at the Information message (if you haven't already turned it off).

3. Click the "SkeletonKey" actor, and then click the Insert Audio tool. In the Book Sounds folder, double-click psycho.wav to add it to the scene. Click OK at the Information message (if you haven't already turned it off). On the Timing toolbar, change the number of play times to 3.0.

To jog the sound effects off just a bit, edit the properties of the sound effects and then increase the Offset value in the Timing tab by 0.5.

Now if you preview your animation in Internet Explorer, you'll hear the new sound effects play half a second after the appearance of their associated objects.

Adding a Mouse-Over Message

Why don't you add some interactivity to this animation? How about a "mouse over" message that tells the viewer to click the key whenever the mouse is passed over the key? Add this suggested mouse-over message (you can make up a different one, if you want):

1. With the "SkeletonKey" actor still selected, click the Insert Text tool.

2. Type **Click the Key!** as the text.

3. Select DialogInput as the Font, Bold as the Style, and 14 as the Size.

4. Click the Color button and select a color for the text. Try the bright yellow color (second color down in the third column). Click OK.

5. Click the Background button and select a color for the text background. Try the bright red color (second color down in the first column). Click OK.

6. Click the Drop Shadow button and select a color for the text's drop shadow. Try the navy blue color (third color down in the sixth column). Click OK.

7. Click the Timing tab and select When Triggered as the Start value. Click Close.

8. Click the "SkeletonKey" actor, then click the Trigger tool. For the Action, select Mouse Moves Over. For the Target, select scene.Inner scene (3).Text (or scene.Inner scene (3).Click the Key!, if that's how it's displayed). Click the Close button.

9. Click the Trigger tool again. For the Action, select Mouse Moves Off. For the Result, select Turn Off. For the Target, select scene.Inner scene (3).Text (or scene.Inner scene (3).Click the Key!, if that's how it's displayed). Click the Close button.

Now if you preview your animation in Internet Explorer, after the rotating skeleton key appears, when you move the mouse over the skeleton key, a message, "Click the Key!," will be displayed, as shown in Figure 6.35. When you move the mouse off the skeleton key, the message disappears.

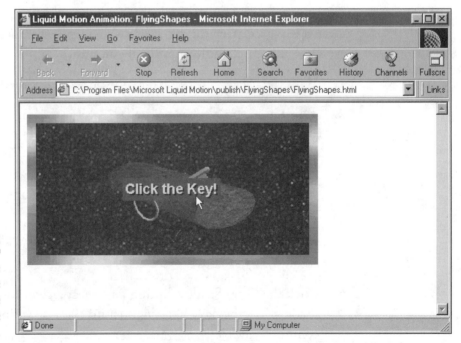

Figure 6.35

When the mouse moves over the skeleton key, the message "Click the Key!" is displayed.

Adding the URL Link

You still need to add the URL link that will be activated when the skeleton key is clicked. For this example, you'll include a relative URL that will link to the Welcome animation you created in the Saturday Afternoon session. Go ahead and add the URL link now to the skeleton key:

1. Click the "SkeletonKey" actor, and then click the URL Link tool.

2. Delete the contents of the URL box, and then type ../**Welcome /Welcome.html** as the URL link. Click Close.

Now if you preview the animation in Internet Explorer, when you click the 3-D skeleton key, you'll jump to the Welcome animation you created in the Saturday Afternoon session. To save your latest changes to your animation's project file, select File, Save.

There's lots more you can do to further customize this animation. For instance, you can try out some different background images in the scenes, or you can try different images for the 3-D object surface textures. You might also insert a text message that is progressively displayed at different points in the animation. You can also add additional inner scenes, transitions, 3-D objects, and sound effects. Your imagination is your limit.

The FlyingShapes animation uses many effects that will only display in Internet Explorer 4.0+. Instead of using it as your front page, you might want to precede it with a page that allows visitors who aren't using Internet Explorer 4.0+ to choose a different page. Hey, that could be another animation project—a couple of animated buttons, one for Internet Explorer 4.0+, the other one for everybody else.

In the Sunday Evening session, "Using Liquid Motion Animations in Web Pages," you'll learn how to create an alternative animation without the Internet Explorer 4+ content, which users of Navigator will see automatically.

Wrapping Up

You covered quite a lot in this session, especially if you managed to do all of the examples. This afternoon you learned how to:

- Use Filters such as Drop Shadow, Wave, Transparency, and others.
- Use Transitions such as Dissolve, Box, Checkerboard, Circle, Split, and others.
- Play Filters and Transitions in sequence.
- Use Filters and Transitions in combination with inner scenes.
- Insert 3-D objects, such as cubes, cylinders, and other 3-D images (skeleton keys and fish, for instance).
- Apply surface textures to 3-D objects and change 3-D light source colors and directions.
- Adjust the attitude and orientation of 3-D objects.
- Change the direction and axis of a 3-D rotation.
- Include WAV and MIDI sound effects.
- Create complex 3-D movements by combining motion paths, growing and shrinking, and rotations.

This is it for the straight animation tutorials. The next session will walk you through including Liquid Motion animations in different kinds of Web pages, as well as give you additional pointers on things you can do with HTML to make your animations more effective. You'll also find information in the appendixes about using Liquid Motion with FrontPage 98

Bonus Session: Using Liquid Motion Animations in Web Pages

- ✿ Editing Liquid Motion Animation Files
- ✿ Displaying Animations Against Background Images
- ✿ Displaying Animations in Tables and Frames
- ✿ Creating Browser-Specific Animations
- ✿ Publishing Multiple Animations

U p until now, you've primarily created stand-alone Web animations. In this bonus session, you'll learn how to optimize your Web animations in HTML Web pages, including:

⬡ Editing Liquid Motion HTML files

⬡ Centering Liquid Motion animations

⬡ Using background images and colors

⬡ Using Liquid Motion animations in tables

⬡ Creating internal hypertext links

⬡ Using Liquid Motion animations in frames

⬡ Creating browser-specific animations

⬡ Creating automatic forwarding links with the META tag

⬡ Using script triggers

⬡ Picking up tips for publishing multiple animations

Editing Liquid Motion HTML Files

Whenever Liquid Motion publishes an animation, it writes an HTML file to the animation's publish folder. If, for instance, you publish an animation called SnackBar to the \Publish\SnackBar folder, an HTML file,

◆◆

If you have no experience with HTML, you may encounter some difficulty with the material covered in the later part of this session. To get the most out of publishing Liquid Motion animations on the Web, at least a basic knowledge of HTML is *highly* recommended. If you want to learn HTML, please check out my *Learn HTML In a Weekend, Revised Edition*. See Prima's Web site (**www.prima-tech.com**) for details. You can also find many online HTML tutorials, guides, and quick references at this book's Web site (**www.callihan.com/liquidmotion/**).

◆◆

SnackBar.html, is written to that folder. You can edit that HTML file, adding a heading, text, links, or anything else with HTML.

The easiest way to edit an animation's HTML file is to open it in Windows Notepad. To run Windows Notepad, click the Start button and then select Programs, Accessories, and Notepad. To open an HTML file in Notepad:

1. Click File, Open. Change the Files of Type selection to All Files (*.*).

2. Go to the folder where the HTML file that you want to edit is stored. To get to the Liquid Motion publish folder, click the Up One Level button to go to the Desktop folder, then double-click My Computer, (C:), Program Files, Microsoft Liquid Motion, and publish. Double-click the folder for your animation (SnackBar, for instance). (If you've installed Liquid Motion elsewhere, you'll need to substitute the actual location of Liquid Motion on your computer.)

3. Double-click the HTML file you want to open (SnackBar.html, for instance).

You can also copy the animation code from SnackBar.html and paste it into another HTML file where you want it to appear. To copy the animation code, after you open the animation's HTML file in Notepad:

1. Click in front of the line beginning with "`<!—WEBBOT bot="lmweb-bot"...`" and hold down the Shift key.

2. Still holding down the Shift key, scroll to the bottom of the animation HTML file and click after the end of the "`<!—WEBBOT bot="HTMLMarkup" EndSpan —>`" line.

3. Release the Shift key. The animation code will be highlighted in blue. Press Ctrl+C to copy the code (or select Edit, Copy from the menu bar).

4. Open in Notepad the HTML file to which you want to copy the animation code. Position the cursor where you want the animation code to be inserted, and then press Ctrl+V to paste in the code (or select Edit, Paste from the menu bar).

NOTE When pasting Liquid Motion animation code into other HTML files, always make sure that you paste it in below the <BODY> start tag, but above the </BODY> end tag. You should also be careful not to paste the code between a "<" character and a ">" character, in that these mark the beginning and end of an HTML tag.

If the HTML file to which you're copying the animation code is in the same folder as the HTML file from which you're copying the animation code, then you don't need to do anything more. The animation will play in the second HTML file just as it did in the first HTML file. However, if the second HTML file is in another folder, you'll need to copy all of the other files in the first folder (SnackBar.jcz and SnackBar.x), plus all of the subfolders in the first folder (audio, dnx, images, and js), to the second folder.

TIP In Internet Explorer 4.0+, you can open the HTML file for any displayed Web page in Notepad by selecting View, Source. You should realize, however, that if you've already opened a copy of the HTML file in Notepad, this will open a second copy.

Previewing HTML Files in Your Web Browser

When you preview an animation's HTML file from inside of Liquid Motion, it automatically runs your default Web browser and loads the animation's HTML file. However, when making changes to a Liquid Motion HTML file, you'll need to follow these steps to preview it in your browser:

1. Open an Animation's HTML file in Notepad (SnackBar.html, for instance).

2. Since any changes you make directly to your animation's HTML file will be wiped out if you republish your animation, it is a good idea to make your changes to a copy of your animation's HTML file, rather than to the original. To do this, resave the HTML file under another name (SnackBar2.html, for instance).

3. Edit the animation file, adding headings, paragraph text, hypertext links, or whatever you want to be displayed in the HTML file in addition to the animation.

4. Save the edited animation file (File, Save).

5. Run your Web browser, preferably without connecting to the Internet. Open the HTML file (SnackBar2.html, for instance) you just saved. To do this in Internet Explorer 4.0+, select File, Open and then click the Browse button. To do this in Netscape Navigator 4.0+, select File, Open Page and then click the Choose File button.

6. Go to the Liquid Motion publish folder (C:\Program Files\Microsoft Liquid Motion\publish), then to the folder where the HTML file you want to open is stored (\SnackBar, for instance) and double-click the HTML file you just edited (SnackBar2.html, for instance). Click OK to open it in your browser.

7. To make further changes to the HTML file, press Alt+Tab to hop back to Notepad. Make any changes you want to the HTML file and then resave it. Press Alt+Tab again to hop back to your Web browser and then press Ctrl+R to reload the HTML file.

■■■

TIP As long as the copy (SnackBar2.html, for instance) remains in the same folder as where you published the original (SnackBar.html), you can republish your animation (using the same location and animation name) without having to recopy the animation codes from the original to your copy. Opening your copy in your browser (or pressing the Refresh or Reload button) will display the changes you just published.

■■■

Centering Liquid Motion Animations

Liquid Motion animations play by default in a Web browser flush against the left margin. To have a Liquid Motion animation play centered in your Web browser, all you need to do is edit the animation's HTML file and insert `<CENTER>` above and `</CENTER>` below the animation code. The animation code is everything starting with "`<!—WEBBOT bot="lmwebbot"...`" and ending with "`<!—WEBBOT bot="HTMLMarkup" EndSpan —>`."

You can also cause a Liquid Motion animation to play flush against the right margin. To do this, just bracket the animation code with a `<DIV ALIGN="right">` start tag and a `</DIV>` end tag.

Using Background Colors and Images

By default, Liquid Motion publishes an animation's HTML file with a plain white background. You can edit an animation's HTML file (either the original or a copy) and assign a background color or a background image.

A background color is included in an HTML file by including a BGCOLOR attribute value in the BODY tag for the file. There are two ways you can include a background color in an animation's HTML file: using either a color name or an RGB hex code. The first way is the simplest, but you are limited to using one of 16 standard color names. The second way allows you to choose from a broader spectrum of colors, but you have to find out what the hexadecimal numerical code is for the color you want to use.

TRANSPARENT SCENE BACKGROUND WORKAROUNDS

The default transparent scene backgrounds Liquid Motion creates are only displayable in Internet Explorer 4.0+. Netscape Navigator and other Java-capable Web browsers display transparent scene backgrounds as white backgrounds. There are two workarounds you can use:

✿ If you want your animation to be displayed transparently against a background image in Java-capable Web browsers, assign the same background image to your animation's root scene (make sure you tile it) that you assign to the HTML file's BODY tag.

✿ If you want your animation to be displayed transparently against a background color in Java-capable Web browsers, click Next twice at the Publish Wizard, then select the background color you want to use when you publish your animation. The same background color will automatically be added to your animation's root scene and its HTML file's BODY tag. (If you copy the animation codes to another HTML file, you need to copy the code for the background color, as well.)

You would include a background color using a color name in the following format:

```
<BODY BGCOLOR="colorname">
```

In this line, *colorname* refers to one of 16 standard color names that can be used in Web pages. These color names are black, white, aqua, blue, fuchsia, gray, green, lime, maroon, navy, olive, purple, red, silver, teal, and yellow. For instance, to specify black as the background color for your Web page, you would edit the BODY tag so that it reads like this:

```
<BODY BGCOLOR="black">
```

When setting a dark background color (or background image), you many need to reset the colors of your text and hypertext links to ensure they'll still be readable (or even visible) against the dark background. You don't want black text against a black background, in other words. You can set these colors the same way as with the BGCOLOR attribute, but instead you use the TEXT, LINK (for hypertext links), VLINK (for visited links), and ALINK (for activated links, where the mouse is pressed on a link, but not yet released) attributes. For instance, to set white text, aqua links, silver visited links, and fuchsia activated links displayed against a black background color, you would edit the BODY tag like this:

```
<BODY BGCOLOR="black" TEXT="white" LINK="aqua" VLINK="silver"
   ALINK="fuchsia">
```

If you'd like to check out what this would look like in a real page, go ahead and open the HTML file for the FlippingBar animation you created in the Sunday Morning session (C:\Program Files\Microsoft Liquid Motion \Publish\FlippingBar\FlippingBar.html) in Notepad, and then edit it like this:

```
<HTML>
<HEAD>
<TITLE>Liquid Motion Animation: FlippingBar</TITLE>
</HEAD>
<BODY BGCOLOR="black" TEXT="white" LINK="aqua" VLINK="silver"
ALINK="fuchsia">
<CENTER>
<!—WEBBOT bot="lmwebbot" PREVIEW="&lt;IMG
SRC='images/lmanimlogo.gif' WIDTH=400 HEIGHT=125&gt;" U-
PREVIMG="images/lmanimlogo.gif" U-MEDIADIR="./" StartSpan —>
[...]
<!—WEBBOT bot="HTMLMarkup" EndSpan —>
<H1>Flipping Bar Animation</H1>
<P>This is just some dummy text. This is just some dummy
text. This is just some dummy text. This is just some dummy
text. This is a <A HREF="dummy.htm">dummy link</A>.</P>
</CENTER>
</BODY>
</HTML>
```

Notice the <CENTER> and </CENTER> start and end tags. Everything between those two tags will be centered on the Web page, including the Liquid Motion animation.

When finished editing the FlippingBar.html file, resave it as Flipping-Bar2.html (in the C:\Program Files\Microsoft Liquid Motion\Publish \FlippingBar folder). If you then open the FlippingBar2.html file in your Web browser, it should look like what is shown in Figure 7.1.

If you press and hold the mouse on the hypertext link, you'll see its color change to fuchsia. When you release the mouse button, your browser will attempt to go to the Web page specified in the link, but because it's a dummy file name, you'll get an error message instead. Just click OK. The color of the link should be changed to the color, silver, that you set in the VLINK (Visited Link) attribute.

Go ahead, if you want, and check out the FlippingBar animation against the black background.

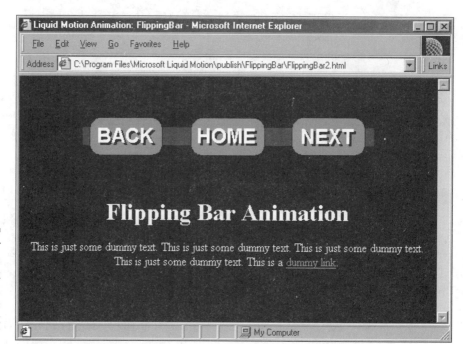

Figure 7.1

The FlippingBar animation is shown against a black background color, with text set to white and the hypertext link set to aqua.

TIP

You can add additional colors to your animation's HTML file by using the FONT tag's COLOR attribute. You can use either color names or hex codes, just as with the BODY tag's BGCOLOR attribute. For instance, to color the level-one heading red in the code example provided earlier, you would bracket the H1 element with the following FONT tags: `<FONT COLOR="red"><H1>Flipping Bar Animation</H1></FONT>`.

Setting Background Colors Using Hex Codes

To be able to select from more than the 16 standard color names, when assigning colors to backgrounds, text, and links, you need to use hexadecimal codes (or "hex codes," for short). The hex code for a background color is inserted in the following format:

`<BODY BGCOLOR="#rrggbb">`

In this line, *rrggbb* refers to two-digit hexadecimal numbers used to specify the red, green, and blue values in an RGB color. For instance, you would specify an orange (not included with the standard 16 color names, by the way) background color like this:

`<BODY BGCOLOR="#FF8000">`

ON THE CD-ROM

Many HTML editors have color pickers that you can use—just click the color you want and they'll insert the hex code for you. There is also a utility included on the CD-ROM, ColorBrowser, that you can use to find out the hex codes for any colors you want to use. Paint Shop Pro, also on the CD-ROM, tells you the hex code for any color selected in its color picker (although you'll have to manually insert it into your HTML file).

If you are wondering why hexadecimal numbers are used instead of decimal numbers to represent numerical color codes in HTML, the reason is simply that you can count from 0 to 255 in hexadecimal entirely in two-digit numbers (00 to FF). Using hexadecimal saves space.

TIP

■■■

For systems that display only 256 colors, most Web browsers use the same palette of 216 colors (often referred to as a "Netscape palette" or a "safety palette"). If you choose a color that is not one of the colors in the palette, although your color will be dithered, actual results can differ strikingly from the colors you intended to display. The trick is to stick to the hexadecimal codes 00, 33, 66, 99, CC, and FF when inserting RGB hex codes, which will limit your color selections only to the 216 colors in the palette.

■■■

ON THE CD-ROM

A copy of the safety palette is included with Paint Shop Pro 5 (included on the CD-ROM). To apply it to an image file, select Colors and Load Palette, then select safety.pal. You should be aware, however, that the quality of images containing more than 256 colors may suffer (and even some images containing only the 256 color Windows palette may suffer, if key colors in the image are not included in the "safety" palette.

Using a Background Image

Using a background image behind a transparent Liquid Motion animation can be quite effective. You specify a background image in an HTML file using the BACKGROUND attribute.

You would include a background image in an HTML file using the following format:

```
<BODY BACKGROUND="filename">
```

In this line, *filename* refers to any background image file (either a .jpg, .gif, or .png file) stored in the same folder as the HTML file. For instance, if you were to copy the background image dark-water.gif from the Book Images folder (in Liquid Motion's Clip Art folder) to the same folder as your animation's HTML file, you would reference it in the BODY tag like this (I've also added the attributes to set the text and links colors):

```
<BODY BACKGROUND="dark-water.gif" TEXT="white" LINK="aqua"
VLINK="silver" ALINK="fuchsia">
```

For instance, assume that you've stored the background image in an images folder that is created in your animation's publish folder, like this:

```
Publish folder
    ¦
    — —  images
```

You would then insert the following in the BODY tag of your animation's HTML file (in your animation's publish folder) to link to the background image (in the images folder):

```
BACKGROUND="images/dark-water.gif"
```

If you made these changes to the FlippingBar2.html file, resaved it as FlippingBar3.html, and copied the background image, it would look like what is shown in Figure 7.2 when opened in your Web browser.

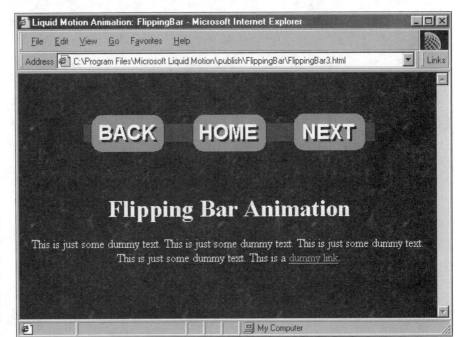

Figure 7.2

The FlippingBar animation is shown against a dark background image, with text set to white and the hypertext link set to aqua.

Assume that you've stored your background image in a parallel folder (both your animation's publish folder and the images folder are located in the same parent folder), like this:

```
Parent folder
  |
  — —  Publish folder
  |
  — —  images
```

You would then insert the following in the BODY tag of your animation's HTML file (in your animation's publish folder) to link to the background image (in the images folder):

```
BACKGROUND="../images/dark-water.gif"
```

NOTE When inserting file or folder names into HTML codes, be sure that they match the case of the file or folder name exactly. The reason for this is that Unix servers are case sensitive, so "myimage.gif" and "MyImage.gif" refer to two different files. This only matters on Unix servers, as servers running under Windows NT interpret these names to be the same file.

Using Liquid Motion Animations in Tables

One of the keys to more sophisticated placement of Liquid Motion animations on Web pages is using HTML tables. In this section, I'll show you a couple of pretty neat things you can do with tables to enhance the display of your Liquid Motion animations:

✪ Wrapping text and other HTML elements around a Liquid Motion animation

✪ Including an animated sidebar menu (like the SidebarMenu animation you created in the Sunday Morning session) that'll run down the left or right side of a Web page.

Wrapping Text and Other HTML Elements around a Liquid Motion Animation

To cause text and other HTML elements included on a Web page to wrap around either the left or right side of a Liquid Motion animation, you need to insert the animation code inside a single-cell table. Here's an example of causing following text and HTML elements to wrap around the SpinAnd-Throb animation you created in the Saturday Evening session:

1. In Notepad, open the SpinAndThrob.html file (from C:\Program Files\Microsoft Liquid Motion\publish\SpinAndThrob).

2. Save the SpinAndThrob.html file as SpinAndThrob2.html (File, Save As).

3. Edit the SpinAndThrob2.html file so that it looks like this:

```
<BODY BGCOLOR="#ffffff">
<TABLE ALIGN="left">
<TR><TD>
<!—WEBBOT bot="lmwebbot" PREVIEW="&lt;IMG
SRC='images/lmanimlogo.gif'
[...]
<!—WEBBOT bot="HTMLMarkup" EndSpan —>
</TD></TR>
</TABLE>
<H1>Spin and Throb Animation</H1>
<P>This is just some dummy text. This is just some dummy
text. This is just some dummy text. This is just some dummy
text. This is just some dummy text. This is just some dummy
text. </P><BR CLEAR="all">
<P>This is just some dummy text. This is just some dummy
text. This is just some dummy text. This is just some dummy
text. This is just some dummy text. This is just some dummy
text.</P>
</BODY>
```

4. Save the SpinAndThrob2.html file (File, Save).

NOTE In the previous code example, the <BR CLEAR="all"> code is inserted to cause following text or elements not to wrap, but to be displayed flush to the left margin below the table. To have both paragraphs wrap around the table, just move the <BR CLEAR="all"> code to the end of the second paragraph, or to a position following any other elements (such as images, headings, etc.) you also want to wrap.

Now if you open the SpinAndThrob2.html file in your Web browser, you'll see that the heading and paragraph text you added will wrap around the right side of the animation (see Figure 7.3).

To have the following heading and paragraph text wrap around the left side of the animation, just substitute <TABLE ALIGN="right"> for <TABLE ALIGN="left"> in the code example.

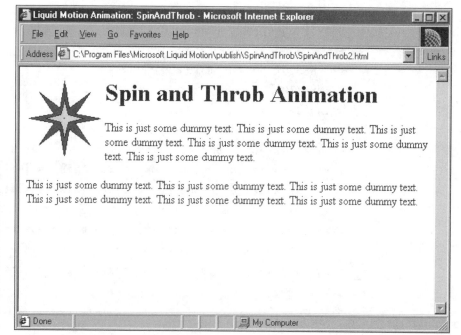

Figure 7.3

With the SpinAndThrob animation inserted inside a left-aligned table, the following heading and paragraph text wrap around the right side of the animation.

Inserting an Animation in a Table Column

One way to create an animated sidebar menu that runs down the left or right side of a Web page is to include the animation code inside a table column. To do this, you need to create a two-cell table and then insert the animation code in either the left or right cell (depending on whether you want the sidebar menu to run down the left or right side of the page). Go ahead and edit the HTML file for the RollOverMenu animation you created in the Sunday Morning session to see how this works:

1. In Notepad, open the RollOverMenu.html file (from C:\Program Files\Microsoft Liquid Motion\publish\RollOverMenu).

2. Save the RollOverMenu.html file as RollOverMenu2.html.

3. Edit the RollOverMenu2.html file so that it looks like this:

```
<BODY BGCOLOR="#ffffff">
<TABLE WIDTH="100%" HEIGHT="100%" CELLPADDING="6"
CELLSPACING="6" BORDER="6">
<TR VALIGN="top">
<TD BGCOLOR="black" ALIGN="center">
<!—WEBBOT bot="lmwebbot" PREVIEW="&lt;IMG
SRC='images/lmanimlogo.gif'
[...]
<!—WEBBOT bot="HTMLMarkup" EndSpan —>
</TD>
<TD BGCOLOR="silver">
<H1>Roll-Over Menu Animation</H1>
<P>This is just some dummy text. This is just some dummy
text. This is just some dummy text. This is just some dummy
text. This is just some dummy text. This is just some dummy
text.</P>
<P>This is just some dummy text. This is just some dummy
text. This is just some dummy text. This is just some dummy
text. This is just some dummy text. This is just some dummy
text.</P>
```

```
<H2>Subsection Heading</H2>
<P>This is just some dummy text. This is just some dummy
text. This is just some dummy text. This is just some dummy
text. This is just some dummy text. This is just some dummy
text.</P>
<P>This is just some dummy text. This is just some dummy
text. This is just some dummy text. This is just some dummy
text. This is just some dummy text. This is just some dummy
text.</P>
</TD></TR>
</TABLE>
</BODY>
```

4. Save the RollOverMenu2.html file (File, Save).

Now if you open the RollOverMenu2.html file in your Web browser, you'll see that the RollOverMenu animation now runs inside a table column with a black background down the left side of the browser window. The rest of the heading and paragraph text you added runs down the remainder of the page inside a table column with a silver background (see Figure 7.4).

If you aren't already familiar with HTML tables, take note of the following:

- The WIDTH="100%" attribute in the TABLE tag specifies that the table will extend across 100 percent of the browser window. The HEIGHT="100%" attribute specifies that the table will extend to the bottom of the browser window. (You can test this in your browser by resizing your browser window—the table will resize itself to fit the new window size.)

- CELLPADDING="6" adds six pixels of space around the inside of the table's cells.

- CELLSPACING="6" adds six pixels of space between the table's cells.

- BORDER="6" adds a six-pixel 3-D border around the table. (BORDER="0" turns off display of the border around a table.)

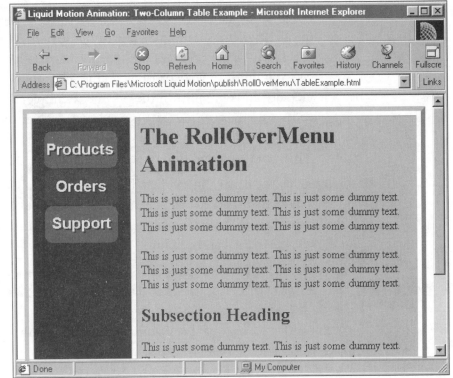

Figure 7.4

The RollOverMenu
animation is
displayed in a table
column running
down the left side
of the page.

○ The VALIGN="top" attribute in the TR tag specifies that the content
of both table cells in the table row will be vertically aligned with the
top of the cells. You can also use the VALIGN="middle" and the
VALIGN="bottom" attributes to align the contents of a table cell with
the middle or top of the table cell.

○ Every table must have at least one row defined (<TR>...</TR>).
The TR tag is always nested directly inside of the TABLE tag. To
add additional rows, you just nest additional TR tags inside the
TABLE tag.

○ In the previous example, two table cells were defined. Table cells
can be defined either using TD (Table Data) or TH (Table
Heading) tags, which can be used interchangeably. (The main difference between these two is that TH tag content is bolded and

centered, while TD tag content is regular left-aligned text.) TD tags (or TH tags) must always be nested inside of a TR tag (<TR><TD> ...</TD><TD>...</TD></TR>, for instance). The number of TD tags you insert in your first row defines the number of columns included in your table. In the previous example, the animation codes are placed inside the first table cell (the left-hand column), whereas the following heading and paragraph text is placed inside the second table cell (the right-hand column).

✪ BGCOLOR="black" in the first TD tag specifies a black background for the first table cell (the left-hand column). BGCOLOR="silver" in the second TD tag specifies a silver background for the second table cell (the right-hand column)

Included with the HTML templates on the CD-ROM is a template that uses a table to create an online newsletter with a masthead, sidebar menu, and main body. You can find the newsletter template at \Examples\HTML Templates\Newsletr on the CD-ROM. To view the template, just open Newsletr.htm in your browser.

Creating Internal Hypertext Links

At some point, you may want to insert an animated menu into an HTML file that will link to other locations in that same HTML file. You may want it to link to the subheadings of a long article, for instance, or to article headings in an online newsletter. To do that, you need to do two things:

✪ Insert "target anchors" to specify the locations where you want your animated menu to jump to (the landing spots).

✪ Add or edit URL links in your animated menu so that they point to the target anchors.

Inserting Target Anchors

A "target anchor" defines a location within an HTML file's text to which a hypertext link can jump. A target anchor has the following general format:

```
<A NAME="anchorname"></A>
```

Each target anchor you insert in an HTML file must be unique. For instance, if you wanted to insert target anchors in front of article headings in an online newsletter, you might insert `<A NAME="article1"></A>` in front of the first heading, `<A NAME="article2"></A>` in front of the second heading, and so on.

Pointing URL Links at Target Anchors

In Liquid Motion, hypertext links are attached to objects with the URL Link tool. To specify the target of a link, you edit the URL box in the properties window for a "URL Link" behavior. To link to another Web page somewhere else on the Web, you only need to specify that page's Web address in the URL box.

However, if you want to link to a location in the same HTML file, you need to specify the name of the target anchor preceded by the "#" character. For the sake of convenience, think of that as a "target reference." For instance, to link to a target anchor `<A NAME="section2">Section 2</A>` in the same HTML file as the animation, you would type the target reference, `#section2`, in the URL box for the link.

Similarly, you might want to link to a location in a different HTML file, but still in the same folder structure as the HTML file from which you're making the link. If that HTML file is in the same folder as the linking HTML file, you would only need to include the file name of the file you're linking to and the target reference identifying the name of the target anchor to which you are linking. For instance, to link to a target anchor, `<A NAME="part3">Part 3</A>` in another HTML file, `MyStory.html`, in the same folder as the linking file, you would type the HTML file's name and the target reference, `MyStory.html#part3`, in the URL box for the link.

It gets a little more complicated if you want to link to a location in an HTML file that is not in the same folder as the linking HTML file. Assume, for instance, that MyStory.html is not in the same folder, but in a subfolder of your animation's publish folder—\MyStories\MyStory.html. You want to link to the same target anchor as before, <A NAME="part3">. To do that, you would type MyStories/MyStory.html#part3 in the URL box for the link.

The forward slash ("/") in the URL link above is a Unix slash, which should always be used when creating URLs, rather than a backward slash ("\," or DOS/Windows slash).

Another situation is when you want to link to a location within another HTML file that is located in the parent folder, or a subfolder of the parent folder, of the linking HTML file. For instance, if the same MyStory.html file were in the parent folder of the linking HTML file, you would type ../MyStory.html#part3 in the URL box for the link. If the same MyStory.html file were in a subfolder of the parent folder of the linking HTML file, such as \StoryFolder of your local hard drive, you would type ../StoryFolder/MyStory.html#part3 in the URL box for the link.

Take a Break?

You've been at this all weekend, and that table section was a bit of a brain buster, so you're probably dying for a break. Get up and walk around the house to get your circulation going. Grab that donut from the cupboard, if you're in need of a sugar fix.

If you are just plain tuckered out, feel free to come back later (like next weekend) to cover the rest of this session's material.

If, however, you're raring to learn more about using Liquid Motion animations in Web pages, I'll see you back in five or ten minutes, when I'll show you how to include Liquid Motion animations in frames.

Using Liquid Motion Animations in Frames

Frames are somewhat similar to tables, except that instead of placing animations, text, and other elements inside of table cells, you create a set of frame windows by creating a file called a "frameset" HTML file. The frameset file defines the layout of the frame page and specifies the HTML files that will be displayed in the frames. In this example, you'll create a two-column frame page. The following is a quick description of what you'll need to do to create this frame page (more detailed instructions are included in the following sections):

1. Open the RollOverMenu animation and revise it, editing the URL links to work within a frameset, after which you'll need to republish your animation (as the FrameMenu animation in the \publish\FrameMenu folder). When you publish the FrameMenu animation, you'll also use the Publish Wizard to add a background image. The FrameMenu.html file will be displayed in the left frame within the frameset.

2. Next, you'll edit the Welcome animation's HTML file and then resave it as Welcome2.html. This file will be displayed in the right-hand frame within the frameset. In editing this file, you'll set background and text colors, center the Welcome animation, and add heading and paragraph text, as well as a link list.

3. Finally, you'll need to create the frameset HTML file that ties it all together and save it in the \publish\FrameMenu folder. This file defines the frame layout and references the initial HTML files that will be displayed in the frame windows. In doing this, you'll define a two-column frameset (a frameset with two side-by-side frame windows). FrameMenu.html file will be specified as the content of the left frame and Welcome2.html will be specified as the content of the right frame.

NOTE The example you'll create in this section uses the RollOverMenu animation from the Sunday Morning session and the Welcome animation from the Saturday Afternoon session. If you haven't created one or both of these animations, you'll need to go back and do so in order to complete the following example.

Creating the FrameMenu Animation

The first thing you need to do is revise the RollOverMenu animation from the Sunday Morning session and republish it as the FrameMenu Animation. In doing this, you'll create a new folder, the /publish/FrameMenu folder, in which you'll also later save the frameset HTML file for the frame page. To create the FrameMenu animation, follow these steps:

1. Start Liquid Motion and open an existing animation file. Double-click the RollOverMenu.jck project file to open it. If the Structure view is not on, click the Structure View tool to turn it on.

2. Click the "+" handle next to the "Rounded Rectangle" actor, then double-click the URL Link behavior ("products_html"). For the URL, replace products.html with **../Welcome/Welcome2.html.** Select Named Frame or New Window as the Frame. In the Name box, type **window.** Click Close.

NOTE The ".." in the URL in step 2 means that the following folder is located up one level in the directory tree from the current folder. In this case, the ".." points to Liquid Motion's publish folder (C:\Program Files\Microsoft Liquid Motion\publish).

3. Repeat step 2 for the other two rectangles ("Rounded Rectangle (2)" and Rounded Rectangle (3)"), editing their URL Link behaviors. For the "orders_html" behavior, type **../FlippingBar/Flipping-Bar.html** as the URL. For the "support_html" behavior, type **../Swimming3DFish/Swimming3DFish.html** as the URL.

4. Next, if you want, edit the three text actors for this animation and substitute more appropriate text (try using "First," "Second," and "Third" as the text for these actors (or, you might substitute "Welcome," "Flip," and "Fish"). Depending on what you use for the text, you may need to adjust the Size value so the text will still fit inside the rectangle button.

5. Now, save your animation as the FrameMenu animation: Click File, Save As. Type **FrameMenu** as the file name for the animation and click Save.

6. Next, publish the FrameMenu animation: Click the Publish tool.

7. At the Publish Wizard, click the Next button twice. Click the Background color button, and choose a color for the HTML file's background (to match the current color of the background scene, choose dark purple, fourth color down in the sixth column. Click OK.

8. Click the Finish button. (The FrameMenu animation will be published to the \publish\FrameMenu folder.)

Creating the Welcome2 HTML File

Next you need to create the Welcome2.html file that is displayed in the right frame of the frame page. Do that now:

1. In Notepad, select File, Open. Select All Files (*.*) in the Files of type box. Go to the C:\Program Files\Microsoft Liquid Motion\publish\Welcome folder and double-click Welcome.html to open it in Notepad.

2. Revise Welcome.html in Notepad, making the changes shown in bold in the following code example (in the address section at the bottom, substitute your own name for *Your Name goes here* and substitute your own e-mail address for *your e-mail address*):

```
<HTML>
<HEAD>
<TITLE>Liquid Motion Animation: Welcome</TITLE>
</HEAD>
<BODY BGCOLOR="#FFFFCC" TEXT="navy">
<CENTER>
<!—WEBBOT bot="lmwebbot" PREVIEW="&lt;IMG
SRC='images/lmanimlogo.gif'
```

```
[...]
<!—WEBBOT bot="HTMLMarkup" EndSpan —>
</CENTER>
<FONT COLOR="red"><H1 AlIGN="center">Welcome to My Animation
Home Page!</H1></FONT>
<P>This is just some dummy text. This is just some dummy
text. This is just some dummy text. This is just some dummy
text.</P>
<H3>Visit My Other Animation Pages:</H3>
<UL>
<LI><A HREF="../FlippingBar/FlippingBar.html">The FlippingBar
Animation!</A>
<LI><A HREF="../Swimming3DFish/Swimming3DFish.html">The
Swimming3DFish Animation1</A>
</UL>
<HR>
<ADDRESS>
<CENTER>
Your Name goes here<BR>
<A HREF="mailto:your e-mail address">your e-mail
address</A><BR>
</CENTER>
</ADDRESS>
</BODY>
</HTML>
```

3. Select File, Save As, and then resave the file as Welcome2.html in
   the C:\Program Files\Microsoft Liquid Motion\publish\Welcome
   folder. (Leave Notepad open. You'll use it again shortly.)

Creating the Frameset File

Finally, you need to create the frameset file that will tie all the pieces
together:

1. In Notepad, start a new file (File, New).

2. Type in the following code to create the frameset file for the frame page:

```
<HTML>
<HEAD>
<TITLE>Welcome to My Animation Home Page</TITLE>
</HEAD>
<FRAMESET COLS="165,*">
<FRAME NAME="menu" SRC="FrameMenu.html" SCROLLING="auto" NORE-
  SIZE MARGINWIDTH=5 MARGINHEIGHT=5>
<FRAME NAME="window" SRC="../Welcome/Welcome2.html"
  SCROLLING="auto" NORESIZE MARGINWIDTH=5 MARGINHEIGHT=5>
</FRAMESET>
<NOFRAMES>
Sorry, this page requires a Frames-capable browser. You can
  download a browser to view Frame pages at <A
  HREF="http://www.microsoft.com">Microsoft's</A> or <A
  HREF="http://home.netscape.com"</A>Netscape's</A> web site.
</NOFRAMES>
</HTML>
```

3. Save this file (File, Save) as FrameExample.html in the C:\Program Files\Microsoft Liquid Motion\publish\FrameMenu folder.

I don't have the time or space to explain everything about creating frames, but here are a few pointers about the frameset HTML file you just created:

✿ The text in the TITLE tag will be displayed on a browser's title bar (and will also be used by search engines to list the page). Feel free to substitute your own name, or substitute another title, if you wish.

✿ The `<FRAMESET COLS="165,*">` line specifies that the frameset will have two columns, the first 165 pixels wide and the second of variable width (depending on the width of the browser window). To specify a frameset with two rows, substitute ROWS for COLS.

- ✪ The FRAME tags (<FRAME>...) define the two frame windows included in the frameset.

  - ✪ The first frame includes a link to the "../FrameMenu/FrameMenu.html" file. You created this file in the "Creating the FrameMenu Animation" section above.

  - ✪ The second frame includes a link to the "../Welcome/Welcome2.html" file. You created this file in the "Creating the Welcome2 HTML File" section above.

- ✪ The NAME attributes in the two FRAME tags are used to identify the frames. When you revised the RollOverMenu animation to create the FrameMenu animation, you specified the "window" frame name so that clicking on any of the rectangle buttons would open the specified HTML file in the "window" frame.

- ✪ SCROLLING="auto" specifies that scroll bars will be displayed for the window only if the contents of the frame are wider or longer than the frame size. NORESIZE specifies that the frames cannot be manually resized in a browser. The MARGINWIDTH and MARGINHEIGHT attributes specify the margins for the frames.

- ✪ The NOFRAMES tag includes text that will only be displayed if a browser does not support frames. The text included in this example directs someone using a non-frames-capable browser to Microsoft's or Netscape's Web site. (You could alternatively include a link here to a non-frames version of your page.)

Run your Web browser. In Internet Explorer 4.0: Select File, Open, and then click Browse. In Navigator 4.0: Select File, Open Page, and then click Choose File. Go to the C:\Program Files\Microsoft Liquid Motion\publish \FrameMenu folder and double-click FrameExample.html. Click OK to open it in Internet Explorer (see Figure 7.5).

Figure 7.5

The FrameExample frameset file in Internet Explorer.

Move the mouse over the buttons in the left frame to see the animation effects and hear the sound effects. Click any of the buttons in the left frame to see its corresponding animation displayed in the right frame (see Figure 7.6).

ON THE CD-ROM

If you want to learn more about using frames, see the frames templates on the CD-ROM. After installing the HTML Templates from the CD-ROM, look in the \Prima Examples\Templates\frames folder inside of Liquid Motion's folder. You'll find two folders there (2frames and 3frames) that include templates for creating a two-frame Web page and a nested three-frame Web page. To view the templates in your browser, just open index.htm in either the 2frames or the 3frames folder.

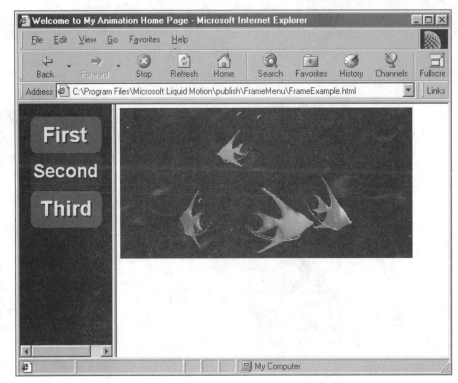

Figure 7.6

Clicking on the "Third" button in the left frame plays the Swimming3DFish animation in the right frame.

 NOTE For links to where on the Web you can find out more about frames, see my Web Links site (**www.callihan.com/weblinks/**). For links to where on the Web you can find software tools for creating frame pages, see my Web Tools site (**www.callihan.com /webtools/**). Also, PRIMATECH's (**www.prima-tech.com**) *Learn HTML In a Weekend, Revised Edition*, includes a tutorial on using Frame-It, a freeware frames utility, to create frame pages.

Take a Break?

That section on frames was pretty intense, so if you want to take another break at this point, please do. Make it a quicky though, because there's lots of good stuff left to go. I'll see you back in about five minutes, when you'll learn how to create animations that'll automatically play in the browser you designate.

Creating Browser-Specific Animations

If you plan to create animations that use effects that can only be displayed in Internet Explorer 4.0+, you may want to create separate versions of your animation file, one for Internet Explorer 4.0+ and the other for any other browsers. Effects that can only be viewed in Internet Explorer 4.0+ are:

- 3-D objects
- Rotations
- Filters and transitions
- Spinning images and text
- WAV, MIDI, and MPEG audio effects
- Panning audio effects
- Transparent backgrounds
- Script triggers

When you publish an animation, Liquid Motion actually creates two versions of the .jck animation file: a .jcz file (used by Java-capable browsers) and an .x file (used by Internet Explorer 4.0+). The trick to creating separate versions is detailed here:

1. Publish an animation created using I.E. 4.0 content. (For instance, you might publish your animation to the \publish\JackNBox folder.)

2. Edit your animation, replacing I.E. 4.0 content with content that can be played in all Java-capable browsers. Replace 3-D objects with 2-D shapes or images. Replace WAV, MIDI, or MPEG audio files with AU audio files. Replace spinning images with spinning 2-D shapes.

3. Republish the animation to a different publish folder. (For instance, you might publish your second animation to the \publish\JackNBox2 folder.)

4. Copy the .jcz animation file from the second folder into the first folder, replacing the .jcz file in the first folder. (For instance, you

might copy JackNBox.jcz from the \JackNBox2 folder to the \JackNBox folder.)

You should now have two animation files in the first publish folder, an .x animation file that includes I.E. 4.0 content, and a .jcz animation file that doesn't include any I.E. 4.0 content.

Creating Automatic Forwarding Links with the META Tag

You can cause another HTML file to be loaded after a specified period of time by using the META tag nested in an HTML file's HEAD tag. (The META tag must be nested inside of the HEAD tag, and won't work if it is inserted anywhere else.) For instance, you could edit an animation's HTML file and include the following code inside the HEAD tag:

```
<HEAD>
<TITLE>Title of HTML File</TITLE>
<META HTTP-EQUIV="Refresh" CONTENT="60;
URL=http://www.callihan.com/liquidmotion/welcome2.html">
</HEAD>
```

This would cause the browser to wait for 60 seconds, after which it would cause the specified Web page (http://www.callihan.com/liquidmotion /welcome2.html) to be opened in the browser. You would need, of course, to substitute the URL here for the actual Web page you want to have opened in the browser.

Because download times for Liquid Motion animations may vary (depending upon the content of the animation, or the distance from which it is being downloaded), you should build in some leeway as to the amount of time you want the browser to wait before loading the second HTML file. You might also want to test the animation on the Web to see how long it will take to download and play, and then add an extra time margin to the CONTENT attribute value to make sure that the animation finishes playing before the browser switches to the other HTML page.

You can't check this out on your local drive, because the load time for the animation is a lot quicker than when you play the animation off of the Web. You'll have to transfer your animation files up onto a Web server to see how this works.

Using Script Triggers

 NOTE Only depend upon using Script Triggers in animations where you've already warned off non-Internet Explorer 4.0+ viewers, or where you've followed the instructions discussed earlier, in "Creating Browser-Specific Animations."

For any actor in a Liquid Motion animation, you can set a script trigger that will activate a JavaScript or VBScript. To include a script trigger, follow these steps:

1. Select the actor to which you wish to assign the script trigger, and then select Interactivity, ScriptTrigger from the menu bar.

2. Specify the Action that will trigger the script (Mouse Click, Mouse Moves Over, Mouse Moves Off, and so on).

3. Specify the Language for the script (JavaScript or VBScript).

4. In the Script Text window, type the JavaScript or VBScript that you want to be triggered by the script trigger. (See the next section for some example scripts you can try.)

Some Example JavaScripts

The following are just a few sample JavaScripts that you could include in a script trigger.

✪ **Displaying a Message on the Browser's Status Bar.** This JavaScript will cause a message to be displayed in the browser's status bar:

window.status="*Type your message here*";

⭘ **Displaying a Pop-Up Alert Message**. This JavaScript will cause a pop-up alert message to be displayed:

alert("Type alert message here");

⭘ **Displaying a Pop-Up E-mail Window**. This JavaScript will cause a Mailto e-mail window to pop up with the address already filled out:

window.navigate("mailto: yourname@yourmail.com");

In this line, just substitute your own e-mail address for "yourname@yourmail.com".

⭘ **Opening an HTML File in Another Browser Window**. This JavaScript will open the specified HTML file in another browser window. The example assumes that its HTML file is in a folder in Liquid Motion's publish folder:

window.open('../Swimming3DFish/Swimming3DFish.html',
'Animation1', 'toolbar=no,location=no,directories=no,
status=no,menubar=no,scrollbars=no,resizable=no,
copyhistory=yes,width=425,height=225');

You could use this script to start any HTML file, including Liquid Motion animation HTML files, in a new window. It also allows you to turn off, or on, any of the browser elements, such as the toolbar, location bar, status bar, menu bar, scroll bars, and so on.

This script actually allows you to do some pretty neat things. For instance, you could use this script in a script trigger attached to the root scene of an animation. When the animation is finished playing, a second browser window will be opened and the specified HTML file displayed.

You're not limited to just doing this with the root scene. You can attach a script trigger to any object, select Stopping as the Action, and a fresh browser window will be opened displaying the specified HTML file.

Another neat thing you could do with this script is first create a menu animation and then attach script triggers, rather than URL links, to the objects or text being used for the menu options or buttons. Set them to be activated when the object is clicked on. You can then include versions of the JavaScript shown previously to display another Liquid Motion animation file in a new browser window, sized to fit the animation. Just change the HTML file that is specified, and reset the dimensions to fit the animation (you want to make them a bit larger than the size of the animation scene). If you created the Swimming3DFish animation in the Sunday Afternoon session, using the example JavaScript in a script trigger would cause the animation to play in a stripped down, resized new browser window, as shown in Figure 7.7. Check on the Web for additional JavaScripts you can use in script triggers. For a partial listing of JavaScript resources available on the Web, check out this book's Web site (**www.callihan.com/liquidmotion/**) for links to where you can find JavaScripts and VBScripts on the Web.

Tips for Publishing Multiple Animations

This section covers some things you can do to help optimize the publishing of multiple animations on a Web page or in a framed Web site.

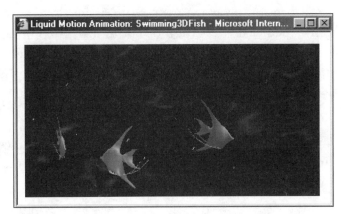

Figure 7.7

You can use a script trigger to open a new browser window, stripped down and resized, and play a specified Liquid Motion animation.

When publishing an animation, in the window allowing you to set a splash image, you can select the Other Animated Elements radio button before clicking on the Finish button. If you plan on using more than just a couple of Liquid Motion animations on a Web page (or in separate windows in a frame page), or if there are other animated elements on the page (such as animated GIFs, scrolling marquees, or streaming audio or video), you might try selecting this option. If you select this option, Liquid Motion will reduce the frame rate for the animation to help optimize its playback performance.

Another way you can help minimize the download time for your animations is to optimize any media files included in your animations.

Using Image Strips for Sequential Display of Images

You can insert several images into Liquid Motion and then set their durations and start offsets so they play in sequence. Because it takes less time to download a single 5KB file than five 1KB files, you may very well be able to improve the download time for your animation by using an image strip, rather than individual images. You can convert individual images into an image strip in two ways.

When Liquid Motion imports an animated GIF file (using the Insert Image tool), it automatically turns it into a "timed strip," which is a special form of an image strip. With a timed strip, you don't have to specify whether it is a vertical or horizontal strip, nor do you have to set the number of frames or the frame rate. Because Liquid Motion uses the animated GIF file to determine the number of frames, the frame rate, and the duration of the timed strip, you don't have to set any of those characteristics for a timed strip.

Thus, a slick way to create an image strip (actually, a timed strip) is to first import the images into a GIF animation editor and then to import the resulting animated GIF file into Liquid Motion. Many GIF animation editors will let you set an absolute frame size and center the animation frames, so you can even include images of dissimilar sizes.

You'll find a couple GIF animation editors in the Multimedia section on the CD-ROM that you can try out. GIF Movie Gear is a stand-alone GIF animation editor. When you install Paint Shop Pro, a companion GIF animation application, Animation Shop, is also installed.

When using a GIF animation editor to create an image sequence, you should be hesitant about adding the transition or panning effects that many of them allow you to include. That's because using these effects can dramatically increase the number of image frames that will be included in the image strip once it has been imported into Liquid Motion.

You can also open your individual images in a graphics editor, and then copy, paste, and position them in a new image window sized to hold all the individual images. For instance, if you have three images that are each 100 pixels wide by 100 pixels high, you would need to open a new blank image window that is 300 pixels wide by 100 pixels high. If your images are not all exactly the same size, you may need to do some experimenting to find the optimum image size, as well as the optimum positions for the images within the image window. The main thing is that the images should be positioned in the new image window so that their centers are equidistant from each other and from the start and end of the image strip (|.[image].|.[image].|.[image].|), for instance).

You insert an image strip into a Liquid Motion animation just like a regular image. In its property window, however, you need to specify whether it is a horizontal or vertical strip, the number of frames (images) in the image strip, and the frame rate at which you want the strip to be played.

Using Liquid Motion Text Instead of Text Included in Images

You can reduce the amount of download time required for an animation by using Liquid Motion's Insert Text tool to add text effects to your animations. You are limited in the different fonts you can select from, plus you are limited to setting fill, background, and drop shadow colors. Using imported graphic text effects (those created in Paint Shop Pro or Adobe PhotoShop, for instance) allows you to select from many fonts, and you can apply more effects to the text, such as gradient or pattern fills, blended drop shadows, and perspective distortions.

Reducing the Number of Image Colors

The fewer colors there are in an image, the smaller the image will generally be. It can pay, therefore, to optimize any images you want to use in a Liquid Motion animation so that they contain no more colors than are required to maintain acceptable image quality. You may want to try doing any of these things:

✪ Reduce the number of colors in an image palette from 16.7 million (true color) to 256 colors (or even to 16 or 4 colors). If image quality is not compromised, this can lead to big savings in image file sizes.

✪ Apply what is sometimes referred to as the "Netscape palette" or "safety palette" to your image. This will convert the colors in your images so that they correspond only to the 216 colors included in this palette (used by Netscape Navigator and Internet Explorer to display images on systems displaying only 256 colors).

✪ Reduce the number of colors in an image palette to only the colors actually included in the image. This is sometimes referred to as creating an "adaptive" palette.

You may need to experiment to find the optimum number of colors for an image. For some images, reducing them from a palette of 16.7 million to 256 colors can degrade image quality to an unacceptable degree, while for other images there will be little or no degradation.

Increasing the Compression Ratio for JPEG Files

The preferred image format for displaying photographic images or other images with continuous tones, or gradient or blend effects, is JPEG. Most image editors allow you to set a compression ratio when you save a JPEG image. The higher the compression ratio, the smaller will be the resulting saved image.

Setting a compression ratio when saving a JPEG image can dramatically reduce the size in bytes of the resulting saved image. A compression ratio that's too high, however, can result in degradation of the image quality. You'll need to experiment to find the optimum compression ratio for a saved JPEG image. First save an uncompressed version of the JPEG, then save a series of additional JPEGs (don't save over your original uncompressed JPEG), progressively increasing the compression ratio for each image (start at a ratio of 20 percent, and then increase it to 30, 40, and 50 percent, for instance). Next, open all of the saved images in your image editor, comparing the results.

Reusing Images, Sound Files, and Other Media in Multiple Animations

You may want to publish multiple animations to the same Web page, frame page, or Web site. One way you can optimize the download time and playback performance for multiple animations that reuse many of the same media (images, sound files, 3-D objects, and so on) is to publish them to the same publish folder. To do this, when publishing the animations, after clicking on Next at the first window, in the Save Published Files In text box, type in the same folder for each of the animations.

Doing this also consolidates the Java player classes all under one folder, allowing them to be reused for multiple animations.

You might want to use the same animation more than one time in the same Web page. For instance, you might create an animated icon that changes colors and pulsates when the mouse is passed over it, and you want to use it as an animated bullet icon to highlight section headings or list items. The trick to doing this is that you need to publish a separate animation for each time you include the animation. If you want to use an animated bullet icon you've created three times in the same Web page, you'd have to save and publish it as AnimBullet1, save and publish it as AnimBullet2, then save and publish it as AnimBullet3. Next, you'd need to copy and paste the animation code from all three animations' HTML files, pasting each animation's code where you want it to appear in your Web page.

Consolidating the Java Player Classes

If you plan on publishing a lot of Liquid Motion animations, you may want to consider consolidating the Java player classes. When Liquid Motion publishes an animation, it also publishes the Java player classes into a subfolder of the publish folder (the \dnx folder). Optionally, you can edit the animation code in the HTML files for your animations so that they all point to the same folder to find the Java player classes. To do this, follow these steps:

1. In Liquid Motion's publish folder, create a new folder to hold the Java class players, such as \classes, for instance.

2. From one of your animations' publish folders, copy the \dnx folder, and then paste it into the \classes folder. The structure of your \classes folder should now be:

    ```
    \classes\dnx
    \classes\dnx\dnxim.cab
    \classes\dnx\lminstall.jar
    ```

3. Delete the \dnx folders in the individual publish folders for your animations.

ORGANIZING THE FOLDERS

You don't have to publish Liquid Motion animations only to its \publish folder. I personally store all my HTML files in c:\pages on my local hard drive, and I publish my Liquid Motion animations to the c:\pages\lm folder. In c:\pages\lm I've created the shared \dnx folder (c:\pages\lm\dnx), into which I've copied the Java player classes. I publish my animations to individual folders within the c:\pages\lm folder (c:\pages\lm\ClickMe, for instance). After publishing the animation, all I have to do is edit the HTML file (as shown in the preceding steps) to point it to the shared folder for the Java player classes. (Publishing to a folder already related to my other HTML folders means that, using relative URLs, I can easily make any URL links I want to other HTML files in my Web site).

---

4. Open the HTML files for each of your animations in Notepad and find the following line (you'll need to visually substitute the name of the animation for *AnimationName*):

```
var AnimationNameCodeDir = AnimationNameMediaDir;
```

5. Change this line to this form:

```
var AnimationNameCodeDir = "../classes/";
```

6. Resave the HTML file.

When you transfer your animation files up onto a Web server, don't forget to transfer the \classes folder, as well. You should also be careful to retain the relationship between the individual animation publish folders and the \classes folder (\pages\lm*AnimationName* and \pages\lm\classes, for instance). For more information on how to transfer your pages up onto a Web server, see Appendix C, "Placing Your Animation Files on a Web Server."

Wrapping Up

This session contained a lot of information you'll want to use for future reference. After reading this session, you should be familiar with how to:

- Edit a Liquid Motion HTML file.
- Center or right-align a Liquid Motion animation in a Web page.
- Set a background image in a Web page.
- Set background, text, and link colors in a Web page using color names or RGB hex codes.
- Wrap text and other elements around an animation by inserting the animation inside of a left-aligned or right-aligned, single-cell table.
- Use animations in a table column.
- Create URL links using internal hypertext links.
- Use animations in frame pages.
- Create an animated menu that controls the contents of another frame.
- Create separate versions of the same animation, one for Internet Explorer 4.0+ and the other for other Java-capable Web browsers (such as Navigator 4.0+, for instance).
- Create automatic forwarding links using the META tag.
- Use script triggers to display a pop-up alert message, a message on the status line, a pop-up Mailto window, and an animation in a customized browser window.
- Optimize your media to improve the download performance of your animations.
- Consolidate the Java class players to improve the download performance of your animations.

This is the end of the weekend! If you made it through everything, then you're simply incredible. If you are human, however, you probably skipped some of the optional bonus examples or sessions along the way. Feel free to come back next weekend to cover any areas that you skipped or would like to do more experimenting with.

Look in the appendixes for additional material covering using Liquid Motion with Microsoft FrontPage 98 and placing your Liquid Motion animations up on the Web so everyone can see your amazing work.

You should be comfortable enough with Liquid Motion now to start creating some of your own Web animations from scratch, without any prompting from me. The main thing is to have some fun, let the creative juices flow. Don't worry too much about the results. Just get in the sandbox and play.

APPENDIX A: Installing Liquid Motion

Liquid Motion is not included on the CD-ROM for this book. To get Liquid Motion, you need to go to the Microsoft Web site and then download and install the 45-day trial version. Optionally, you can purchase and download the licensed version of Liquid Motion at the Microsoft Web site, or you can purchase the licensed version of Liquid Motion online at the Microsoft site any time after downloading the trial version.

Minimum Requirements

Microsoft Liquid Motion is currently only available for the English language versions of Windows 95, 98, or NT.

According to Microsoft, a Pentium PC with 16MB of RAM is required to run Liquid Motion. I've successfully installed and run Liquid Motion on a 66 Mhz 486 with 20MB of RAM (it is woefully slow, but it runs).

A super-VGA graphics board capable of 800X600 screen resolution and 16-bit color resolution ("high color" or a palette of about 32,000 colors) is recommended.

For a minimal install of Liquid Motion, you will need at least 30MB of free disk space.

AOL users must have Microsoft Internet Explorer 3.02+ or Netscape Navigator 3.0+ to download and install Liquid Motion.

NOTE Due to legal restrictions, only residents of the United States can download and install Liquid Motion from the Microsoft Web site. If you reside in Canada, you should call the Microsoft Canada Order Centre at 888-296-6582 to order Liquid Motion. If you reside in the United Kingdom, you should call Microsoft Connections at 0345 00 2000 to order Liquid Motion. If you reside in some other country, contact your local Microsoft subsidiary to find out if you can obtain Liquid Motion (see **www.microsoft.com/worldwide/** on the Web for links to all of Microsoft's international subsidiaries).

You should close any nonessential applications or services before starting the download and install process. This will help to ensure that the download and install process will not get hung up part way. If you are also purchasing Liquid Motion, you should have a blank floppy disk on hand to create the backup license disk (you'll need it if you later need to reinstall Liquid Motion).

Which Browser Should You Use?

I recommend that you download and install Internet Explorer Version 4.0 (or greater) before trying to install Liquid Motion from the Web. You can download the latest version of Internet Explorer at **http://www.microsoft.com/windows/ie/ie40/.**

Although most animation effects that you can create using Liquid Motion can be viewed in both Internet Explorer and Netscape Navigator (in fact, in any Java-capable browser), some animation effects, such as filters and transitions, 3-D objects, rotating objects, and spinning text, can only be viewed in Internet Explorer 4.0. If you want to do the sections of the book that cover these effects, you'll need to have Internet Explorer 4.0+ installed.

Installing Liquid Motion from the Web

You need to install Microsoft Liquid Motion directly from the Microsoft Web site. Here are general instructions for installing Liquid Motion from the Web:

1. Run your Web browser and go to the Microsoft Liquid Motion Web site at **www.microsoft.com/liquidmotion/.** (If you get an HTTP 404 error, just click on the Refresh or Reload button until the page is displayed.)

2. Click on the "FREE TRIAL!" animation on the right.

3. At the Try & Buy page, click on one of the buttons to select a reseller.

4. If you're using Netscape Navigator 4.0, you will be instructed to download and install the InstallFromTheWeb Client for Netscape. Just follow the instructions provided. (After installing the InstallFromTheWeb Client and then activating it at the reseller's download page, you will see a blue InstallFromTheWeb button. Just click on it to install Liquid Motion.

5. If you're using Internet Explorer 4.0, an ActiveX control is automatically downloaded and installed (this can take a few minutes), so there is no need to do anything to begin installing Liquid Motion from the Web. If you get a "Security Warning" asking if you want to install the "InstallFromTheWeb Client," just click

on Yes to accept the Verisign certificate. When you can see the InstallFromTheWeb button, just click on it to install Liquid Motion.

NOTE When you first download Liquid Motion, you have the option of buying the licensed version. Just click on the TryAndBuy button at the reseller's download page. You can also return at any time after installing the 45-day trial version and click on the TryAndBuy button to purchase the licensed version.

If You Have Problems

If you run into any difficulties installing Liquid Motion from the Web, a FAQ at **www.digitalgoods.net/lm/mw/faq.htm** covers some of the basic problems that can arise when installing Liquid Motion.

Microsoft does not offer direct technical support for the 45-day trial version of Liquid Motion, but you can bring up a form at **www.digitalgoods.net/lm/twsupport.htm** to submit queries about any problems you may run into.

Microsoft also has an online support page available for Liquid Motion at **support.microsoft.com/support/liquidmotion/default.asp.** After registering, you'll be able to access Microsoft's FAQ (different from the FAQ mentioned earlier), search the Microsoft Knowledge Base, read about using Liquid Motion with FrontPage, and get information on Liquid Motion newsgroups.

If you've purchased the licensed version of Liquid Motion, you can call Microsoft Liquid Motion support at 425-635-3103. If you've purchased the CD-ROM version available to Canadian users, you can call 905-568-3503 for support.

Reading the Liquid Motion Newsgroups

Microsoft has set up some newsgroups for providing peer-group support from other Liquid Motion users. These newsgroups are:

microsoft.public.liquidmotion

microsoft.public.liquidmotion.discussion

To access these newsgroups, you'll need to have a newsreader installed and configured. For Internet Explorer 4.0+, you'll need Internet Mail and News from the Microsoft

Internet Explorer Web site. For Netscape Navigator 4.0+, you'll need Netscape Communicator (rather than the stand-alone version of Navigator) and Netscape Messenger.

These newsgroups may not be available from the news server provided by your ISP (Internet service provider). If they aren't, you'll need to add Microsoft's news server, msnews.microsoft.com, to your newsreader's list of news servers and then subscribe to the newsgroups from that server.

Setting Internet Explorer 4.0+ as Your Default Browser

In order to automatically preview your Liquid Motion animations in Internet Explorer, it must be your default browser. If Internet Explorer 4.0+ isn't set as your default browser, you won't be able to directly preview your animations from Liquid Motion in Internet Explorer. If Navigator comes up when you preview an animation, you know that Navigator is your default browser.

Setting Internet Explorer as your default browser will not interfere with your continuing to use Netscape Navigator as your main browser. The only difference you'll see is that when you double-click an HTML file in Windows Explorer, the HTML file will be displayed in Internet Explorer, rather than in Navigator.

Here are the steps to specify Internet Explorer 4.0+ as your default Web browser:

1. In Internet Explorer 4.0+, select View, Internet Options.

2. Click on the Programs tab and then select the check box at the bottom of the window ("Internet Explorer should check to see whether it is the default browser").

3. Exit and rerun Internet Explorer. At the prompt asking you if you want Internet Explorer to be your default browser, click Yes.

NAVIGATOR AND ACCELERATOR

If you are using Netscape Navigator 4.0+, when installing Liquid Motion you may be prompted to install the Liquid Motion Accelerator. Installing the accelerator is necessary if you want to get optimum playback of Liquid Motion animations in Navigator. If you opt to install the Liquid Motion Accelerator (highly recommended), you may be warned that doing so may pose a security hazard. To install the accelerator, you'll have to grant the privilege of installing the software on your local hard drive.

Netscape Navigator 4.0+ users who haven't already installed Liquid motion will be prompted to install the Liquid Motion Accelerator when they first view a Liquid Motion animation from the Web. The accelerator is automatically included the first time a Liquid Motion animation is downloaded using Navigator 4.0+, but it doesn't have to be downloaded again once it is installed.

APPENDIX B:
Using Liquid Motion with FrontPage 98

If you are a FrontPage 98 user, you should find Liquid Motion easy to learn and use, since the two applications share toolbars, buttons, and shortcut keys, and they have similar menu items.

• •

FrontPage 98 is not included on this book's CD-ROM. For information on ordering FrontPage 98, see the FrontPage 98 Web site at **www.microsoft.com/frontpage/**.

• •

FrontPage 98 users can take advantage of the following capabilities:

✪ Publish Liquid Motion animations directly to a FrontPage Web.

✪ Drag and drop Liquid Motion animations to FrontPage 98.

✪ Use Easy-Authoring Templates that are specially designed for use with FrontPage 98 themes.

Checking for the Liquid Motion Component in FrontPage 98

If FrontPage 98 is already installed on your computer when you install Liquid Motion, a special DLL (.dll) file is installed under the FrontPage folder (look in the \Program Files\Microsoft FrontPage\bots\lmwebbot folder for lmwebbot.dll). You can also check that this DLL file has been installed by opening the FrontPage Editor and then selecting Insert, FrontPage Component. In the list of components, you should find "Liquid Motion Animation" listed as one of the components. If you double-click it, you'll see a pop-up message giving you information on using Liquid Motion with FrontPage 98. Just click OK to close the message window.

Publishing Animations to a FrontPage Web

There are three ways you can publish a Liquid Motion animation in a FrontPage 98 Web:

✿ Publish an animation directly to a FrontPage Web.

✿ Publish an animation to a location in a Web page open in the FrontPage Editor.

✿ Drag and drop an animation into the FrontPage Explorer (or to a location in a Web page open in the FrontPage Editor).

Publishing an Animation Directly to a FrontPage Web

To publish a Liquid Motion animation directly to a FrontPage Web, do the following:

1. Open or create an animation in Liquid Motion.

2. Click the Publish tool, and then select the FrontPage 98 (or newer) Web radio button. Click Next.

3. Select the second radio button (a new folder in any FrontPage web). Click Finish or Next.

4. If you clicked on Next, you can specify another location to save the published files. To accept the default location, click Finish or Next.

5. If you clicked on Next, you can specify another name for the animation's HTML file. To accept the default HTML file name, click Finish or Next.

6. If you clicked on Next, you can specify a splash image that will be displayed while your animation is being downloaded. To not specify a splash image, just click Finish.

7. At the Getting Started window, you can select the FrontPage Web you want to publish to. This can include a local FrontPage Web on your hard drive or a Front-Page Web that is located on a Web server. You can also choose to create a new FrontPage Web.

Publishing an Animation to a Web Page Open in the FrontPage Editor

Another option is to publish a Liquid Motion animation to a specified location in a Web page open in the FrontPage Editor. To do this, follow these steps:

1. Open a Web page in the FrontPage Editor and position the cursor at the location where you want the Liquid Motion animation to be inserted.

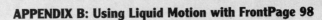

2. Run Liquid Motion and open or create an animation.

3. Click the Publish tool, and then select the FrontPage 98 (or newer) Web radio button. Click Next.

4. Select the first radio button (the page currently open in the FrontPage editor). Click Finish or Next.

5. If you clicked on Next, you can specify another location to save the published files. To accept the default location, click Finish or Next.

6. If you clicked on Next, you can specify another name for the animation's HTML file. To accept the default HTML file name, click Finish or Next.

7. If you clicked on Next, you can specify a splash image that will be displayed while your animation is being downloaded. To decline to specify a splash image, just click Finish.

You'll see a Microsoft Liquid Motion placeholder inserted at the location of your cursor in the Web page open in the FrontPage Editor (see Figure B.1), dimensioned to the size of the animation scene. You won't actually be able to see the animation until you publish the Web page to your FrontPage Web.

Dragging and Dropping Animations into FrontPage 98

You can drag and drop a Liquid Motion animation into the FrontPage Explorer or into a Web page open in the FrontPage Editor.

To drag and drop a Liquid Motion animation into the FrontPage Explorer, do the following:

1. Run FrontPage 98, and then run Windows Explorer.

2. In Windows Explorer, open the folder where the animation's HTML file is stored (for instance, to drag and drop the Wave banner from the Easy-Authoring Templates, open the C:\Program Files\Microsoft Liquid Motion\Projects\Templates\Banners\wave folder).

3. Click and hold the mouse on the HTML file (wavebanner.html, for instance) in Windows Explorer, and then drag it to the destination folder in the FrontPage Explorer. Drag the animation's HTML file until it is positioned on top of the destination folder in the FrontPage Explorer window.

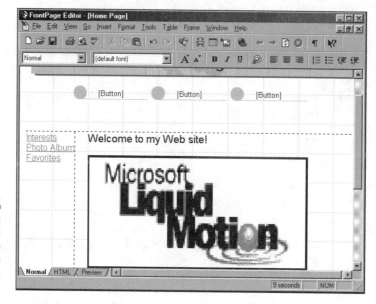

Figure B.1

You can publish a
Liquid Motion
animation directly to
a location in a Web
page open in the
FrontPage Editor.

If the folder in FrontPage Explorer into which you want to drop the animation is obscured by the
Windows Explorer window, while still holding down the mouse button, hold down the Alt key and press
the Tab key to bring the FrontPage Explorer window to the foreground.

4. Release the mouse button to drop the animation into the folder located under the
mouse cursor.

If the Liquid Motion component was installed in FrontPage, the other files and folders
required for the animation will automatically be added to the FrontPage folder.

Alternatively, you can drag and drop an animation directly into a Web page open in the
FrontPage Editor.

1. Run FrontPage 98 and open a Web page in the FrontPage Editor. Run Windows
Explorer.

2. In Windows Explorer, open the folder where the animation's HTML file is stored (for
instance, to drag and drop the Wave banner from the Easy-Authoring Templates, open
the C:\Program Files\Microsoft Liquid Motion\Projects\Templates\Banners\wave
folder).

3. Click and hold the mouse on the HTML file (wavebanner.html, for instance). In the FrontPage Editor, drag the mouse to the location in the Web page you want the animation to appear. (If necessary, while still holding down the mouse button, press Alt+Tab to bring the FrontPage Editor window to the foreground.)

4. Release the mouse button to drop the animation into the location under the mouse cursor.

Moving Animations in a FrontPage Web

You can move an animation added to a FrontPage Web by either dragging and dropping it or copying and pasting it.

Dragging and Dropping an Animation

You can drag and drop an animation to a new location in a FrontPage Web using these steps:

1. In FrontPage Explorer, if the Folders view is not turned on, select View, Folders.

2. If the folder to which you want to drag and drop the animation doesn't exist yet, select File, New, Folder. Type the name of the new folder and press Enter.

3. Open the FrontPage Web folder where the animation's HTML file is stored. In the folder contents window (the right window), click and hold the mouse on the animation's HTML file, and then drag it to the folder in the folder tree window (the left window) where you want to drop the animation.

4. Release the mouse button to drop the animation into the folder under the mouse pointer.

5. Open the animation's HTML file (from the folder where you've dropped it) into the FrontPage Editor. You'll probably see a broken image placeholder in place of the Liquid Motion placeholder. If you try to preview the Web page, you'll get a script error.

6. To fix this, right-click the broken image icon, and then select FrontPage Component Properties.

7. The Liquid Motion placeholder image should now be visible (this tells you that all the attendant files and folders required by the animation are copied to the new location).

NOTE

If you haven't previously opened the original animation file in FrontPage, you may get a message window saying that FrontPage can't find the Liquid Motion files. You'll need to type the relative path from the new location of the HTML file you've opened in the FrontPage Editor and the location from which you dragged and dropped the HTML file. For instance, if you dragged and dropped the animation's HTML file from the PushButton folder in the root of your FrontPage Web to another folder also in the root of your FrontPage Web, you need to type ../PushButton/ and then click OK.

Copying and Pasting an Animation

This is similar to dropping and dragging, except you copy and paste the animation. Just right-click the HTML file of the animation you want to move, and select Copy. Right-click the folder where you want to copy the animation, and select Paste. The rest here is the same as if you had dragged and dropped the animation's HTML file. See steps 3 through 7 (and the note) in the previous section, "Dragging and Dropping an Animation."

Getting FrontPage 98 Help

If you have further questions about using Liquid Motion with FrontPage 98, you may be able to get answers by calling Microsoft's FrontPage support numbers:

In the U.S.: (425) 635-7088

In Canada: (905) 568-3503

You may also be able to get answers to FrontPage 98/Liquid Motion questions at the FrontPage newsgroup:

microsoft.frontpage.client

This newsgroup may not be available from the news server provided by your ISP (Internet service provider). If it isn't available, you'll need to add Microsoft's news server, msnews.microsoft.com, to your newsreader's list of news servers and then subscribe to this newsgroup from that server.

APPENDIX C:
Placing Your Animation Files Up on a Web Server

Once you've put the finishing touches on that great animated Web site on your local drive, you'll want to put it up on the Web so that everybody else can see it too. Actually, it is probably a good idea to preview your animations on a Web server *before* you've completely developed a whole animated Web site. You can't tell how an animation is going to play until you actually test it out on the Web.

Finding a Web Host

The first step is to find a server to host your page. If you are a student, your school might be able to host your pages. If you are a subscriber to one of the online services such as CompuServe or AOL, it also might provide some Web space.

Most local access providers (providing dial-up access to the Internet) now provide Web space to you at nominal cost (or no cost). Many provide up to 10MB of free Web space.

If you want to create a commercial Web site, you hope to generate a considerable amount of traffic, or you just want access to a fuller range of features and services, consider finding a Web host that focuses on providing raw Web space. For a list of affordable presence providers, see my Web site, the Budget Web Host List, at **www.callihan.com /budget/.** Be sure to check out the "More Lists" link in the sidebar menu for links to many other lists of low-cost and free Web space providers.

You may also consider getting a domain name. The easiest way to get a domain name is to have your Web space provider register and maintain it for you. Web space accounts that include the registration and maintenance of a domain name are usually referred to as "virtual host" accounts. Many Web space providers have a link where you can check and see if the domain name you want is still available or not (if they don't have a link, you can do a WHOIS search at InterNIC's Web site at **http://www.internic.net/.**) You should be aware that after you register a domain name through your Web space provider, you'll be billed $70 by InterNIC to cover the first two years, and will be billed $35 each year after that, as long as you choose to keep the domain name. These fees are separate from any setup fee you may pay to your Web space provider for registering and maintaining your domain name.

Finding a FrontPage Web Host

If you use FrontPage 98 to create your Web pages, you'll probably want to find a Web host that supports the FrontPage 98 server extensions. Microsoft has a list of Web presence providers that support FrontPage 98 at **microsoft.saltmine.com/frontpage /wpp/list/.** Alex Chapman's BudgetWeb Index also has a list of Web space providers, at **budgetweb.com/budgetweb/windowshosting.html.** The providers he lists use Windows NT servers, most of which support FrontPage 98.

The Microsoft list of FrontPage presence providers is organized by state, but you shouldn't feel constrained to stick to providers in your local area. If you plan on primarily generating local traffic to your site, you may benefit from selecting a local Web host for your pages. Otherwise, feel free to shop around to find the best deal.

NOTE The instructions provided in this appendix for using WS_FTP to transfer HTML files and Liquid Motion animation files to a Web server are for you if you don't use FrontPage 98.

If you're a FrontPage 98 user and your Web pages are located on a Web server with the FrontPage Server Extensions installed, you should probably just stick to using FrontPage 98 to transfer your files to your FrontPage server.

If you're a FrontPage 98 user but your Web pages are located on a server that doesn't have the FrontPage Server Extensions installed, when you publish your FrontPage Web pages to your server, FrontPage 98 actually uses FTP to transfer your files to your Web server. Optionally, you could just as easily use WS_FTP LE, or any other FTP program of your choosing, to transfer your files.

For more information, see Appendix B, "Using Liquid Motion with FrontPage 98."

Connecting to a Web Server

Your Web host should provide you with FTP access to your Web pages. This means providing you with a user ID and a password, as well as assigning you a password-protected directory on its server where you can store your pages. You might also be assigned an

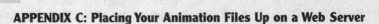

account name, although usually not. This allows you to access your directory (and any directories you create within that directory) through FTP, copying files to or from it, while keeping everyone else out.

Before you can use FTP to transfer Web pages to your Web host's server, you need to find out the following information from your Web space provider:

🔧 **Host name.** The host name of your Web host's server. This must identify a fully qualified Internet host name or IP address that belongs to a real server; it cannot be a virtual host name. Your Web host should provide you with this information.

🔧 **User ID.** This is a unique user name that identifies you to your server. If you receive your Web space from a local ISP or a commercial online service, this will very likely be the same as the user name you use to log on. Otherwise, your Web host will ask you to specify a preferred user name when you get your Web space account.

🔧 **Password.** You need to have a password so that only you can access your Web pages on the server. Your Web host will ask you to specify a password when you get your Web space account. As with your User ID, if you receive your Web space from a local ISP or a commercial online service, your password will likely be the same as the password you use to log onto the Internet.

🔧 **Account.** Most Web hosts do not provide an account name—only a user name (User ID) and a password are usually required. If they require an account name, they should let you know.

🔧 **Remote directory path.** This is the directory path to where your files are located on your server. In most cases, you won't need to provide this information—most Web hosts automatically switch you to your own root directory on your server when you log on with your User ID and password. If a remote directory path is required, it needs to be the actual full path on your server, and not your alias. You need only be concerned about this if you are not automatically switched to your directory on the server. That should only rarely be the case, but if it is, and they haven't already provided you with the information, you'll need to query your provider for the full path to your directory on their server.

NOTE On Unix servers, the Host Name and User ID are case-sensitive. So if you chose "JBlow," for instance, as your User ID (rather than "jblow"), you'll need to enter it exactly as shown. Windows NT servers, however, are not case-sensitive, so you could enter your User ID in any combination of upper- and lowercase letters.

Setting Up WS_FTP LE

To transfer your Web pages from your local computer to your Web server, you need to use an FTP program. The following examples all use WS_FTP LE for Windows 95/98/NT, version 4.6, which is on the CD-ROM that comes with this book. Earlier versions of WS_FTP LE should all be quite similar, except that the arrangement of the Properties and Options menus might be somewhat different. Other FTP programs should work similarly, although I can only speak here for WS_FTP LE.

You can also download WS_FTP LE 4.6 directly from this book's CD-ROM. Just click Utilities, WS_FTP LE, then Install. There is also a trial version of WS_FTP Pro that you can install and try out on your computer (the instructions in this appendix, however, are written with WS_FTP LE in mind).

You can download WS_FTP LE directly from the Ipswitch Web site at **www.ipswitch.com/downloads/ws_ftp_LE.html**. It is free to qualified noncommercial users.

I assume that you have a connection to the Internet, that you have been provided with or have rented some space on a Web server to store your Web pages, and that you have password-protected access to your directory. I also assume that you know the information detailed earlier under "A Few Things You Need to Know" and that you have installed WS_FTP LE.

Starting WS_FTP LE

You can run your dialer to log onto the Internet, then run WS_FTP LE, or you can do it the other way around (you'll be prompted later to log onto the Internet).

To run WS_FTP LE, click on the Start button and then select Programs, Ws_ftp, and WS_FTP95 LE.

Figure C.1 shows the opening screen of WS_FTP LE for Windows 95, version 4.6, displaying the General tab section of the Session Properties window (earlier versions of WS_FTP LE might combine the General and Startup tab sections in one window). Follow the steps outlined in the subsequent sections to define a new session profile.

The General Tab

1. In the Profile Name box, type a name for your session profile. This can be whatever you want. For instance, you might define "MySite" as your profile name. Just make it something you can remember.

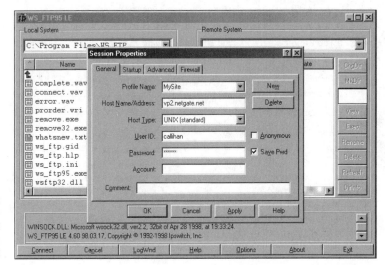

Figure C.1

The General tab section of the WS_FTP Session Properties dialog box

2. In the Host Name/Address box, type the host name of the Web host server where your Web space is located. This is a fully qualified Internet host name or IP address—mine, for instance, is **vp2.netgate.net.** This is not your virtual host name, if you happen to have one (my virtual host name is **www.callihan.com,** for instance).

3. In the Host Type box, you should leave "Automatically detect" enabled. If that doesn't work, try "UNIX (standard)"—the majority of Web servers are still Unix machines. In most cases, one or the other of these two settings should work. If neither works, you need to find out the actual host type from your Web space provider so that you can select one of the other options.

4. In the User ID box, type your user name.

5. To disable anonymous login, click on the Anonymous check box so that it is unchecked (blank). To save your password so that you won't have to type it in every time you log in, click on the Save Pwd check box to check it.

NOTE You only do an anonymous login if you are connecting to an FTP site that is open to all comers. Since you are logging into your own private FTP account, using a user name and password, you need to turn anonymous login off here.

◆◆◆

CAUTION If you are on a network, you should be aware that checking the Save Password check box will save your password to your hard drive in an encrypted form. It is, however, not difficult to decrypt for someone who is determined to do so—a hacker, for instance. If you don't save your password here, you must type it in each time you use FTP to log on to your Web server. It's your pick—security or convenience. If you are not on a network, however, security shouldn't be as much of an issue, as a hacker would have to sit at your keyboard to get at your password.

◆◆◆

6. Type your password in the Password box. Your password appears as a row of asterisks. (Don't type a row of asterisks!)

7. Leave the Account box blank unless your Web host has provided you with an account name. Refer to Figure C.1 for an example of how your filled-out General tab section should look (substituting your own information, of course).

8. Click on the Startup tab.

The Startup Tab

1. You don't need to type anything in the Initial Remote Host Directory box—your Web host should automatically switch you to your root directory (based on your user name). If your Web host doesn't automatically switch you, you'll need to type the full path to your folder on your Web server. Your Web page folders may also be in a "www" folder on your server. If that is the case, you may want to enter www here, so you can go directly to the root folder for your Web pages. (Don't enter this, however, until you've actually connected to your server and can confirm that this is the case.)

2. In the Initial Local Directory box, type the path of your local directory (folder), such as c:\pages, for instance, where your HTML files are stored on your hard drive.

3. Click on the Apply button to save your new session profile. (In some earlier versions of WS_FTP, this is a Save button, instead.)

4. Leave the rest of the fields blank (see Figure C.2).

The Advanced Tab Section

You need to change the settings here only if the default settings don't work. For instance, if you're having trouble connecting, you might increase the number in the Connection

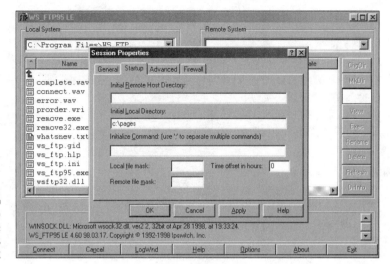

Figure C.2

The Startup tab section of the Session Properties dialog box

Retry box. You could also increase the Network Timeout entry if you are timing out before you connect. Finally, a port number other than 21 (which is the standard port number for an FTP server) might need to be set in the Remote Port box, although this is unlikely.

● ●

There is no need to fill out the Firewall tab section unless your Web directories are located behind a firewall, which is unlikely. If you do need to fill out this section, find out from your Web space provider the information you'll need to type in here.

● ●

Connecting to Your Server

To connect to your server, click on the OK button. If you're not currently connected, you'll be prompted to connect to the Internet. If your settings are correct, you'll see the root directory on your server displayed in the right-hand window. If it is present, double-click on the "www" folder (your server may use a different folder name) to open the root folder for your Web pages (see Figure C.3).

If this hasn't worked, you'll need to go back to the drawing board. You may need to specify a host type (you'll probably have to e-mail your Web host to find out what this is). Make sure that the host name of your Web server is correct. You should double-check that your user ID, password, and account name (if you have one) are correct.

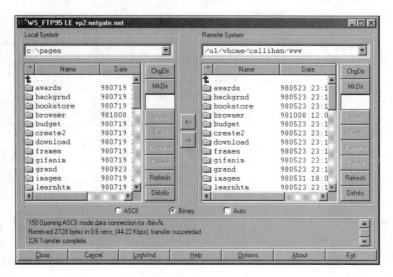

Figure C.3

Once you connect to your server and open the root folder for your Web pages, WS_FTP displays your local directories on the left and your directories on your server on the right.

If it still doesn't work, under the same Advanced tab, try increasing the Network Timeout amount or the number of connection retries. If none of this works, check with your Web host to make sure you're using the correct user name, password, and so on. Also make sure you have the right remote directory path, if that is required.

NOTE

The whole battle to being able to use FTP to update your Web pages on your server is simply getting these settings correct. So make sure you find out from your Web space provider the exact settings you need to provide here. Once you get them right, it is as easy as pie. (But it's pretty much pie in your face if you don't get them right! So be patient if you can't get this to work right off the bat.)

TIP

You'll notice in Figure C.3 that the folders in the left window (on my local hard drive) and the folders in the right window (in the WWW folder on my remote server) mirror each other exactly. As long as your local and remote folders mirror each other in this fashion, and you use relative URLs for all internal links, you can thoroughly check out your HTML files and Liquid Motion animations on your local drive and then transfer them up to your Web server without having to change any of the links.

Using WS_FTP LE

In WS_FTP LE's main screen, the window on the left shows the local folder (directory) on your hard drive that you specified in the Initial Local Directory box under the Startup

tab. The window on the right shows the directory on your Web server (you left this blank) that you specified in the Initial Remote Host Directory box, also under the Startup tab.

You'll notice that I have quite a few directories already set up in the right-hand window. That's because I've been a busy chipmunk and have managed to create quite a few Web pages. In order to keep track of them, I have organized them into separate directories. Because you're just getting started, you might not have any directories or files set up yet, unless your provider has already created some sample directories or files for you.

Navigating WS_FTP LE's Main Window

Navigating WS_FTP's main window, you can do the following:

- Move up or down the directory structure in either window. Double-clicking on a folder will open that subdirectory. Double-clicking on the two periods (..) will move you up one directory level. You also can use the ChgDir button in either window to change the directory.

- Use the MkDir button to create a directory in either window. You can use the Delete button to delete a directory.

- Transfer files from the directory on your local PC to the directory on your Web server (you can also do this the other way around). For instructions for transferring files from your local computer to your sever, see "Transferring Your Files to Your Server."

- Of the remaining buttons, the ones you are most likely to use are the View button and the Rename button, which (unsurprisingly) let you view and rename files, and the DirInfo button, which gets information on the files in a directory (such as size and date).

Transferring Your Files to Your Server

Transferring your files onto your server is fairly simple. Just follow these steps:

1. On your local PC (the window on the left), change to the folder that contains the files you want to transfer to your server. Highlight the files.

2. Check the radio button of the type of file you transfer. If you transfer HTML files or any other text files, you must click on the ASCII radio button so that it is filled. If you transfer graphics files, such as GIF or JPEG images, you must click on the

Binary radio button so that it is filled. (Before you select the Auto button to transfer files or folders, read the next section of this appendix, "Setting File Extensions for Auto Mode Transfer.")

3. To transfer the highlighted files from the local PC directory (the left window) to the currently displayed directory on your Web server (the right window), click on the right-arrow button. (To copy a file the other way, from your Web server to your local PC, you would click on the left-arrow button.)

Be patient. If you copy several files, or if any of them are large (such as a banner graphic file, for instance), it might take a minute or so before the files transfer.

Setting File Extensions for Auto Mode Transfer

When transferring Liquid Motion animation files, you'll want to transfer the whole folder for an animation. You might think that by selecting Auto as the transfer mode, WS_FTP would automatically transfer ASCII files (such as HTML files or other text files) in ASCII mode and transfer binary files (such as GIF, JPEG, or other executable files) in Binary mode. That's not the case, however—selecting Auto as the transfer mode will cause all files to be transferred in Binary mode, unless the file extension is listed in WS_FTP's list of ASCII file names and extensions. When you first install WS_FTP, however, only the .TXT extension (for text files) is listed. To make sure that ASCII files created by Liquid Motion are transferred in ASCII mode when using the Auto transfer mode, you'll need to add their extensions to WS_FTP's list:

1. At WS_FTP's main window, click on Options, and then select the Extensions tab.

2. In the text box, type the following extensions, then click on Add to add them to the list one by one:

    .HTM
    .HTML
    .JS

3. Click on the Apply button to make the new settings the default (see Figure C.4). Click on OK.

Important: Don't Force Lowercase File Names

When using WS_FTP to transfer Liquid Motion animation files and folders to a Unix Web server, you should *not* set Liquid Motion's option to force lowercase file names. On a Unix server, the case of a file name in a URL (for a hypertext link or inline image) *must*

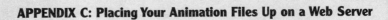

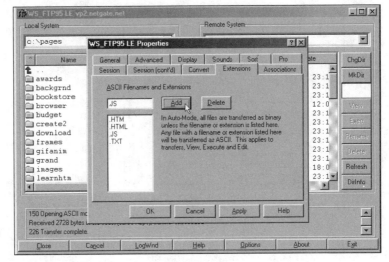

Figure C.4

The .HTM, .HTML, and .JS file extensions are added to WS_FTP's list of ASCII file extensions.

agree with the case of the actual name of the file (on a Unix server, MyPage.html and mypage.html would refer to two different files). Liquid Motion includes many mixed-case file names in the files it automatically creates when you create an animation. Forcing lowercase file names when transferring your Liquid Motion files to a Unix Web server could result in your animations not working. The default after installing WS_FTP LE is to have this option not selected. To make sure this option has not been reset as the default:

1. Click on Options. Select the Session tab (in earlier versions of WS_FTP LE, you might need to select Session Options here).

2. Check to see that the Force Lowercase Remote Names check box is *not* checked (see Figure C.5).

3. If the check box is checked, click on it to uncheck it. To set it as the default, click on the Set as default button and click on OK.

You may still want to use this option when transferring non-Liquid Motion files onto a Unix Web server. What I do, for instance, is make sure in my HTML files that all file names are lowercase, regardless of their case on my local hard drive (Windows 95/98 has a penchant, for instance, for initial-capping file names). I then make sure the option is set in WS_FTP to force lowercase file names when transferring my HTML and other attendant files (graphics, for instance) up onto my Web server. That way, both the file names in my URLs and the actual file names of the files on my Unix Web server are always lowercase.

Figure C.5

When using the Auto mode to transfer Liquid Motion files and folders, you must ensure that the Force Lowercase Remote Names check box is unchecked.

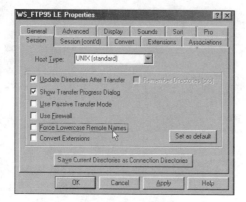

If you want to set this option as the default, you'll need to deselect it whenever you want to transfer Liquid Motion animation files and folders. Since I transfer a lot of non-Liquid Motion HTML files up onto my Unix server on a regular basis, I leave this as the default, but I always remember (or try to remember!) to uncheck this option when transferring Liquid Motion files and folders.

Closing and Exiting WS_FTP

When you are through transferring files to or from your server, you should always close your FTP session before exiting WS_FTP. To do this, just click on the Close button, wait for the "Goodbye" message to be displayed in the lower activity window, and then click on the Exit button.

PROGRAM DETAILS

WS_FTP LE by Ipswitch, Inc.

www.ipswitch.com/

E-Mail: sales@ipswitch.com

Other Ipswitch products: WS_FTP Pro (professional version); VT320 Telnet Terminal Emulator (DEC VT320 terminal emulator and Telnet communications program).

APPENDIX D: What's on the CD-ROM

You'll find on the CD-ROM all of the example images and sound files used in this book's animation examples (apart from those already included with the trial version of Liquid Motion). You'll also find a wide assortment of other resources to assist you in your Web animation efforts. Here's a rundown of the contents:

✿ All the example images and sound files used in the animation examples that are not included with Liquid Motion. Additionally, a wide assortment of additional images and sounds are included that you can use to create your own animations from scratch, including quite a few .au-format sound files that'll play in all Java-capable Web browsers.

✿ A collection of sample Liquid Motion animations that you can preview directly from the CD-ROM (if you have a fast enough CD-ROM drive) or from your own local hard drive. These include most of the example animations covered in the book, plus quite a few extra sample animations you can check out for new ideas or use as templates for getting a jump start on creating your own animations.

✿ A wide assortment of evaluation, shareware, and freeware software tools, such as paint and drawing programs, HTML editors, a sound editor, and utilities for creating forms, frames, image maps, GIF animations, style sheets, Java applets, and more.

✿ A selection of HTML templates into which you can easily plug the animations you've created with Liquid Motion . Make a few changes to customize the templates to suit your own purposes, add an animation or two, and you've created your own animated Web page or site. Included are templates for creating framed Web sites, an online newsletter, a genealogy Web site, and more.

Running the CD-ROM

The CD-ROM is designed to run under Windows 95/98 or Windows NT. If you haven't disabled Autorun, the CD-ROM will run automatically after you insert it into your CD-ROM drive.

If you've disabled AutoRun, perform the following steps to run the CD-ROM:

1. Insert it in the CD-ROM drive.

2. From the Start menu, select Run.

3. In the Open text box, type **D:\prima.exe** (where *D* is the CD-ROM drive).

4. Click on OK.

NOTE If you don't have a CD-ROM, all the example images and sound files used in the animation examples, as well as the additional collections of Web art, audio files, fonts, and HTML templates, are all available for download from this book's Web site at **http://www.callihan.com/liquidmotion/**.

Using PRIMA TECH's User Interface

PRIMA TECH's user interface is designed to make viewing and using the CD-ROM contents quick and easy. It contains four category buttons[em]Examples, Web Tools, Multimedia, and Utilities[em]that allow you to install, explore, and view information on the CD-ROM, or to visit the Web site for any of the example files or tools that the CD-ROM includes. To install any of the example files or software tools included on the CD-ROM, select these options:

- **Examples:** You'll find here all the example files contributed by the author, including images and sound files used in the book's animation examples (plus a lot of extra ones), a set of sample animations, and HTML templates you can use to enhance your Web animation endeavors.

- **Web Tools:** You'll find here a wide assortment of software tools (including HTML editors) for creating and managing Web pages and Web sites, plus tools for creating image maps, forms, frames, and style sheets.

- **Multimedia:** You'll find here a selection of multimedia tools, including paint and draw programs, graphic viewers and converters, and GIF and Java animation tools.

- ✿ **Utilities:** You'll find here a miscellaneous selection of other tools, including FTP programs, zip/unzip utilities, a mail list manager, and other utilities. Be sure to check out Top Ruler (it works great for lining up actors in Liquid Motion, which doesn't include any rulers).

When you select any of the examples or tools from the category windows, you can execute the following options:

- ✿ **Install:** Selecting this option allows you to install the example or tool on your hard drive.

- ✿ **Explore:** Selecting this option allows you to explore the folder for the example or tool on the CD-ROM.

- ✿ **View Information:** Selecting this option allows you to view any README text file or, alternatively, any Help file that accompanies the example or tool.

- ✿ **Visit Web Site:** Selecting this option launches your Web browser (Internet Explorer or Navigator only) at the associated Web site. This is a good way to check later if an updated version of the program or utility is available on the Web.

On the left panel of the CD-ROM interface screen are five additional options:

- ✿ **Navigate:** This provides options to return to the main menu, go to any of the category windows, or visit the Prima Web site.

- ✿ **Explore:** This lets you explore the current folder on the CD-ROM.

- ✿ **Exit:** This lets you exit the CD-ROM interface.

- ✿ **< and >:** These options move you backward or forward between the different windows in the CD-ROM's interface.

Installing the Example Files

At PRIMA TECH's main window, clicking on the Examples option gives you access to all of the images and sound files used in the book's animation examples, the sample animations, and a set of HTML templates. In the Examples window, you have these options:

NOTE If you choose to install any of the following options, a folder, Prima Examples, will be installed in the Liquid Motion folder (C:\Program Files\Microsoft Liquid Motion\). For this reason, I recommend that you not install any of these options until after you have installed Liquid Motion. For information on installing Liquid Motion, see Appendix A, "Installing Liquid Motion."

Book Examples: Click here to install all of the image files and sound files that are used in this book's animation examples, as well as a wide assortment of additional images and sounds you can use to create your own animations from scratch. Installing the book examples will create two folders (\Prima Examples\Book Images and \Prima Examples\Book Sounds) inside the Microsoft Liquid Motion folder. You can also explore this area of the CD-ROM or view information about the book examples.

Sample Animations: Click here to install a collection of sample animations to your hard drive. Installing the sample animations will create a folder (\Prima Examples\Samples) inside of the Microsoft Liquid Motion folder. You can also explore this area of the CD-ROM, view information about the sample animations, or view the sample animations directly from the CD-ROM.

HTML Templates. Click here to install a collection of HTML templates to your hard drive. Installing the HTML templates will create a folder (\Prima Examples\Templates) inside of the Microsoft Liquid Motion folder. You can also explore this area of the CD-ROM or view information about the different templates that are included.

◆◆

The Sample Animations option in the Examples section has an additional option you can select: View Sample Animations. Selecting this option will open an HTML file in your Web browser from which you'll be able to preview the sample animations directly from the CD-ROM.

Some computers may have difficulty previewing the sample animations directly from the CD-ROM, especially if you have a slower CD-ROM drive. If this is the case, you should install the sample animations to your hard drive and then preview them from there. The sample animations take up about 15MB of space.

Since the HTML file for previewing the sample animations also includes several animations, some slower computers may also run into difficulty trying to preview the sample animations, even after installing them to the local hard drive. For slower computers, I've included an alternative HTML file (without the front-end animations) that you can use to preview the sample animations. Just start your Web browser and open index2.html from the C:\Program Files\Microsoft Liquid Motion\Prima Examples\Samples folder. (Note: I reused the same sidebar file of links in index2.html that I used for index.html, so feel free to use any of the links to the animations, but don't use the Home link[md]it'll take you back to index.html, instead of index2.html.)

If you use Netscape Navigator as your Web browser, you may be prompted to install the Liquid Motion Accelerator when you first preview a Liquid Motion animation. The LM Accelerator is automatically downloaded the first time a Liquid Motion animation is played in Navigator. If you choose to install it, it doesn't have to be downloaded again.

You must install the accelerator if you want decent playback performance from Navigator when previewing Liquid Motion animations. You may be warned that installing the accelerator is a security hazard (the accelerator needs to be installed to your hard drive), but since this is signed as provided by Microsoft, you shouldn't be concerned that any damage will result. Because the accelerator is included with every animation, no additional download time is required to install it.

◆ ◆

Using the Software on the CD-ROM

A wide range of freeware, shareware, and trialware applications and utilities is included on the CD-ROM. You're expected to register any shareware programs or evaluation versions if you wish to continue using them beyond their evaluation periods. Some evaluation versions will stop working after their evaluation periods are up, whereas others may give you extra time after the evaluation period is up to decide if you want to register the software (Paint Shop Pro 5, for instance, gives you an extra 30 days after its 30-day evaluation period is over). Yet other evaluation versions may just pester you with nag screens. You are free to use freeware programs as long as you wish, although some restrictions may apply (some programs are free to use only for noncommercial purposes, for instance).

● ●

Notice: Any shareware distributed on this disk is for evaluation purposes only and should be registered with the shareware vendor if used beyond the trial period.

● ●

The following are brief descriptions of some of the software that you'll find on the CD-ROM:

✪ **ColorBrowser:** A great utility for specifying those pesky hexadecimal codes used in HTML to specify background and text colors

✪ **CoolEdit96:** A great shareware sound editor that you can use to create sound files for Liquid Motion. Also available on the CD-ROM is an evaluation version of CoolEdit Pro (select the Explore option to go to its folder and install it).

✪ **Frame-It:** A great freeware utility for creating Web sites using frames. Use Frame-It in combination with Liquid Motion to create an animated frame page. (Although Frame-It is now freeware, the program still says you have only 14 days to evaluate it. Use the Visit Web Site option to go to Frame-It's Web site and get a user name and password that will allow you to continue using Frame-It for free.)

✪ **GIF MovieGear:** An easy-to-use, relatively compact, but thorough GIF animator program

- ✿ **HTML Power Tools:** A collection of powerful HTML utilities, including a spell-checker, a syntax analyzer, a rule-based editor, and more

- ✿ **Character Builder:** A means to liven up your Web site with animated 3-D characters

- ✿ **CoffeeCup HTML Editor++,** Image Mapper++, and StyleSheet Maker++: A great collection of programs that edit HTML files, create image maps, and create cascading style sheets

- ✿ **ImageCommander:** A fast and powerful image viewing and file conversion program for Windows-based computers

- ✿ **Liquid Characterz:** Animated figures with embedded behaviors and intelligence

- ✿ **LView Pro 2.0:** A full-featured 32-bit image processor program that handles the image formats found on Microsoft Windows environments and Internet Web pages

NOTE Lview software is Copyright (C) 1993-1998 by Leonardo Haddad Loureiro

- ✿ **MediaBlaze.** The Swiss army knife of multimedia tools. Organize and keep tabs on all your multimedia files.

- ✿ **Paint Shop Pro 5:** One of the leading graphics editors, with features rivaling commercial graphics editors, such as Adobe PhotoShop or Corel Photopaint, costing hundreds of dollars more. Installed with Paint Shop Pro 5 is a companion program, Animation Shop, which is a great GIF animation program.

- ✿ **Top Ruler:** A great utility that gives you onscreen rulers that you can use to line up Liquid Motion actors. You can use it up to 50 times before having to register it.

- ✿ **WinZip:** One of the most popular file compression utilities around. It makes working with ZIP files and many other file compression formats in Windows a breeze.

- ✿ **WS_FTP LE:** A great FTP program that is free to qualified noncommercial users. An evaluation version of WS_FTP Pro is also available on the CD-ROM (if you are not a qualified noncommercial user, you are expected to use WS_FTP Pro instead of WS_FTP LE.

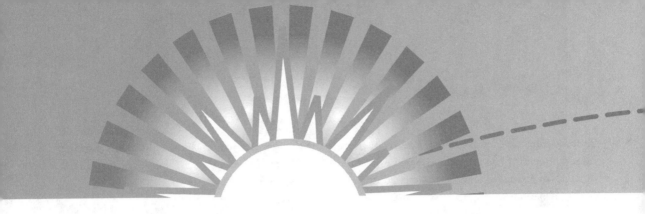

GLOSSARY

2-D shape. A two-dimensional shape in Liquid Motion. 2-D shapes that can be used in Liquid Motion include preset geometric shapes (rectangles, squares, ovals, circles, polygons, stars, banners, arrows and speech balloons), user-drawn shapes (angular or freeform), and 2-D shapes that can be imported from Macromedia Freehand. Preset geometric shapes can be reshaped and altered using either preset or freeform editing controls. User-drawn shapes can either be angular or freeform shapes. Imported Macromedia Freehand shapes can be .fh4, .fh5, and .fh7 files that contain a single shape or shape group.

3-D light. Light falling directly on a 3-D shape from a 3-D light source. In Liquid Motion, the color and position of a 3-D light source relative to a 3-D shape can be controlled. More than one 3-D light source can be created for a single 3-D shape. *See also* 3-D shape *and* ambient light.

3-D shape. A three-dimensional shape in Liquid Motion. 3-D shapes are created using DirectX technology and are displayable only in Internet Explorer, Version 4.0 or greater.

absolute URL. A complete path, or address, of a file on the Internet (such as, http://www.some-server.com/somedir/somepage.html). It is also called a "complete URL." *See also* relative URL.

active content. Content on a Web page, implemented through ActiveX controls, that changes over time or in response to user actions.

ActiveX. Microsoft's set of programming technologies for creating interactive software components in a networked environment.

ActiveX controls. Software components incorporating ActiveX technology that can be used to add animation, pop-up menus, interactive forms, and other features to Web pages. ActiveX controls can be written in several languages, including C, C++, Visual Basic, and Java. They are currently only supported in Microsoft's Internet Explorer browser, Version 4.0 and greater.

actor. An object in a Liquid Motion animation, such as an image, text, sound effect, 2-D shape, or 3-D object.

adaptive palette. A color palette reduced to only the colors present in the image.

ambient light. Reflected light from surrounding objects displayed on a 3-D shape. In Liquid Motion, the amount of ambient light falling on an object can be adjusted. *See also* 3-D light.

animate color. In Liquid Motion, a behavior that causes the colors of an actor to be cycled from an initial to an ending color. It is also referred to as "color animation."

antialiasing. The blending of colors to smooth out the jagged stair-stepped edges (jaggies) in fonts.

applet. A client-side program, usually Java or ActiveX, that is downloaded from the Internet and executed in a Web browser.

ASCII. The American Standard Code for Information Interchange, defining a standard minimum character set for computer text and data. ASCII files are sometimes called "DOS text" files, or "plain text" files.

AU. A file format for audio files. In Liquid Motion, AU files (8-bit, mono, 8000Hz, mu-Law) can be played by all Java-compliant Web browsers.

AutoEffect. In Liquid Motion, an automatically generated effect that can be played in an animation. AutoEffects include Sparkles, Twirlers, Bubbles, Filled Bubbles, Drifting Clouds, and Billowing Smoke. AutoEffects can play over time or be activated by moving, dragging, or pressing the mouse.

AVI. Audio Video Interleaved, a multimedia format for sound and video that is common on the Windows platform.

avoid. A behavior in Liquid Motion that causes one actor to avoid another. *See also* follow.

bandwidth. The transmission capacity of a network, but also the amount of capacity consumed by a connection. A Web page containing many graphics will consume more bandwidth than one containing only text.

behavior. A function (such as shrinking, growing, spinning, color animation, and so on) that can be assigned to an actor.

binary file transfer. Transfer of an eight-bit file, such as an executable program or graphics file, either over the Internet using an FTP program or over regular phone lines using a communications program. Binary code consists of program instructions compiled into a machine-readable form. When transferring files, you have to specify whether they are binary or ASCII. ASCII files, such as regular text files and HTML files, are seven-bit files.

bookmark. A means, in Netscape Navigator, for marking the URLs of favorite Web sites so that they can easily be returned to. Bookmarks are saved by Navigator as HTML files, BOOKMARK.HTM. A similar feature in Microsoft Internet Explorer is called "Favorites" (but the URLs are saved as separate files, rather than in a single file).

Cascading Style Sheets. Means for defining styles, using the STYLE tag, for controlling display of HTML elements. A style sheet can either reside inside of the HTML file or in a separate file downloaded along with the HTML file. Current versions are Cascading Style Sheets, level 1 (CSS1), and Cascading Style Sheets, level 2 (CSS2). You can find out more about Cascading Style Sheets at the World Wide Web Consortium's site at **www.w3.org/Style/**.

CGI. The Common Gateway Interface, an interface to a gateway through which a Web server can run programs and scripts on a host computer.

client. A computer on a network that makes a request to a server.

clipboard. An area in memory, on the Windows platform, for instance, to which data can be copied or cut from one program or location and then pasted into another program or location.

definition list. A glossary list in HTML, created using the DL (Definition List) element.

DHTML. *See* Dynamic HTML.

DirectX. A software technology for Windows 95/98 that allows applications, such as games and animations, to directly access a computer's graphics and sound hardware. Liquid Motion's 3-D effects make use of DirectX technology. You can find out more about DirectX at Microsoft's Web site at **www.microsoft.com/directx/**.

dithering. A method for smoothing out color and tonal transitions. Dithering helps to eliminate "color banding" that is often evident in lower-resolution images displaying fewer than 256 colors or shades of gray. *See also* antialiasing.

domain category. A major grouping of domain names (such as .com, .org, .net, .edu, .mil, and .gov), as well as many national domain categories (.us, .uk, .ca, and so on).

domain name. An alphanumeric alternative to an IP address, registered with the InterNIC (Internet Network Information Center).

download. To transfer files from a server to a client. *See also* upload.

DPI. Dots per inch, used in combination with the number of pixels in an image to determine the size of an image. For instance, an image scanned at 75 DPI will be smaller than the same image scanned at 150 DPI.

Dynamic HTML. Various means of providing dynamic Web content that respond interactively to user actions, such as producing on-the-fly Web pages, starting and stopping animations, and so on. (Microsoft refers to its rendition of this as "Dynamic HTML" (or DHTML), while Netscape refers to its rendition as "dynamic HTML.")

embedded animation. A Liquid Motion animation that is saved and then imported into another animation.

end tag. The end of a nonempty HTML element (...</P>, for example). *See also* start tag.

extension. A nonstandard extension to HTML implemented by a particular browser (as in "Netscape extension" or "Microsoft extension") that may or may not be displayable in other browsers.

filter. In Liquid Motion, an effect that can be applied to the root scene which affects the entire scene, such as a Drop Shadow, Glow, Gray, Negative, Transparency, or Wave filter. *See also* transition.

follow. A behavior in Liquid Motion that causes an actor to follow another actor.

fragment identifier. A string at the end of a URL preceded by a "#" character, used to identify a target anchor name. It allows a hypertext link to jump to a specific location in another or the same Web page.

frames. An extension to HTML that allows multiple HTML documents to be displayed at the same time in separate frame windows within a web page.

FrontPage web. A Web site created and maintained in FrontPage, either on a local hard drive or on a remote Web server.

FTP. File Transfer Protocol, the protocol used for downloading or uploading both ASCII and binary files on the Internet.

GIF. Graphics Interchange Format, a popular Web graphics format developed by CompuServe. Each image can include up to 256 colors, transparency, interlacing, and multiple frames (GIF animation). *See also* JPEG.

GIF animation. A GIF-format image file containing multiple images that cumulatively create an animation. Such an animation is usually only viewable in a Web browser.

grow. In Liquid Motion, a behavior that causes an actor to grow in size.

hot link. Another term for a hypertext link.

HTML. HyperText Markup Language, a markup language for preparing documents for display on the World Wide Web. The current standard version of HTML is HTML 4.0 (previous versions were HTML 1.0, HTML 2.0, and HTML 3.2).

HTML editor. A software program that edits HTML files. HTML editors cover a wide spectrum, from fairly simple Notepad-like editors, in which HTML codes can either be typed or selected using toolbars, menus, or wizards, to fancy WYSIWYG (such as FrontPage 98, for instance) that shield you from having to do any of your own hand-coding. An HTML editor, however, isn't necessary for creating HTML files—Windows Notepad works just fine.

HTML element. Everything encompassed within a start and end tag in HTML. Stand-alone tags (such as the HR or IMG tag) are both tags and elements.

HTML tag. A markup code in HTML. There are two types of tags in HTML: container tags and empty tags (or stand-alone tags). Container tags start with a start tag (<H1>, for instance) and end with an end tag (</H1>, for instance). End tags always begin with a "/" (</P>, </B>, and so on). Everything between a start tag and an end tag is also called an "HTML element." Empty tags (also called "stand-alone" tags) are single tags that don't have end tags (<HR>, for instance).

HTTP. HyperText Transfer Protocol, the protocol used to exchange Web pages and other documents across the Internet. A Web server, for instance, may also be called an HTTP server, in contrast to an FTP (File Transfer Protocol) server.

hypermedia. A term coined by Ted Nelson, the inventor of hypertext. It generally refers to the interlinking of multiple media (text, images, sound, animation, video).

hypertext. Described by Ted Nelson, its inventor, as "non-sequential writing." Hypertext links allow non-sequential linking of information within a "docuverse" (also one of Ted Nelson's coinages).

hypertext link. A means, using the A (Anchor) element in HTML, for jumping from a location in an HTML document to another Web page or object file on the Web, to a location in another Web page, or to a location in the same Web page. It is also called a "hot link."

image link. An inline image inserted inside a hypertext link, usually displayed with a blue border to show that it is an active link.

image map. An image displayed in a Web browser with hidden "hot spots" that can be clicked on to link to their designated URLs. Older browsers only supported server-side image maps (image maps executed from a server), whereas newer browsers also support client-side image maps (image maps executed from the desktop, or client).

image strip. Also called an image sequence. In Liquid Motion, a GIF or JPEG image including a series of images, arrayed either horizontally or vertically, that can be played sequentially at an assigned frame rate. When animated GIFs are imported into Liquid Motion, they are automatically converted into a special form of image strip, a timed strip. (You can specify the number of frames and the frame rate in a regular image strip, but not in a timed strip, where these properties are predetermined based on the imported animated GIF.)

inline image. An image (GIF, JPEG, or PNG) that is displayed on a Web page.

inner scene. In Liquid Motion, a scene created within another scene, either inside the root scene or inside another inner scene. *See also* root scene.

interactive behavior. In Liquid Motion, a behavior that responds to user actions, such as triggers, URL links, script triggers, avoid, and follow.

interlaced GIF. A GIF-format graphics file that can be gradually displayed in a browser while still being downloaded. On each pass, only some of the lines of the image are displayed, allowing a viewer to see what the image is going to be long before it has been downloaded completely.

Internet. A set of protocols for transmitting and exchanging data among networks.

IP address. An Internet Protocol address. A unique number, such as 185.35.117.0, that is assigned to a server on the Internet.

IPP. An Internet presence provider, also often called a "Web host" or "Web space provider." A company that rents Web space.

ISP. An Internet service provider, also often called an "access provider." A company that provides dial-up access to the Internet.

jaggies. In lower-resolution images, the "stairstep" appearance displayed by curved or diagonal lines. Also termed "aliasing." *See also* antialiasing.

Java. Sun Microsystem's object-oriented programming language, designed to create programs that can be run securely on any platform, making it the ideal programming language for the World Wide Web. Because programs distributed across the Web need to be small (because of bandwidth constraints), Java programs, as well as ActiveX controls, are often called "applets."

Java player classes. A set of files that must accompany any Liquid Motion animation so that they can be played in a Java-capable Web browser.

JavaScript. A scripting language developed by Netscape and Sun that is loosely based on Java. Useful for adding behaviors to a Web page, such as mouse-over effects, for instance. *See also* Jscript *and* VBScript.

JPEG. Joint Photographic Experts Group. Besides GIF, the most common graphics format for the display of images on the Web. Images can use a palette of up to 16.7 million colors. Unlike GIF images, however, JPEG images cannot be transparent, interlaced, or animated. Often referred to as JPG format images, because the file extension for JPEG images under DOS/Windows is ".jpg." JPEG images are generally best for images that require more than 256 colors, such as continuous tone photograghs or images that make use of gradient fills. GIF images are best for images that have fewer than 256 colors. *See also* GIF.

JScript. A version of JavaScript developed by Microsoft for its Internet Explorer browser. It works with ActiveX controls, unlike JavaScript.

jump. In Liquid Motion, a behavior that causes an actor to jump from one place to another in an animation scene.

link list. A list of hypertext links, sometimes also called a "hotlist."

link text. The text displayed in a hypertext link, usually in blue and underlined.

marquee. An HTML element supported only by Microsoft Internet Explorer that displays scrolling text in a Web page. It is not included in standard HTML.

MathML. Mathematical Markup Language, the proposed standard for displaying equations and mathematical symbols on the Web. You can find out more about MathML at the World Wide Web Consortium's site at **www.w3.org/Math/**.

MIDI. In Liquid Motion, an audio format often used for music that can only be played in Internet Explorer, Version 4.0 or greater. Files have an extension of .mid.

motion path. A behavior in Liquid Motion that is created by recording the motion of an actor as you drag it around a scene.

MPEG. In Liquid Motion, an audio format that can only be played in Internet Explorer, Version 4.0 or greater. Files with extensions of .mpg, .mp2, or .mpa can be used. Liquid Motion does not support using .mp3 files.

named anchor. *See* target anchor.

Netscape palette. A color palette composed of the 216 colors used by Netscape Navigator to display images on a computer displaying 256 colors. It is also called a "safety palette."

object. In Liquid Motion, an actor or a behavior—anything for which properties can be defined (such as duration, play times, size, color, and so on).

offline browsing. Browsing HTML files on a local hard drive, without connecting to the Internet.

ordered list. A numbered list created in HTML using the OL (Ordered List) tag.

pixel. Short for picture element. Identifies a "point" in a graphic image but also includes bytes that represent its color depth. The number of pixels does not determine the size of an image, but only the resolution of the image. The size of the image (whether printed or displayed) is determined by the *DPI* (dots per inch).

PNG. Portable Network Graphics, the newest standard graphics format for the display of images on the Web. It supports up to 48-bit true color (JPEG supports up to 24-bit true color), as well as transparency and interlacing.

POP3 server. A Post Office Protocol, version 3, or "incoming mail," server (e-mail is received from a POP3 mail server). *See also* SMTP server.

publish. In Liquid Motion, to save an animation to its publish folder, along with all the attendant files required for it to be displayed in a browser.

relative URL. A Web address stated in relation to the current (or linking) page—"images/mypic.jpg" would link to "mypic.jpg" in an "images" folder that is a subfolder of the folder where the linking HTML file is located, while "../frames/myframe.html" would link to a "myframe.html" file in a "frames" folder that is a subfolder of the parent folder of the folder where the linking HTML file is located. Internal links within a Web site should always use relative URLs, which allow the linked files to be uploaded onto a server or moved to another location without the need to change the links.

root scene. The initial scene created in a Liquid Motion animation. *See also* inner scene.

rotate. In Liquid Motion, a behavior that causes a 3-D shape to be rotated three-dimensionally in space.

server. A computer on a network that responds to requests from clients. *See also* client.

SGML. Standard Generalized Markup Language, the parent markup language of HTML. SGML is primarily intended for marking up electronic documents for printing (while HTML is intended for marking up electronic documents for publishing on the Web).

shrink. In Liquid Motion, a behavior that causes an actor to shrink in size.

SMTP server. A Simple Mail Transfer Protocol, or "outgoing mail," server (e-mail is sent to an SMTP mail server). *See also* POP3 server.

spin. In Liquid Motion, a behavior that causes a 2-D shape, image, or text actor to spin in a clockwise or counterclockwise direction.

splash image. An image displayed in a browser while a Liquid Motion animation downloads.

start tag. The start of a non-empty HTML element (<P>..., for instance).

structure view. In Liquid Motion, a hierarchical presentation of the actors and behaviors in an animation. In the structure view, you can right-click on an actor or behavior to edit its properties.

surface texture. In Liquid Motion, a texture that can be applied to the surface of a 3-D shape.

tables. Displaying data in a tabular format in HTML by using the TABLE tag. Table rows are defined by the TR (Table Row) tag, whereas table cells are defined by the TD (Table Data) tag. Inserting Liquid Motion animations in tables is a great way to control the positioning of an animation relative to other elements on a Web page.

tag. A code in SGML, HTML, and XML used to define a document element. Tags can either be the start and end tags of a "container" element (such as a paragraph or a heading) or stand-alone tags that define an "empty" element (such as an inline image or a horizontal rule).

target anchor. A hypertext anchor that defines the "landing spot" for a link.

TCP/IP. The Transmission Control Protocol/Internet Protocol, the standard protocol set for transmissions across the Internet.

throughput. *See* bandwidth.

timeline slider. In Liquid Motion, a control, composed of the timeline and the slider button, that can be used to play an animation and manipulate an animation's timeline. The slider button moves along the timeline to indicate the progress of an animation. By moving the slider button to it, the content of the animation at any one point in time can be displayed in the scene. The start offset for any object can be set by first moving the slider button to a point on the timeline before the object is inserted into the scene.

toolbar. Onscreen buttons or icons in a graphical user interface (GUI) that usually provide shortcuts to menu and other program functions.

transition. In Liquid Motion, an effect that can be applied to the root scene, such as a Dissolve, Fade, Random, Blinds, Box, Checkerboard, Circle, Random Bar, Split, Strips, or Wipe transition. *See also* filter.

trigger. In Liquid Motion, an interactive behavior that responds to an action—such as a mouse action (clicking, pressing, releasing the mouse, or moving over or off a part of the scene)—by turning on or off another behavior, actor, or trigger.

Unix. A multi-user, multitasking operating system originally developed by AT&T Bell Laboratories. Versions include Linux, Xenix, AIX, and A/UX. The majority of servers on the World Wide Web run Unix, although Windows NT servers are also numerous.

unordered list. A bulleted list created in HTML using the UL (Unordered List) tag.

upload. To transfer files from a client to a server.

URL. Uniform Resource Locator; an address on the Web.

URL link. In Liquid Motion, a behavior that causes the launching of a Web address (URL) when the actor to which it is assigned is clicked on.

VBScript. Visual Basic Scripting Edition, Microsoft's scripting language for use on the World Wide Web. It is similar to JavaScript but only runs on Internet Explorer.

Visual J++. Microsoft's implementation of the Java programming language.

VRML. The Virtual Reality Modeling Language, a language used to describe 3-D scenes and models. A free utility, the VRML to X Converter, is available at **www.thirddimension.com/third/util.htm**. It will convert VRML .wrl files to Liquid Motion .x files.

WAV. An audio file format common to Windows. WAV format sound files included in Liquid Motion animations can only be played in Internet Explorer, Version 4.0 or greater.

Web browser. A software program that browses (or "surfs") HTML and other files on the World Wide Web.

XML. eXtensible Markup Language. Slated by the w3C (World Wide Web Consortium) as the next-generation markup language for display of documents and data not only on the Web, but in all manner of media. Using XML, a single document can be marked up to be displayed on the Web, read in a Braille reader, printed in a book, or spoken by a speech application. In many ways, XML is intended as the strict subset of SGML that HTML was *supposed* to have become. You can find out more about XML at the World Wide Web Consortium's site at **http://www.w3.org/XML/**.

INDEX

2-D shapes. *See also* specific shapes.
    animating colors, 84, 87
    growing, 81, 85, 87–88
    inserting, 80, 83, 86
    shrinking, 85, 87–88
    spinning, 81, 85, 88
2-D Shapes tool, 83
3-D animation
    Drop Shadow Filter, 232–237
    Flying Shapes, 249–265
    Swimming 3-D Fish, 206–230, 296
    Transitions, 238–248
3-D Light behavior, 226, 253
3-D shapes
    cube, 250–254
    cylinder, 255–259
    fish, 206–230
    skeleton key, 259–262
    sound effects and, 262–263
    URL links and, 265
    Web browser considerations, 206, 248
4-pointed star shape, 86–88
8-pointed star shape, 83–85

A

absolute URL, 40
Abstract button, 12–15
acceleration
    actor, 219
    Grow behavior, 90–91, 219
    motion path, 219
    Spin behavior, 88

Accelerator, Liquid Motion, 314
account name, Web server, 323
activated links, 275
actors
    defined, 26–27
    determining display sequence of, 36
    dragging and dropping, 36, 122
    editing properties of, 68
    identifying, 26–27
    lining up, 335
    moving in structure view tree, 122
    selecting, 34
Adobe PhotoShop, 304
Alex Chapman's BudgetWeb Index, 322
alignment, Web animation, 128, 273
ALINK attribute, 275
America Online, 311, 321
Animate Color tool, 67, 78, 79
Animate features, menu bar, 27
animated color bar, 97–101, 105–106
animation. *See also* 3-D animation; interactive animation; Web animation.
    DirectX, 5
    GIF, 3, 302–303
    software tools, 3–4, 334
animation files
    browser-specific versions, 297–298
    download considerations, 298–299, 302, 303–306
    editing, 269–272
    internal hypertext links in, 286–288
    naming, 228, 280
    organizing, 307
    previewing in Web browser, 272–273

animation files (continued)
transferring to Web server, 307, 329–330
using background colors and images in, 273–280
Animation Shop, 303, 338
AOL, 311, 321
applets, 5
.au files, 110, 111, 181, 182, 195–196, 206
audio files. *See* sound effects; specific file types.
Audio folder, 181
audio panning, 206
Auto Mode Transfer, 330, 332
AutoEffects, 65, 105, 154–156

B

back bar, 149–150, 157–158
BACK button, 153–154, 165–167, 169–170
background
panning, 184–188
transparent, 206, 274
BACKGROUND attribute, 278–280
background color, 44, 51, 62, 79, 273–274
background image, 44, 62, 134, 225, 278–280
balloons, speech, 189–193, 199
Banner animation, 61–82
banner templates, 10–12
Behavior toolbar, 28–29
behaviors. *See also* specific behaviors.
defined, 26–27
dragging and dropping, 36
expanding and collapsing lists of, 34–35
identifying, 34, 39
selecting, 35
BGCOLOR attribute, 273–274, 286
Blinds transition, 238
Blue Bar banner
editing, 36–41
playing, 42
previewing, 10–12, 43–47
BODY tags, 271
"boing" sound effect, 144, 156–157, 197
Book Examples, CD-ROM, 181, 225, 336
Book Images folder, 193, 199, 225, 336

Book Sounds folder, 181, 182, 195, 227
BORDER attribute, 284
Box transition, 238, 240–241
BR CLEAR tag, 282
browser. *See* Web browser.
bubbles
image, 210–212
sound effect, 227
Budget Web Host List, 321
BudgetWeb Index, Alex Chapman's, 322
Burma Shave signs, 127
button templates, 12–16, 89
buttons
adding to animations, 89
adding to navigation bar, 150–152
adding URL links to, 169–170, 182–183
copying and pasting, 151
creating text for, 152–154
growing/shrinking, 90–91
roll-over, 173
buzzwords
DirectX, 5
Dynamic HTML, 230
Java, 5
JavaScript, 5
parent folder, 137
URL, 135

C

cache, Web browser, 12
Callihan Web site, 7, 270, 296, 301
Canada Order Centre, Microsoft, 311
Car Honk animation, 106–113
carhonk.au file, 110, 195–196
catalogs, product, 8
CD-ROM
installing example files, 335–336
programs and files, 333, 336–338
Animation Shop animation editor, 303, 338
ColorBrowser utility, 277, 336
CoolEdit 96 sound editor, 111, 337
frames template, 295
GIF Movie Gear animation editor, 303, 337

CD-ROM (continued)
  newsletter template, 286
  Paint Shop Pro 5, 190, 277, 278, 303
  sample Liquid Motion animations, 21
  sound files, 181, 182
  WS_FTP LE, 47, 322, 324–332, 338
running, 334
user interface, 334–335
CELLPADDING attribute, 284
CELLSPACING attribute, 284
CENTER tags, 128, 273, 275
centering Web animations, 128, 273, 275
Character Builder, 338
Checkerboard transition, 238, 243–244
Circle transition, 238, 245
classes, Java player, 306–307
Click Me! animation, 133–149
"Click me" balloon, 19
clip art, 28, 195, 199
Close button, 63
CoffeeCup HTML Editor, 338
color
  for animations, 67–69, 77–79, 101, 157–158,
      277
  background, 44, 51, 62, 79, 273–278
  safety palette, 278, 304
  for shapes, 64
  Web browser considerations, 278, 304
Color Bar animation, 97–101, 105–105
color codes, 273, 277–280
color pickers, 277
ColorBrowser utility, 277, 336
compression ratio, for image files, 305
compression tools, 335
CompuServe, 321
CONTENT attribute, 298
CoolEdit 96, 111, 337
Copy command, 35
Create Your First Web Page In a Weekend, 7
cube, 3-D, 250–254
Cut command, 35
cutting-edge Web sites, 5–6

cylinder, 3-D, 255–259

D
definitions. *See* buzzwords.
Delete command, 35
dial-up access, Internet, 321
dimensions, scene, 62–63, 107, 114, 175
Direction arrows, 32
directory path, remote, 323
DirectX, 5
Dissolve transition, 206, 240
.dll files, 315
domain name registration, 321–322
DOS/Windows slash (, 136, 288
"double-click" sound effect, 144–145
download time, for animation files, 298–299,
      302, 303–306
downloading
  Easy-Authoring Templates, 20, 21
  Internet Explorer, 312
  Liquid Motion, 312
  Web animations, 21, 298–299, 302, 303–306
  WS_FTP LE, 324
dragging and dropping
  actors, 36, 122
  animations to a FrontPage 98 Web page, 319–320
  behaviors, 36
drop shadow
  filter, 206, 231, 232, 233–234, 236–237
  for shapes, 114–115
  for text, 55–56
Duration control, 32, 63, 66, 70, 74, 76–77
dynamic content
  examples, 7–8
  reasons for using, 5–6
  software tools, 3–5
Dynamic HTML, 230, 237

E
Easy-Authoring Templates. *See also* specific tem-
      plates.
  finding additional, 21, 286
  previewing, 9–10, 20–21
Edit Colors window, 52

Edit features, menu bar, 27
Edit URL Link window, 41
editing
    actor/object properties, 35, 41, 68
    animation files, 269–272, 303
    background image strips, 200
    Blue Bar banner, 36–41
    filter properties, 236
    GIF animations, 302–303
    HTML files, 237, 269–271
    Letters banner, 47–54
    sound files, 111
    Waves banner, 54–56
Effects features, menu bar, 27
eight-pointed star shape, 83–85
embossed buttons, 89
end state, setting, 63
error message, "HTTP Error 404," 147
Expanding Circle transition, 245
Extras, template, 16–20

F
fades, 206
File features, menu bar, 27
file folders. *See* folders.
file names
    animation files, 228, 330–332
    Web page, 170, 280
File Transfer Protocol. *See* FTP; WS_FTP LE.
filters
    editing properties, 236
    previewing in Web browser, 233
    running in sequence, 235–236
    specific types available, 206, 231
    timing, 231, 234–235
    tips for using, 230–231
Fish animation, Swimming 3-D, 206–230, 296
Flipping Navigation Bar animation, 149–172, 276, 279
Float properties, 66–67
Flying Shapes animation, 249–265
folders
    naming, 280

    organizing, 307, 328
    parent, 137
    specific
        Audio, 181, 195
        Book Images, 193, 199, 336
        Book Sounds, 181, 182, 195, 227, 336
        Clip Art, 195
        Program Files, 48
        Projects, 48, 53
        Publish, 43–44, 269–270, 306
fonts, 52
four-pointed star shape, 86–88
Frame Menu animation, 290–296
frame rate, 45
FRAME tags, 294
Frame-It, 296, 337
frames, 185, 190, 288–296
frameset file, 289, 292–295
freeware, 336. *See also* specific programs.
FrontPage 98
    installing, 315
    Liquid Motion component, 315
    moving animations, 319–320
    newsgroup, 320
    ordering, 315
    publishing animations with, 43, 47, 316–319
    Server Extensions, 322
    technical support, 320
    themes, 21
FTP, 43, 47, 136, 322, 324–332
Full Circle radio button, 101
Future Splash, 4

G
gallery, Liquid Motion animations, 21
Getting Started dialog box, 9
GIF animation, 3, 302–303, 303
GIF Movie Gear, 303, 337
Gleam effect, 68, 102–103
Glow effect, 68, 102–103
Glow filter, 231
graphics. *See also* images.
    clip art collections, 28, 195, 199

graphics (continued)
  editors, 303
Gravity properties, 66–67
Gray filter, 231
Grow tool, 27, 71, 77, 81, 85, 87

H
hardware requirements, Liquid Motion, 311
Help button, 15–16
Help features, menu bar, 28
hexadecimal color codes, 273, 277–280, 336
hexagon shape, 137–140
Hold End check box, 32–33, 63
HOME button, 152–153, 159–164, 169–170
Honking Car animation, 106–113
host name, 323
hosting services, Web, 321–322
.htm/.html files, 330
HTML
  attributes
    ALINK, 275
    BACKGROUND, 278–280
    BGCOLOR, 273–274, 277, 286
    BORDER, 284
    CELLPADDING, 284
    CELLSPACING, 284
    CONTENT, 298
    MARGINHEIGHT, 294
    MARGINWIDTH, 294
    NAME, 294
    NORESIZE, 294
    SCROLLING, 294
    TEXT, LINK, 274
    VALIGN, 285
    VLINK (Visited Link), 274
    WIDTH, 284
  color pickers, 277
  cutting and pasting animation code, 6–7, 105
  Dynamic, 230, 237
  files
    editing, 237, 269–271
    frameset, 289, 292–295
    organizing, 307

  previewing in Web browser, 272
  recommended books on, 7, 270, 296
  relative URLs/links, 137
  tables, 280–288
  tags
    BODY, 271
    BR CLEAR, 282
    CENTER, 128, 273, 275
    FRAME, 294
    META, 298–299
    NOFRAMES, 294
    TABLE, 285
    TD (Table Data), 285–286
    TH (Table Heading), 285–286
    TITLE, 293
    TR (Table Row), 285
  tutorials, 270
HTML Power Tools, 338
"HTTP Error 404" message, 147
hypertext links. *See* links.

I
IE. *See* Internet Explorer.
image maps, 7, 334, 338
image sequence, 185
image strips, 184–185, 200, 302–303
ImageCommander, 338
images
  background, 44, 62, 134, 225, 278–280
  color considerations, 304
  compression ratio, 305
  inserting in animation, 72–74, 89
  preferred format for photographic, 305
  reusing, 305–306
  shrinking and growing, 73–74, 108–109
  splash, 44–45, 302
  viewing and converting, 338
inner scenes, 115
Insert Audio tool, 110
Insert AutoEffect tool, 65
Insert 2-D/3-D tools, 212
Insert features, menu bar, 27
Insert Image tool, 72, 89

Insert Text icon, 37
Insert Text tool, 74, 303–304
installation
    CD-ROM example files, 335–336
    FrontPage 98, 315
    Liquid Motion, 8–9, 311–313
interactive animation. *See also* Web animation.
    examples, 7–8
        Click Me! animation, 133–149
        Flipping Navigation Bar, 149–173, 276, 279
        Roll-Over/Sidebar Menu, 173–184,
            283–286, 289–296
        Running Man, 184–200
    reasons for using, 5–6
    software tools, 3–4
Interactivity features, menu bar, 27, 299
interface, Liquid Motion user, 25–36
internal hypertext links, 286–288
Internet Explorer
    3-D animations and filters support, 201
    downloading, 312
    Dynamic HTML features, 230, 237
    Java features, 206
    Liquid Motion and, 4, 311
    setting default browser, 10, 314
    sound-file formats, 110
Internet service providers, 321, 324
InterNIC, 321
Ipswitch, 324, 332
ISPs, 321, 324

J
Java
    defined, 5
    Internet Explorer-only features, 206
    player classes, 306–307
    supported sound-file formats, 110
    Web browser considerations, 4, 206
JavaScript
    defined, 5
    resources on the Web, 301
    triggers, 299–301
    Web browser considerations, 4–5

.jck files, 297
.jcz files, 297
JPEG files, 305
.js files, 330
Jump tool, 27

L
Learn HTML In a Weekend, Revised Edition, 7,
    270, 296
Letters banner
    changing color and typeface, 51–54
    editing, 47–49
    playing, 49
    previewing, 12, 13
light source, 252–253
links, 135–137, 169–170, 182–183, 265,
    274–275, 286–288
Liquid Characterz, 338
Liquid Motion
    Accelerator, 314
    animation examples, 7–8
    FAQ, 313
    installing, 8–9, 311–314
    Microsoft order centers, 311
    minimum system requirements, 311
    newsgroups, 313–314
    sound file formats, 110
    technical support, 313
    Try and Buy version, 312–313
    user interface, 25–36
    Web site, 20–21
lowercase file names, 330–332
LView Pro 2.0, 338

M
Macromedia Flash, 4
MARGINHEIGHT attribute, 294
MARGINWIDTH attribute, 294
marquee, scrolling, 113–128
MediaBlaze, 338
menu bar, 26, 27–28
menus, creating, 173–184
messages, scrolling, 113–128
META tags, 298–299

Microsoft
    Internet Explorer (*See* Internet Explorer)
    Liquid Motion Web site, 311, 312
    ordering Liquid Motion from, 311
    technical support, 313
.mid files, 110, 206
Mirrored Box transition, 240–241
motion path
    for 3-D Swimming Fish animation, 207–208,
          213–214, 217–218, 221–222
    for Honking Car animation, 107–108
    for Running Man animation, 194–195
    for Scrolling Marquee animation, 117–119
    for Welcome Banner animation, 72–73
mouse-over effects, 5, 7, 173, 263–264
.mp2 files, 110
.mpa files, 110
.mpg files, 110, 206
multimedia tools, 334, 338

N

NAME attributes, 294
names
    animation file, 228, 330–332
    text actor, 70, 120, 141
    Web page file, 170, 280
navigation bar, interactive animated, 149–172
Navigator. *See* Netscape Navigator.
Negative filter, 231
Netscape Navigator
    3-D animations and filters support, 201
    Dynamic HTML features, 230
    Liquid Motion and, 4, 311, 312, 314
    setting default browser, 10
Netscape palette, 278, 304
newsgroups
    FrontPage 98, 320
    Liquid Motion, 313–314
newsletter template, 286
NEXT button, 154, 167–170
No Change radio button, 101
NOFRAMES tag, 294
NORESIZE attribute, 294

Notepad, Windows, 270

O

Object toolbar, 28, 29
objects
    defined, 26–27
    editing properties, 41, 66, 68
    working with, 35–36
Offset value, 77, 79, 86
online support, Microsoft, 313
oval shape, 64–65

P

paint program, 190, 200, 277, 278, 303, 304, 334
Paint Shop Pro 5, 190, 277, 278, 303, 304, 338
panels, image strip, 184–188
panning, audio, 206
panning background, 184–188
parent folder, 137
password, Web account, 323
Paste command, 35
Pause tool, 30
performance considerations, 298–299, 302,
    303–306, 314
photographic images, 305
PhotoShop, Adobe, 304
Play control, 32
Play Forward/Backward arrows, 74
Play tool, 42, 49
Player features, menu bar, 28
Player toolbar, 26, 29, 30, 42
polygon shape, 137–140
position indicator, 187
presence providers, 321–322
Preview in Browser tool, 43, 46, 50, 53, 79–80,
    105
Prima Tech
    user interface, CD-ROM, 334–335
    Web site, 7, 270, 296
product catalogs, 8
Program Files folder, 48
programs, Web animation, 3–4
Projects folder, 48, 53

properties
defined, 26–27
editing, 35, 41, 66, 68
Publish folder, 43–44, 269–270, 306
Publish tool, 46, 105
Publish Wizard, 43–47
publishing
to a FrontPage 98 Web page, 316–319
tips for using multiple animations, 301–307

Q
quizzes, animated, 8

R
Random Bar transition, 238
Random transition, 238
Record Motion tool, 72–73, 108
Record tool, 30
rectangle shape, 114–115
Refresh button, 46
registration, domain name, 321–322
relative URL, 40, 135, 136, 265
Reload button, 46
remote directory path, 323
RGB hex codes, 273, 277–280, 336
roll-over buttons/effects, 5, 7, 173–184
Roll-Over Menu animation
creating, 173–183
previewing in Web browser, 183
suggestions for using, 184
frameset example, 289–296
HTML table example, 283–286
root scene, 115, 230
Rotate 3-D tool, 27, 209–210, 215, 224–225, 252, 257
rulers, for lining up actors, 335
Running Man animation
creating
extra frames, 190
image strip, 189, 232
panning background, 184–188
sound effects, 195, 196, 199
speech balloon, 189–193, 199

traffic, 193–198, 199
previewing in Web browser, 198
setting duration, 198
using in other Web pages, 200

S
safety palette, 278, 304
sample animations
2-D Star with Throbbing Button, 82–92
Click Me! animation, 133–149
Color Bar, 97–101, 105–106
Drop Shadow, 232–237
Flipping Navigation Bar, 149–172, 276, 279
Flying Shapes, 249–265
Frame Menu, 290–296
Honking Car, 106–113
Liquid Motion gallery of, 21
Roll-Over/Sidebar Menu, 173–184, 283–286, 289–296
Running Man, 184–200
Scrolling Marquee, 113–128
Sparkles effect, 101–103
Swimming 3-D Fish, 206–230, 296
Transitions, 238–248
Welcome Banner, 61–82, 289–296
Save tool, 53
saving Web animations, 53, 62, 129
scene dimensions, 62–63, 107, 114, 175
scenes, 26, 34, 115
script triggers, 299–301
scripting language, 5. *See also* JavaScript.
SCROLLING attribute, 294
Scrolling Marquee animation
creating marquee and messages, 113–118, 119–121, 125–126
recording motion paths, 118–119
setting Duration controls, 123, 124
using in other Web pages, 127–128
server. *See* Web server.
Server Extensions, FrontPage, 322
shadow. *See* drop shadow.

shapes, working with, 64–65, 80–82, 206. *See also* 2-D shapes; 3-D shapes.
shareware, 336. *See also* specific programs.
Shrink tool, 27, 64, 65, 73–75, 85, 87
Sidebar Menu animation
    creating, 173–180
    inserting in table, 283–286
    previewing in Web browser, 183
    sound effects for, 181–182
    suggestions for using, 184
    URL links in, 182–183
skeleton key, 3-D, 259–262
sky background image, 239–240
Skydiver Extra template, 16–17, 18
slashes, DOS/Windows *vs.* Unix, 136, 288
Slider button, 29–31, 50
software, Web animation, 3–4, 334
software requirements, Liquid Motion, 311
sound editor, CoolEdit 96, 111, 337
sound effects
    adding to transitions, 245–247
    attaching to 3-D shapes, 262–263
    interactive, 144–145, 181–182
    specific
        "boing" sound, 144–145, 156–157, 197
        bubbles, 227
        car engine, 110
        car honk, 110–111
        double-click, 144–145, 181–182, 197
    triggering, 145
sound files
    common formats, 110–111
    Internet Explorer formats, 206
    supplied on CD-ROM, 181
Sparkles effect
    animation example, 101–103
    attaching to mouse movements, 154–156
speech balloons, 189–193, 199
Spin and Throb animation, 82–92, 281–282
Spin behavior, 27, 81
Spin tool, 85, 88
Spinning Logo animation, 82–92, 281–282

splash image, 44–45, 302
Split transition, 238, 249–250
Standard toolbar, 28, 29
star shape, 82–92
Stop tool, 30, 42, 49
Strips transition, 238
structure view, 33–36, 65, 66, 68
style sheets, 334, 338. *See also* templates.
Sun Microsystems, 5
surface textures, 251–252, 257–258
Swimming 3-D Fish animation
    creating, 206–224
        adding background image, 225
        adding Rotate behaviors, 224–225
        adding sound effects, 227
    playing in frames, 296
    previewing in Web browser, 228–229
    setting 3-D Light color, 226
    suggestions for using, 229–230

T

TABLE tag, 285
tables, HTML, 280–288
tags, HTML
    BODY, 271
    BR CLEAR, 282
    CENTER, 128, 273, 275
    FRAME, 294
    META, 298–299
    NOFRAMES, 294
    TABLE, 285
    TD (Table Data), 285–286
    TH (Table Heading), 285–286
    TITLE, 293
    TR (Table Row), 285
target anchors, 286–288
taxi cab image, 193
TD (Table Data) tag, 285–286
teaching tool, Web animations as, 8
technical support
    FrontPage 98, 320
    Liquid Motion, 313

templates. *See also* Easy-Authoring Templates.
  banner, 10–12
  button, 12–16, 89
  frames, 295
  newsletter, 286
testing animations. *See* Preview in Browser tool.
text
  adding to templates, 36–38
  changing color and typeface, 51–54, 55
  creating for interactive animation, 140–142
  for roll-over buttons, 176–178
  in scrolling marquee messages, 123
  shrinking, 74–75
  for speech balloons, 191–193
  wrapping, 281–282
TEXT, LINK attribute, 274
text actors, 37, 70, 120, 141. *See also* actors.
textures, surface, 251–252, 257–258
TH (Table Heading) tag, 285–286
three-dimensional animation. *See* 3-D animation.
tiling background image, 134, 239
TimeEffects tab, 88
Timeline Slider, 29–31, 63
Timing toolbar, 31–33, 63, 123
tips
  accepting Publish Wizard defaults, 45
  adding colors to animation HTML files, 277
  attaching sound files to 3-D shapes, 262
  bringing FrontPage Explorer window to fore-
     ground, 318
  checking HTML files and animations before
     transferring to server, 328
  choosing colors for Web animations, 278
  coordinating actor/behavior with start of scene,
     247
  copying and pasting triggers, 181
  dealing with "HTTP Error 404" message, 147
  editing object properties, 41, 66
  opening HTML files in Internet Explorer, 271
  positioning actors in a scene, 187
  previewing animations, 104
  republishing an animation, 273

  selecting colors for animations, 102
  using FTP program to transfer animations to
     another location, 47
TITLE tag, 293
toolbars, 26, 28–29, 31–33
Top Ruler, 335, 338
TR (Table Row) tag, 285
transitions
  applying to inner scenes, 241–245
  classes of, 237–238
  defined, 237
  setting end state, 247
  sound effects and, 245–247
  specific types, 206, 238
  Web browser considerations, 230
Transitions animation, 238–248
Transparency filter, 231
transparent backgrounds, 206, 274
triggers
  interactive, 27
  script, 299–301
  sound effect, 181, 227
troubleshooting, 80, 313
Try and Buy version, Liquid Motion, 312–313
tutorials
  frames, 296
  HTML, 270
  Liquid Motion, 28
Twirlers, 65–69
two-dimensional shapes. *See* 2-D shapes.

U
Uniform Resource Locator. *See* URL.
Unix slash (/), 136, 288
URL
  assigning to buttons, 38–41, 169–170
  defined, 135
  links, 135–137, 169–170, 182–183, 265
  relative *vs.* absolute, 40, 136
URL Link tool, 287
user ID, 323
user interface, Liquid Motion, 25–36

users guide, 28

V

Valentine Extra template, 17, 19
VALIGN attribute, 285
VBScript, 299
View features, menu bar, 27
views
    structure, 33–36, 65, 66, 68
    workspace, 33, 65, 66
virtual host account, 321
VLINK (Visited Link) attribute, 274
voice-over, 8

W

.wav files, 110, 111, 206
Wave filter, 231
Waves banner
    editing, 54–56
    playing, 56–57
    previewing, 12, 14
Waves button, 16, 17
Waves Extra template, 18, 20
Web address. *See* URL.
Web animation. *See also* 3-D animation; interactive animation.
    basic types of, 97
    centering, 128, 273
    creating
        with Easy-Authoring Templates, 25
        from scratch, 61–63
    defined, 3
    editing HTML file, 269–271
    examples
        2-D Star with Throbbing Button, 82–92
        Click Me! animation, 133–149
        Color Bar, 97–101, 105–106
        Drop Shadow Filter, 232–237
        Flipping Navigation Bar, 149–172, 276, 279
        Frame Menu, 290–296
        Honking Car, 106–113
        Liquid Motion gallery of, 21

        Roll-Over/Sidebar Menu, 173–184, 283–286, 289–296
        Running Man, 184–200
        Scrolling Marquee, 113–128
        Sparkles effect, 101–103
        Swimming 3-D Fish, 206–230, 296
        Transitions, 238–248, 249–265
        Welcome Banner, 61–82, 289–296
    playing, 42, 49, 56–57
    previewing in Web browser, 43–47, 50, 79–80, 104
    publishing, 43–45, 105, 301–307, 316–319
    saving, 53, 62, 129
    software tools, 3–4, 334
    viewing structure of, 33–36
    ways of using, 7–8
        in frames, 288–296
        in tables, 280–288
    wrapping text around, 281–282
Web browser. *See also* Internet Explorer; Netscape Navigator.
    3-D animation and filters support, 201
    adjusting window dimensions, 11
    cache, 12
    color considerations, 278
    Java-capable, 4–5, 206
    Liquid Motion and, 4–5, 297
    previewing animations in, 43–47, 50, 79–80, 104, 272
    setting default, 10, 314
    sound-file support, 110
Web hosts, 321–322
Web page file names, 170
Web server
    connecting to, 322–323, 327–328
    transferring animation files to, 307, 329–330
Web sites
    characteristics of cutting-edge, 5–6
    competition for visitors, 5–6
    specific
        Alex Chapman's BudgetWeb Index, 322
        FrontPage 98, 315

Web sites (continued)
    InterNIC, 321
    Ipswitch, 324
    Liquid Motion, 20–21
    Microsoft, 311
    PRIMA TECH, 7, 270, 296
    Steve Callihan's, 7, 270, 296, 301
    Web Tools, 296
  ways of using Web animations in, 7–8
Welcome Banner animation, 61–82, 289–296
WHOIS search, 321
WIDTH attribute, 284
Windows Notepad, 270
Windows/DOS slash, 136, 288
WinZip, 338
Wipe transition, 206, 238
Wizard, Publish, 43–47
workspace view, 33, 65, 66
wrapping text, 281–282
WS_FTP LE, 47, 322, 324–332, 338

X
"x" button, 63
.x files, 297

Z
zip/unzip utilities, 335, 338

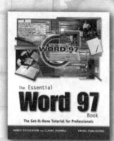

Channel SEEK

100% Webcasting Program Guide

Check out ChannelSEEK for up-to-the-minute program information on all streaming media on the web.

 Concerts

 Movies

 Radio Programs

 Music Videos

 Sporting Events

WEBCASTERS! Check out our affiliate network at www.ChannelSEEK.net and find out how you can add the ChannelSEEK concert applet to your webpage, FREE!

for more information

ChannelSEEK, Inc. • P.O. Box 501135 • Indianapolis, IN 46250 • 888-871-5819 x100
email: info@ChannelSEEK.com

www.ChannelSEEK.com

License Agreement/Notice of Limited Warranty

By opening the sealed disk container in this book, you agree to the following terms and conditions. If, upon reading the following license agreement and notice of limited warranty, you cannot agree to the terms and conditions set forth, return the unused book with unopened disk to the place where you purchased it for a refund.

License:

The enclosed software is copyrighted by the copyright holder(s) indicated on the software disk. You are licensed to copy the software onto a single computer for use by a single concurrent user and to a backup disk. You may not reproduce, make copies, or distribute copies or rent or lease the software in whole or in part, except with written permission of the copyright holder(s). You may transfer the enclosed disk only together with this license, and only if you destroy all other copies of the software and the transferee agrees to the terms of the license. You may not decompile, reverse assemble, or reverse engineer the software.

Notice of Limited Warranty:

The enclosed disk is warranted by Prima Publishing to be free of physical defects in materials and workmanship for a period of sixty (60) days from end user's purchase of the book/disk combination. During the sixty-day term of the limited warranty, Prima will provide a replacement disk upon the return of a defective disk.

Limited Liability:

THE SOLE REMEDY FOR BREACH OF THIS LIMITED WARRANTY SHALL CONSIST ENTIRELY OF REPLACEMENT OF THE DEFECTIVE DISK. IN NO EVENT SHALL PRIMA OR THE AUTHORS BE LIABLE FOR ANY OTHER DAMAGES, INCLUDING LOSS OR CORRUPTION OF DATA, CHANGES IN THE FUNCTIONAL CHARACTERISTICS OF THE HARDWARE OR OPERATING SYSTEM, DELETERIOUS INTERACTION WITH OTHER SOFTWARE, OR ANY OTHER SPECIAL, INCIDENTAL, OR CONSEQUENTIAL DAMAGES THAT MAY ARISE, EVEN IF PRIMA AND/OR THE AUTHOR HAVE PREVIOUSLY BEEN NOTIFIED THAT THE POSSIBILITY OF SUCH DAMAGES EXISTS.

Disclaimer of Warranties:

PRIMA AND THE AUTHORS SPECIFICALLY DISCLAIM ANY AND ALL OTHER WARRANTIES, EITHER EXPRESS OR IMPLIED, INCLUDING WARRANTIES OF MERCHANTABILITY, SUITABILITY TO A PARTICULAR TASK OR PURPOSE, OR FREEDOM FROM ERRORS. SOME STATES DO NOT ALLOW FOR EXCLUSION OF IMPLIED WARRANTIES OR LIMITATION OF INCIDENTAL OR CONSEQUENTIAL DAMAGES, SO THESE LIMITATIONS MAY NOT APPLY TO YOU.

Other:

This Agreement is governed by the laws of the State of California without regard to choice of law principles. The United Convention of Contracts for the International Sale of Goods is specifically disclaimed. This Agreement constitutes the entire agreement